the
spirituality
revolution

– the emergence of contemporary spirituality –

DAVID TACEY

Routledge
Taylor & Francis Group

LONDON AND NEW YORK

First published 2004 by Routledge
27 Church Road, Hove, East Sussex BN3 2FA

Simultaneously published in the USA and Canada
by Routledge
270 Madison Avenue, New York NY 10016

Reprinted 2004, 2005 and 2007

Routledge is an imprint of the Taylor & Francis Group, an informa business

First published in Australia in 2003 by HarperCollins*Publishers* Pty Limited,
Sydney, Australia

This edition published by arrangement with HarperCollins*Publishers*.

Printed and bound in Great Britain by TJ International Ltd, Padstow,
Cornwall

British Library Cataloguing in Publication Data
A catalogue record for this book is available from the British Library
Library of Congress Cataloging in Publication Data
Tacey, David J. (David John), 1953-
   The spirituality revolution : the emergence of contemporary
spirituality / David Tacey.
       p. cm.
Includes bibliographical references and index.
   ISBN 1-58391-873-6 (alk. paper) — ISBN 1-58391-874-4 (pbk. : alk.
paper)
   1. Spirituality. I. Title.
BL624 .T33 2004
204—dc22

                                    2003025319

ISBN 978-1-58391-874-6 (pbk)

Contents

Whatever side one takes in this debate about the 'return of the religious' . . . one still must respond. And without waiting. Without waiting too long.
Jacques Derrida, *Religion.*

To the surprise of many, the term spirituality has become democratised. Ideals that for centuries an elite viewed as virtually unattainable now prompt spiritual growth in everyone. In a word, a 'spirituality revolution' during the past thirty years has democratised pursuit of holiness.
William Johnson, *Recent Reference Books in Religion.*

So the secular, this present, empirical epoch, this phenomenal world, studied by science, does not eliminate the sacred after all; to the contrary, it urges us on a spiritual quest.
Holmes Rolston, *Spirituality and the Secular Quest.*

The 'soul of Britain' project found that seventy-six per cent of people in the UK admitted to having had a religious or spiritual experience. The figures contrast radically with statistics showing how church attendance is declining in all the mainstream Christian denominations. But if one looks at the figures on spiritual experience, they might suggest that we are in the midst of an explosive spiritual upsurge.
David Hay and Kate Hunt, *The Tablet.*

Spirituality has rarely enjoyed such a high profile, positive evaluation, and even economic success as it does among Americans today. If religion is in serious trouble, spirituality is in the ascendancy and the irony of this situation evokes puzzlement and anxiety in the religious establishment, scrutiny among theologians, and justification among those who have traded the religion of their past for the spirituality of their present.
Sandra Schneiders, *The Santa Clara Lectures.*

The spirituality revolution

What is the spirituality revolution? It is a spontaneous movement in society, a new interest in the reality of spirit and its healing effects on life, health, community and well-being. It is our secular society realising that it has been running on empty, and has to restore itself at a deep, primal source, a source which is beyond humanity and yet paradoxically at the very core of our experience. It is our recognition that we have outgrown the ideals and values of the early scientific era, which viewed the individual as a sort of efficient machine. We now have to revise our concepts of life, society, and progress, while preserving the advances that technology and science have given us. Significantly, the new revolution is found at the heart of the new sciences, where recent discoveries in physics, biology, psychology, and ecology have begun to restore dignity to previously discredited spiritual visions of reality. Science itself has experienced its own revolution of the spirit, and is no longer arraigned against spirituality in the old way.

This book presents an image of the spiritual situation of our time. It is my attempt to explore what is happening today in the West in our experience of the spirit; and to suggest ways in which we might uncover a universal spiritual wisdom that could transform our fractured world. The spiritual life is no longer a specialist concern, confined to the interests of a religious group. No membership is required to relate to spirit. Spirituality is now the concern of everyone, religious or secular, young or old, atheist or believer, educated or otherwise, because we inhabit a different world in which spirit is making new and quite extraordinary demands.

The spirituality revolution thrusts us into a new social situation. We have not only outgrown the values and assumptions of mechanistic science and humanism, but we can no longer situate ourselves comfortably in the containment of the traditional religions. We need spiritual guidance, but for a variety of historical and social reasons we cannot return to organised religion or dogmatic theology in their old, premodern forms (this is explored in Chapters 2 and 8). This makes some people shudder with horror, while others rejoice at the new feeling of liberation and freedom from the strictures of the past. But Western society cannot be expected to return to antiquated systems of meaning that have not themselves been part of the long line of historical changes and revolutions that society has experienced over the recent period.

We are caught in a difficult moment in history, stuck between a secular system we have outgrown and a religious system we cannot fully embrace. We are feeling the sting of the ancient Chinese curse: 'may you live in interesting times'. However the birth of the new has never been easy, and our experience testifies to the agony and disruption of changing times. At this point, regression to fundamentalism is always a real but counter-revolutionary possibility. Nevertheless, I remain optimistic about the future, and I believe the creative potentials of spirit will break through. We see this already, not only in the new sciences and the arts, but in education (Chapter 4), personal experience (Chapter 7), contemporary philosophy (Chapter 8), and popular feeling for the environment (Chapter 11).

The spirituality revolution is also discovered in the recent upwelling of spiritual feeling in young people throughout the world, who increasingly realise, often with some desperation, that society is in need of renewal, and that an awareness of spirit holds the key to our personal, social, and ecological survival (Chapters 3 to 6). It is expressed in students of all ages including spiritual themes in their essays and discussions, and secular-trained staff not quite knowing how to respond (Chapter 4). It is found in afflicted patients and suicidal youth often telling health authorities that 'spirituality' might have something to do with their malaise, their lack of orientation and their radically compromised sense of wellbeing (Chapter 13).

The fields of public health, social work and psychology are now facing a crisis situation, where secular-trained therapists are no longer sure how to respond to this new and urgent cry for spiritual meaning. Psychiatrists are speaking about a 'spirituality gap', a discernible schism between the professionals who are trained in secular knowledges and methods, and the wider soul-searching community who are no longer content with reductive answers to human problems. Some educators and social scientists fear that this new cry for spirituality is itself part of the sickness of society, that we are becoming deluded and losing the plot. But this is not the case; instead, some of our established social attitudes have been mistaken: as a community we have forgotten, buried, or repressed too much of our human heritage, too much of our ancient past (Chapter 14).

In our arrogance, we have imagined that we have outgrown the sacred, and that notions of soul and spirit are archaisms of a former era. When the hunger for the sacred erupts in our time, we don't know how to respond, and are often unable to determine what is sickness or health, what is wisdom or delusion, in ourselves or others. It is we who must change the myths and narratives that we live by, we who must invent a better form of sanity, a new kind of normality, so that spirit and soul can be included again in the common understanding of what it means to be human. In this time of transition, many people are the victims of deep structural change. Some have their concepts of reality overturned, others cling to former notions of sanity and order, while others succumb to depressive illness when they see through the lie of the modern world. Spirituality is a major social issue and requires immediate attention if we are to creatively respond to the spiralling outbreaks of depression, suicide, addiction, and psychological suffering.

A DEMOCRATIC MOVEMENT FROM BELOW

Is the spirituality revolution the same thing as the New Age? No, it is larger, broader, and more encompassing than the New Age, which is a specific and highly commercialised 'wing' of the new spiritual movement. What is called the 'New Age' is a kind of parody of the new world about to be born. The New Age, as this term is currently used, is frequently an exploitation of the new public interest in the spirit, rather than a creative response to it. The spirituality revolution is rising from below, and not from above. As such, it is vulnerable to commercial manipulation and unscrupulous interest. There are many organisations and groups that seek to capitalise on the shifts taking place in society, and we have to be alert at every turn to possible abuse, violation, and distortion of the spiritual impulse.

This is a people's revolution. It is taking place because society's loss of meaning is becoming painfully obvious, especially to the young, the disenfranchised and to all who suffer. It is a counter-cultural revolution, a romantic rebellion against the rise of materialism, inhumanity, and economic rationalism. Because this interest is rising from below, it may take some time before the mainstream institutions in health, education, politics, journalism, and religion are able to catch up with it. To date, there has been much suspicion and resistance, and a tendency to lump everything spiritual into the category 'New Age', where it is damned and forgotten. There has not been enough discrimination, because we do not know how to see this blurred and repressed area of our own experience.

Most of our public institutions are secular and are not prepared for a revolution of spirit. The mainline churches are apparently unable to take up a dialogue with the new spirit of our time, partly because they only acknowledge conventional ideas of the sacred (Chapters 10–12). Things may change, and I certainly hope they do. But the field of spirituality is wide open and largely unexplored: we have yet to see any committed institutional response to the challenges posed by the new spirituality.

This revolution involves a democratisation of the spirit. It is about individuals taking authority into their own hands, and refusing to be told what to think or believe. It is about personal autonomy and experimentation, with the use of direct experience of the world as a kind of laboratory of the spirit. There is a new desire to observe, create theories, and test these against the facts of our experience. We seem to be applying the scientific method to our spiritual lives. Not all this investigation is happy or profitable, and this is all the more reason why public institutions must eventually take up a dialogue with popular spirituality.

The spirituality revolution is also about finding the sacred everywhere, and not just where religious traditions have asked us to find it. Things previously considered worldly or even unholy are being invested with new spiritual significance, such as the body, nature, the feminine, sexuality, and the physical environment. This is not an escapist or otherworldly movement, but a direct political and philosophical challenge to traditional notions of sacredness and the holy. It therefore belongs to the long line of democratic revolutions, and is the spiritual counterpart to former and continuing revolutions in politics, society, law, race, education, and gender. It is a forward movement of civilisation, even though it is an advance that is paradoxically achieved by revisiting and reconnecting with the ancient past.

BEYOND FUNDAMENTALISM

The regressive appeal of the religious fundamentalisms has to be taken seriously at this time. After 11 September 2001, and the collapsing of the World Trade Center in New York, all of us should be concerned about the rising tide of fundamentalism, especially within the three monotheisms: Islam, Judaism, and Christianity. In the contemporary world, where so much is open and uncertain, where traditions have been shaken or overturned, where we stand almost naked before the spirit, there is a strong counter-revolutionary force: a desire for absolute certainty, religious security, and nostalgic traditionalism (Chapters 1, 8, 9). Fundamentalisms offer us a parodic version of our need to turn back to the past, only here the turn back is a full-blown regression, a deliberate and systematic retreat from the demands and revolutions of the modern period. This is not going back in order to move forward, but going back to escape the tensions and complexities of a difficult present.

Fundamentalism also supplies a distorted version of the past: its past is largely invented, a projection of regressive social values and anti-modern perspectives into an imagined former era. In the same way that the New Age seeks to ape our spiritual future, so fundamentalism seeks to mimic our past. Today ersatz formulas, escapisms, parodies, fakes, phony gurus, false prophets, and frauds surround us. It is hard for the earnest seeker to steer a successful course through the pitfalls and dangers of the spiritual landscape.

My main interest here is to reach behind the clashing ideologies and fundamentalisms that threaten to dehumanise and destroy the world, and access a mystical source from which all belief systems emerge. This is our immediate hope: to retreat from the rivalry of dogmatic beliefs and uncover a universal spiritual wisdom that might transform us from within. If we dare to enter the mystical ground of our being, we might find a source from which peace and compassion arise. This is the hope of the mystical traditions: to withdraw from the social violence of claim and counter-claim to access the life-giving currents that flow beneath a divided world, offering it an opportunity for healing and renewal.

WHERE I STAND

I write this report on the spiritual situation of the West from a place in the East which pretends to be West: Australia. Here I witness the gradual disintegration of the colonial West, and its transmutation into new forms. On the one hand, there is the powerful influence of the East and the great Asiatic religions; on the other, there is the challenge of the Aboriginal people, and their concern for a spiritual relationship with the earth. From the East we are learning the art of interiority and the psychological basis of faith. From indigenous people we are learning to bring divinity out of the clouds and into earthly experience. The East is teaching us how to transcend the ego, and indigenous people are showing us how to overcome our otherworldliness.

The influence of the East and of indigenous cultures is felt everywhere, perhaps most strongly in new world countries like America, Canada and Australia, where such forces seem to rise from the soil and from surviving local traditions. But the old countries of Europe are experiencing similar processes: established religions are being overturned, deconstructed, and forces long suppressed or banned are awakening with new and surprising power. The 'very ancient' is now contemporary, and the established is being displaced. It is a time of enormous spiritual turbulence, and the spirit has spilled out of old vessels, and surprises us with its capacity to reveal itself in new ways.

I would describe my own personality as mystical, anti-fundamentalist, and humanist. I was born in Melbourne, of Anglo-Irish ancestry, and I received a Western education and a British colonial upbringing. At twelve years of age, the time of initiation in tribal cultures, my family moved to Alice Springs, central Australia, a town of seven thousand people of mixed racial origins, in the middle of a vast desert with few signs of European civilisation. Here, in a place long ruled by Aboriginal law and cosmology, my Western ideas of divinity and reality were challenged and transformed by the local indigenous traditions. I tell the story of this dramatic upheaval and reorientation in another book, *Edge of the Sacred.*

In my spiritual journey I started with the Christian West, and this was challenged by the ancient indigenous world. Then, after a tertiary education that proved disappointing in its inability to engage the sacred, I felt the need to become psychological, and I moved to the United States, where psychology is a dominant cultural force, a kind of modern mythology. Religion had taught me to find God in heaven, Aboriginality had shown me to find the sacred on earth, and now I wanted psychology to reveal to me the possibility of finding the sacredness within.

I was attracted to the Jungian tradition of depth psychology, and a Harkness Fellowship from New York enabled me to work in Texas under the supervision of James Hillman, and with the support of Thomas Moore. Texas may seem like the most unlikely place on earth to search for the sacred, but spiritual experience is always full of paradox and contradiction. Depth psychology proved remarkable, and provided a dimension that neither theology nor indigenous religion could deliver. But by itself psychology and therapy are not enough. They give us access to the internal process, but we tend to lose the world, community, nature, and the environment, not to mention the transcendent dimension of the sacred. Hillman and Moore have themselves outgrown psychology in its narrow form, and have contributed enormously to a more expansive and environmental sense of soul.

It seems to me that no one path can give us the full picture, we have to travel on many roads, invite many perspectives, to see the spiritual life in its totality. My university degrees were in literature, philosophy, and art, and I followed these with post-doctoral studies in Jungian psychology and mythology. Then I felt the need to educate myself in the fields of theology, sociology, and the history of religions. I have explored seven or eight areas of thought in my bid to follow the spirit in our time. Like an outback tracker in a desert landscape, I have gone in search of spirit in the wilderness of secular society, finding hints and clues along the way, and motivated by the belief that spirit is alive and present in our midst.

I appear to some people to be optimistic, given my conviction that we exist in a living connection with a spiritual reality, whether or not we notice it. We might not see spirit directly, but indirectly we have enormous evidence, especially in the domains of culture, history, and human feeling and intuition, which by themselves are not considered 'scientific' proofs, but nevertheless constitute the main foundations for belief in the spiritual. I am no longer sceptical about the existence of spirit, although I have lived through periods of doubt and questioning. Suspicion and doubt yield poor rewards, but if we enter into life with an open heart and a recovered innocence, the world of spirit unfolds before us.

In August 2000, I attended the Millennium World Peace Summit of Religious and Spiritual Leaders, at the United Nations in New York. It was interesting to notice at this Summit the concern among religious leaders for a universal language of the spirit, a new language that is respectful of traditions, but capable of reaching people who are outside religious structures and who belong to the expanding secular society. Something new and different is emerging in our globalised planetary culture, and everywhere I observe a general sense of expectation and awe: something is taking its course, but what?

In the present global culture, with the need for common values and visions in a multicultural and plural world, the time is propitious for the discovery of a universal spirituality. To this end, not dogmatic religion but mystical and poetic vision is needed to release the potentials of spirit in an increasingly secular society. Spirituality is by no means incompatible with religion, but it is existential rather than creedal. It grows out of the individual person from an inward source, is intensely intimate and transformative, and is not imposed upon the person from an outside authority or force.

David Tacey
September 2002

PART 1

The

present

situation

CHAPTER 1

Rising waters of the spirit

The spiritual awakening that is taking place counterculturally
will become more of a daily norm as we willingly break
mainstream cultural taboos that silence or erase our passion
for spiritual practice.

Bell Hooks[1]

A spirituality revolution is taking place in Western and Eastern
societies as politics fails as a vessel of hope and meaning. This
revolution is not to be confused with the rising tide of religious
fundamentalism, although the two are caught up in the same
phenomenon: the emergence of the sacred as a leading force in
contemporary society. Spirituality and fundamentalism are at opposite
ends of the cultural spectrum. Spirituality seeks a sensitive,
contemplative, transformative relationship with the sacred, and is able
to sustain levels of uncertainty in its quest because respect for
mystery is paramount. Fundamentalism seeks certainty, fixed answers
and absolutism, as a fearful response to the complexity of the world
and to our vulnerability as creatures in a mysterious universe.
Spirituality arises from love of and intimacy with the sacred, and
fundamentalism arises from fear of and possession by the sacred. The
choice between spirituality and fundamentalism is a choice between
conscious intimacy and unconscious possession.

Spirituality ultimately produces a state of mind that the poet John Keats called 'negative capability':

when a man is capable of being in uncertainties, mysteries, doubts, without any irritable reaching after fact and reason.[2]

This is surely a condition to aspire to in our torn and broken world, especially since the 'sacred' is being invoked by warring parties and hostile forces who are absolutely sure that God is on their side. If we were less certain of our beliefs, and more receptive to mystery and wonder, we would paradoxically be closer to God, more intimate with the spirit, and more tolerant of our fellow human beings and their differing conceptions of the sacred.

SECULARISM UNDER PRESSURE

The confusion of spirituality and religious fundamentalism causes many reasonable people to reject both, in the belief that humanity is better off without the sacred, since it seems to be at the heart of contemporary conflicts. This desire to distance society and its institutions from the sense of the sacred has underpinned the creation of the modern secular state, which has chosen to put 'religious matters' to one side, so that the business of living, educating, informing and governing the people can take place 'unimpeded' by irrational impulses. But the ideals of secularism, however well intended, are inadequate for life, since our lives are not rational and we are hugely implicated in the reality of the sacred, whether or not this is acknowledged.

What we are seeing in so-called 'secular' or worldly societies is a return of the spiritual impulse, which can cause a great deal of strife and turmoil if it is not consciously integrated into social reality. The purely secular condition has proved inadequate to contain, nurture or transform the spiritual impulses in human lives, and if the fundamentalist state represents an appropriation of the religious instinct for political gain, the secular state represents a repressive denial of the same instinct, also for the sake of political control. We urgently need to discover new ways of being political and social, new ways of defining, describing and living human reality.

Secular nations of the world are feeling the strain and seeking to hold back the tides of spiritual water. Some of our best minds are suspicious and cynical about the eruption of spiritual feeling, as commentators fear we are reverting to the premodern past, regressing to outmoded forms of thinking and losing our grasp on rational civic order. Churches notice an explosion of spiritual interest, but fear it could be an outbreak of gnosticism, while universities complain that people are retreating into the solace of ancient superstition. The waters of the spirit are rising, and this is disturbing to social institutions that thought they had reached an understanding of the human condition.

FACTS, FIGURES, TRENDS

In practical terms, how do we know that spirituality is rising? Initially, it may be easier to notice the radical decline in organised religion and in political idealism than it is to actually quantify the rise of interest in spirituality. Part of the problem is that our established institutions are not very concerned with this social phenomenon. Spirituality which is not attached to church or state is seen as too vague to be of interest, or too threatening for organisations to take seriously enough to analyse and interpret. Church life surveys are usually concerned about which 'denomination' or 'tradition' individuals or families belong to. But the majority of people in secular societies are not bothered about such forms of designation or belonging. They are mostly on individual quests for meaning, so that the questions asked by the religious surveys are frequently out of touch and inappropriate.

Similarly, the secular state is not interested in learning about the spiritual strivings of its citizens. It is content to know that citizens belong to this or that church or tradition, but if they have fallen out of traditions, it is simply assumed that they are secular and therefore have no spiritual interests. Dealing with spirituality 'outside' tradition is too scary, dangerous and annoying for secular nations, for it suggests that spirituality might not be contained in its old forms, and may even be inherent in the nature of human experience. If that is true, where does this leave the secular beliefs of the state and its humanist philosophy? And what of the disruptive possibilities of free-floating spiritual urges to the social and political order?

The nation state is happy to remain with the conventional idea that spiritual interest can be handled by the old religions, and it is pleased to hand such interest over to those traditions, rather than be sullied by it itself. Typically, census forms invite citizens to tick the box that corresponds to their affiliation, whether Baptist, Mormon, Catholic, Orthodox, Muslim, Jewish, and so on. One of my students said she was forced to tick the 'Anglican' box in a recent census questionnaire, because she could not find anything which came even remotely close to her own spiritual identity. 'Why', she said to me, 'do these forms never assume that the citizen can think for herself? Why is it always assumed that personal spiritual identity and religious affiliation are the same thing? Why is there no recognition that people could be on spiritual journeys outside the formalised traditions?' The honest answer is that the government offices that invent these forms do not have the creativity or imagination to understand what its own citizens are doing with their lives.

In my own case, I found out about the extent and popularity of spiritual interest simply by talking to people. We sometimes have to resort to anecdotal evidence, if the revealing statistics are not available, or if they are not made public. In March 1998, I surveyed fifty of my students who had enrolled in one of my literature and psychology courses. An impressive forty-seven students indicated that personal spirituality was a major concern in their lives, while only two students said that religion was important. In 2002, I surveyed 125 students in my undergraduate subject, and 115 expressed personal concern for 'spirituality', while only about ten said they were pleased to be designated as following one of the religions. If our social institutions want to stay in touch with the people they are supposed to serve or govern, they ought to kick themselves out of their lethargy and pay attention.

There are statistics available about the spirituality revolution, but they are frequently buried in academic journals and not made public, because institutions do not like to notice them. Surveys of students in the religious schools indicate widespread defection from faith practices in favour of personal quests for meaning. In Australia, Catholic students who abandon formal worship within eighteen months of graduating from school amount to a staggering 97 per cent of the student body.[3] These are not figures that any institution would be proud of, and consequently they are not broadcast.

But even in so-called 'religious' countries such as the United States, the defection rate from the formal religions, among both the young and the mature-aged, is astronomical. The defection rises dramatically with increased exposure to educational opportunities, so that today the number of people in the States who espouse personal spirituality far exceeds the number who subscribe to formal religious denominations. The best I can do here is refer the interested reader to the statistical sources, especially to the *Journal for the Scientific Study of Religion*, and in particular to the useful study by Brian Zinnbauer, 'Religion and Spirituality: Unfuzzying the Fuzzy'.[4] The situation in the United States is best summarised by Sandra Schneiders, theologian at the Jesuit Theology School, Berkeley, California:

> Spirituality has rarely enjoyed such a high profile, positive evaluation, and even economic success as it does among Americans today. If religion is in trouble, spirituality is in the ascendancy and the irony of this situation evokes puzzlement and anxiety in the religious establishment, scrutiny among theologians, and justification among those who have traded the religion of their past for the spirituality of their present.[5]

Across the Atlantic, the situation is similar and even more compelling, because of the dramatic rise of popular interest in 'spirituality' among the British in recent years. The British are unlike the Americans; they are generally not known for their interest in spiritual or mystical matters. And yet extraordinary figures have been released quite recently. Researchers David Hay and Kate Hunt, based at the University of Nottingham, have been monitoring these changes:

> Something extraordinary appears to be happening to the spiritual life of Britain. At least that's what we think, after a first look at the findings of the 'Soul of Britain' survey recently completed by the BBC. The results show that more than 76 per cent of the population would admit to having had a spiritual experience. In hardly more than a decade, there has been a 59 per cent rise in the positive response rate to questions about this subject. Compared with 25 years ago, the rise is greater than 110 per cent.[6]

These figures seem to defy logic, given the typical reticence that the British often feel toward things that are non-empirical and hidden, and also given the continued dramatic demise of public participation in and membership of the churches. While 76 per cent of the population are interested in spirituality, only about 7 per cent remain committed to regular church attendance. Hay and Hunt continue:

> The figures [on spiritual interest] are startling if only because our lengthy research experience at the Centre for the Study of Human Relations at Nottingham University tells us that English people are very shy about admitting to spiritual experience. This makes it even more remarkable that the responses were obtained in the relatively uncongenial circumstances of a national telephone poll. Why might this be happening? Is it to do with the move away from the materialism of the 1980s? Is there more social permission today for admitting in public what was until recently something too intimate or embarrassing to be shared?[7]

THE COMING AEON

We are entering a new aeon, governed by a new ethos and a new spirit. The secular period has peaked and is drawing to a close. The dry, arid wasteland of the modern era is being eclipsed by something new, and it is still too early to determine exactly what it is.[8] For decades there have been various intimations of a coming age. In the 1960s, the hippies claimed that an Age of Aquarius was about to dawn, but this myth was so highly idealised and based on such grandiose expectations about a future of love and peace that it lost credibility. In the same decade, French intellectuals felt we had entered a postmodern stage, in which the values and certainties of the 'modern' period had been shaken.[9]

Although postmodernism became an elite enterprise that few citizens could understand, it did signify that the familiar world was over. From a spiritual point of view it loosened the structures of rationality and provided openings for the return of mystery and spirit.[10] And while the 'Age of Aquarius' is a faded ideal of a bygone decade, it too can provide clues to our present condition, especially if we look at the significance of Aquarius as a metaphor.[11] The symbol of Aquarius is the Waterbearer who pours the water of life upon a thirsty world. The Waterbearer holds the upturned jug aloft, and humanity is renewed by what he pours forth.

Strangely, years after the hippy dream has faded, we see signs of spiritual renewal in ordinary people and mainstream society. The idea of spirituality and personal contact with cosmic forces is no longer confined to the eccentric fringe or to dropouts, but is experienced and discussed by ordinary citizens in secular societies that have not seen such interest in spiritual matters in living memory. We have become so used to the secular dryness of modernity, or to the non-spiritual aridity of institutional religion, that we have forgotten what spirituality is and what blessings it can bring. We do not know whether to celebrate the rise of these waters of spirituality, or to guard ourselves against them. Neither 'postmodernism' nor 'Aquarius' can define the radical shift that is taking place, but these ideas do contribute intuitions about our world and its departure from the previous sense of social order.

Our institutions are troubled, since they are not in control of these floodwaters, and they worry that people will be carried away by them. They worry also about their own survival, since so much appears to be happening outside their boundaries and without their 'permission'. Because they do not control this revolution, the faith institutions can deem it heretical and dangerous and the knowledge institutions mad and regressive. The mainstream media only becomes interested when something controversial or crazy takes place, in which case the rise of 'irrationality' can be lamented, or the 'New Age' can be bitterly attacked. For the most part the new spirit of the time does not even appear on the radar screen of social reporters, who are either oblivious to the changes or are deliberately repressing what they find too difficult to understand.

RECOVERING THE SACRED

The consequences of the spirituality revolution are far-reaching, and they are being registered most profoundly in the human heart and personal identity. We live in an unstable and even anarchic phase of history, where significant dimensions of human experience are not contained by institutions, and where individuals have to move beyond conventions to meet the challenges of the time. Poets, philosophers, artists and reflective people can see what is happening and what is to come. In particular, the spiritual challenges of the time are discerned most dramatically by the young, since they are the ones who are most directly exposed to the zeitgeist and show the least resistance.

But why is the secular structure of society breaking down? Why are so many people recovering a sense of the sacred and a primal thirst for the waters of the spirit? There are several historical reasons.

We are by nature religious beings, and the secular modern period has witnessed a general repression of our sense of the spirit. After a self-imposed ban we are remembering our sacredness and our dormant religious life is awakening As David Hay and Kate Hunt said of the situation in Britain:

> **We suspect that the spiritual awareness we are uncovering has always been there, but is only now coming to light as we witness the breakdown of a taboo.**[12]

We are in the presence of a great historical shift, as the secular period which arose with humanism and the intellectual enlightenment draws to an end. Most of our knowledge institutions are products of the enlightenment, and as such they do not reach out beyond the present or show us a way into the future. They are frustratingly inadequate, with little to tell us about our situation. The old cultural wineskins cannot contain the new wine of the spirit, and that is why we have so much instability, uncertainty, disruption, and anxiety. We need to make a new pact with the sacred and its archetypal forces. How do we do this when society still operates as if God is dead and spirituality mere superstition?

THE COLLAPSE OF IDOLS AND FALSE GODS

Why are the waters of spirituality flooding their banks now? It could be that our religious substitutes and our false gods are failing us. The secular society worshipped reason and enshrined logic and science. It proclaimed that rationality would deliver us from the superstitions of religion and liberate us from mythological thinking. Science, logic, and reason (*logos*) would eradicate the old gods (*mythos*) and create a brave new world, where we would feel free and satisfied. But what happened? We became free of religion, but we did not feel freer. Instead, we masked our spiritual urges and gave them new names, and new social and political outlets. A host of liberation ideologies, beginning with the natural sciences, progressive economics, and Marxian communism, were invented to cure our ills and overcome our afflictions. For a while, we told ourselves that these ideologies would work, that they simply needed more time and a better chance to prove themselves. Politics would deliver liberation to the people, and economics would bring about a better world. Science and reason would triumph over unreason, and utopia was just a little way ahead.

Our liberation ideologies did not set us free, but just produced monsters. Socialism produced totalitarian fascism, repression, subjugation, mass murder and tyranny. Western liberalism produced gigantic industries, globalism, terrifying levels of consumerism, social exploitation, pollution and the desecration of the environment. Our various forms of cultural materialism were meant to deliver a better and more humane world, but instead we fell victim to new kinds of enslavement and oppression, and old mythology has become reality as giants (in the form of monstrous corporations) stalk the earth.

Do we need to turn beyond the human in order to discover a more humane world? Paradoxically, it may be the extra-human and the spiritual that delivers the liberation and justice that we seek. We might need to draw from the transcendental and its lofty ideals so that we can become more fully human. Certainly, it has become increasingly difficult for people to have a faith in politics, science or humanism. We can see evidence of this in the decline in voter turnout in the United States and United Kingdom, and disillusionment in party politics in most of the democracies. We know that the promises secular authorities make are inadequate, that they cannot be trusted, that they fall prey to corruption. We can no more invest our hopes and dreams in utopian political programs.

The state or political cause has little to offer the desire for liberation and freedom, for unconditional love and support. The secular world is running on empty, and it has run out of answers. Every one of our institutions has 'experts' and futurists who claim to see the way through this depressed phase to a brighter future, but few of us are taken in by their claims. In this depleted state, with less to believe in, we are ready to reconsider what we had once thrown out: religion and spirituality.

CAN RELIGION RESPOND TO THE NEW LONGING?

Formal religion is somewhat dazed and confused by these turbulent times and by this shift of social direction. Religion is so used to being self-protected, to smarting under the attacks of science, reason and secularism, so deeply withdrawn into its defensive cocoon, that it can hardly imagine that the people really do need the gifts of the spirit.

The conservative elements in religion are quite suspicious of what is currently taking place. They suspect that this new taste for spiritual nourishment is just another consumer fad or fashion of a desperate society. Western religion is extremely judgemental of the new rise of spirituality, especially as this popular movement is not 'churchy' and does not fit in with formal religious expectations. It looks upon the wider community and sees confusion, witchcraft, occultism, esoterica, and various kinds of archaic or atavistic enchantments.[13] The new revolution rarely consults religious doctrines or seeks the counsel or authority of religion. It appears to the church to be wild, feral, and derailed. As one clergyman said to me, 'How can the churches get excited about the new spirituality if it is not putting bums on church seats?'

This is a short-sighted response to the present social predicament. How ironic if the ball of Western civilisation is now back in the religious court, but the court of religion does not know about it, or has stopped playing ball with the world. What if it ignores the present challenge or does not care enough to take up a dialogue with the world? The yearning for sacredness, spiritual meaning, security, and personal engagement with the spirit are the primary needs and longings of the contemporary world. What is happening if the institutions of faith are so bound up in themselves and resistant to change that they cannot make some contribution to these needs? Our contemporary situation is full of ironies and paradoxes. Chief among these is that our secular society has given birth to a sense of the sacred, and yet our sacred traditions are failing to recognise the spiritual potential.

The historian of religions, Mircea Eliade, was not especially sanguine about the ability of formal religion to recognise the sacred in secular society. Writing about the youth culture of the 1960s, Eliade commented that the religious impulse was making a new and genuine appearance in the cultural forms of the day, but that religious tradition seemed incapable of recognising it:

> In the most radically secularised societies and among the most iconoclastic contemporary youth movements (such as the hippy movement, for example), there are a number of apparently non-religious phenomena in which one can decipher new and original recoveries of the sacred; although, admittedly, they are not recognisable as such from a Judeo-Christian perspective.[14]

The fact that religious tradition fails to recognise another expression of the religious instinct is hardly a recent phenomenon. The old religious form often despises the new, not only because the new revelation challenges the authority of the old, but because the old religion thinks of itself as complete and absolute. Religion is sometimes 'full of itself', and this is what Paul Tillich, the influential theologian, referred to accurately as 'the sin of religion'.[15]

The ruling tradition in any era does not grasp the fact that if God is alive and active in the world, then God will be creative in the world, beckoning us to new transformations. The old tradition may in some ways prefer God to be 'dead', because then the sacred body of God can be laid out, dissected by systematic theologians and pedants, and pinned down in precise and scientific ways. But if God is alive, our experience of the sacred is going to be uncertain, creative, imprecise and full of surprise and astonishment. If God is alive, God will always be revealed as mysterious, unknowable and unable to be contained and captured.

RISING WATER IN THE WASTELAND

We might get a better understanding of our present predicament if we return to the metaphor of spiritual water and explore it for its social meaning. In 1867, in the poem 'Dover Beach', Matthew Arnold proclaimed that the 'sea of faith' was at low tide, and seemed to be ebbing away from the dry land of consciousness.

> The Sea of Faith
> Was once, too, at the full, and round earth's shore
> Lay like the folds of a bright girdle furled.
> But now I only hear
> Its melancholy, long, withdrawing roar,
> Retreating, to the breath
> Of the night-wind, down the vast edges drear
> And naked shingles of the world.[16]

Arnold laments the sadness and misery wrought by the sudden loss of faith in his day. It had been replaced with natural science, economics, and a positivist belief in progress and social advancement.

Today, I would argue, we are in the opposite situation. We are at high tide again, only the sea is somewhat chaotic and unruly, the water is murky and polluted, and it is not the crystal clear water of spirit that could be recognised by an ethical religion or a puritanical awareness shaped by 19th-century religiosity. Our social scene is full to the brim with individual and esoteric spiritualities, with personal searches for meaning and sacredness, most of which bear little resemblance to the conventional experience of religious faith. The waters of the spirit that subsided and withdrew during the secular period, are now rising with a tremendous force, perhaps even with a vengeance.

When I think about the dramatic rise of popular spirituality in our world, I sometimes think about the flooding of a river in a desert landscape. When I was a boy growing up in the arid regions of central Australia, I occasionally witnessed a wonderful phenomenon. After we had experienced significant rains and storms near Alice Springs, the normally dry and sandy bed of the Todd River would suddenly be transformed into a raging torrent, and the people of the town would behold the mystery of a gushing stream rising up from what seemed like nowhere. The high school I attended stood on the banks of the river bed, and after storms we sometimes received an announcement from the headmaster that we were to walk quickly and quietly to the banks of the Todd, to watch the river coming into flood. This might occur only once or twice a year. During drought the river might not flow for several years. It was a spectacular and unusual event, which brought a great sense of renewal to the town and its people.

We were told by our geography teachers that the Todd River was actually flowing all the time, but that we could not see it. Just below the ground and beyond our sight, there were bodies of moving water or underground streams, and in times of flood the water-table would rise from its subterranean depths and become a visible river. Students and workers alike would cheer, whistle and applaud when the wall of water appeared. To the people of the town this was something of a mystical experience, a kind of apparition, and a dramatic event that brought excitement, interest and unity to the district.

CYCLES OF THE SPIRIT

I am reminded of the flooding Todd River when I think of the rising waters of spirituality. After a long season of spiritual dryness, in which faith and intuition have atrophied, a new river of spiritual possibility is rising from below, with potentially great benefits to society and life. The river of spiritual life is paradoxical. In one sense it is always present and available to those who wish to gather at its banks, but sometimes whole societies and periods of time choose not to see it or be replenished by it. This rhythmic cycle of spiritual life is something that has puzzled many philosophers, including Hegel, Nietzsche and Derrida. Hegel wrote about our contemporary thirst for spiritual water in these terms:

> The spirit is profoundly desiccated, and like a wanderer in the desert it craves for the merest mouthful of water. By the little which can thus satisfy the needs of the human spirit we can measure the extent of its loss.[17]

In his recent essay, 'Faith and Knowledge', the French philosopher Jacques Derrida speaks of 'the return of the religious', of 'its interminable and ineluctable return'.[18] The reasons for the strange appearance and disappearance of spirit are many, but postmodern thinkers are recognising that spirit is on its way back again.

In the past, our spiritual water was contained by, and made visible in, religious rituals, liturgies and sacred observances. Indeed, the word 'ritual' is from Latin *ritus*, meaning 'to flow, run, rush or stream'. A 'rite' is a river; *rivus*, a rushing stream. As Thomas Moore said, 'To be in ritual is to be in the river', and to gather in sacred community is to gather at the river.[19] In religious rituals, we are told of the living water that we do not see, but which, once we allow ourselves to taste it, would give us eternal life and replenish our souls. The widespread demise of religion throughout the educated countries of the world has brought with it a great impoverishment and aridity to the human soul, which thirsts again for living water. The river of spirit is becoming evident partly because our resistances are breaking down and our thirst is so great.

MURKY WATER AND THE RETURN OF THE REPRESSED

According to St John the Divine, the revelation of the glory of God on earth will be occasioned by rising waters of spiritual life:

> Then the angel showed me the river of the water of life, rising from the throne of God and of the Lamb, and flowing crystal-clear down the middle of the city street.

(Revelation 22:1)

I can see spiritual waters flowing down our city streets today, but our waters are not clear. As those who live in desert areas know, a river that bursts into flood, after leading a life below the surface, carries ahead of it a lot of froth and bubble, brown debris and murkiness. The rising water pushes ahead trash that had been dropped in the dry river bed, and the water is, for many hours and days, brown, colloidal and full of silt and dirt. The river of spiritual interest in our society is also murky, dark, impure, and certainly not 'crystal-clear'. But that is no reason why religion should not take up a dialogue with it. Formal religion looks at the murky stream rising in secular society, and it is inclined to throw up its arms in horror and cry, 'God help us'.

What we are witnessing is the return of the repressed, and such a return, as Freud knew, is anything but glamorous or civilised.[20] What Freud discovered about the repression of sexuality can just as easily be applied to the repression of spirituality. As the visionary Marxist, Joel Kovel, has said: 'The denial of spirituality, like any form of denial, tends to distort spirit'.[21] The return of the repressed is not a pretty sight, and it is attended by many distortions and aberrations. We must be patient and sift through the mess to the potential within it.

As we stood on the banks of the Todd River and craned our heads to see the miracle of water, it was not all romantic or mystical. We could see empty cans and bottles bobbing in the froth and foam, together with plastic bags, used condoms, and other odd bits of rubbish. It is the same with our spiritual river today. Many of our emerging spiritual impulses and ideas are archaic, malformed, nascent or ugly. These longings have been buried for centuries, and many have acquired a 'gothic' appearance. Some have reverted to archaisms of the past and are premodern, uneducated and silly. When cultural contents are buried, they often regress to the ancient past, which Freud referred to as the atavistic regression to type. That is, contents that are repressed seem to turn 'primitive', so that when spirit is repressed we will notice its reappearance in forms that take us back to ages past. Hence the popularity today of archaic and esoteric forms of spirit that predate modernity by thousands of years.

We see this especially in the New Age spiritual interests and industries, some of which are positively infantile and deeply regressed.[22] By 'infantile', I mean that the world of the spirit is taken literally, as a kind of supernatural wonderworld similar to that imagined by late night television shows. And some New Age methods are regressive, in that they strive for the extinction of consciousness and its problems in an oceanic realm of bliss. The New Age movement is to some extent a parody of the Coming Age, and in this movement we see the most nascent, literal and crude interpretations of the living spirit. However, we must not condemn the New Age movement, but strive to educate it beyond its crudity. We must not condemn the river because of the rubble and mess it is forced to carry.

What wells up from secular society is not dressed in the costume of formal religion, but sometimes seems to draw on pre-theological contents. Hence in popular spirituality, we find people who are interested in primordial religious movements, in ancient esoteric sects, in long-forgotten initiatory or mystery cults. There is great interest in indigenous tribal religions, in paganism and wicca, in ancient Egypt, Greece and Tibet, in hermeticism, alchemy and astrology, and in long-buried divinatory systems and gnostic traditions. These ancient realities do not emerge from the secular unconscious as pure spiritual contents, but they come tinged with our narcissism and power-drives, with impure motives and consumerist desires. In the New Age market of technologies, everything is filtered through our pathologies and complexes, and is designed to appeal to egotism and pride. There are gems of wisdom buried there, but they are contaminated with infantilism and encrusted with hubris. The task of religion is not to stand on dignity and rail against the inferiority of spirituality. Instead, it has to get down to ordinary experience and build bridges of communication between the new flood and traditional mystery.

DANGER IN THE WATER

In his essay 'The spiritual problem of modern man', Jung offered an explanation for the rise of spirit in our time which is of interest, especially in view of the metaphor of the rising waters and their freight of 'rubble':

> Through his scepticism [about the rational organisation of the world] modern man is thrown back on himself; his energies flow towards their source, and the collision washes to the surface those psychic contents which are at all times there, but lie hidden in the silt so long as the stream flows smoothly in its course.[23]

Under stable social conditions, our energies move outward into life and the world, and the 'heavier' contents fall to the bottom of the stream of life and 'lie hidden in the silt'. But when our forward flow is blocked by disappointment, wars, depression and doubt, then our energies 'flow towards their source', libido is reversed, and the 'collision' between our introversion and life's stream 'washes to the surface' those psychic contents that normally lie hidden.

This is a fascinating argument as to why spirituality should arise at critical periods of history, indicating that spirituality is not itself a sign of decadence or decay, but a consequence of enforced inwardness and the withdrawal of hopes and dreams from the world. This also gives us a psychological basis for the sudden lifting of the bans against the spiritual dimension of life. The lifting of these bans is not actually our own conscious doing, rather we are reluctantly forced to lift them because there is so much 'new' material that is rising up from within, compelling us to take notice of what we would normally forget.

Although Jung was viewed as a mystic or romantic by his Freudian detractors, he certainly held no romantic illusions about what was being brought to the surface by our inner turmoil. He saw clearly the murkiness, darkness and danger of the post-Christian unconscious, as he wrote in his essay on the Aquarian Age, in *Aion*:

> **What is now welling up from the unconscious [is] the end-result of the development of Christian consciousness. This end-result is a false spirit of arrogance, hysteria, woolly-mindedness, criminal amorality, and doctrinaire fanaticism, a purveyor of shoddy spiritual goods, spurious art, philosophical stutterings, and Utopian humbug. That is what the post-Christian spirit looks like.**[24]

Jung recognised that the post-Christian unconscious was not a thing of beauty. It would take some getting used to, which is why he introduced the idea of 'befriending the shadow' as the first stage in the process of coming to terms with the unconscious.[25] 'To rediscover his spiritual life, modern man is obliged to struggle with evil, to confront his own shadow, to integrate the devil. There is no other choice.'[26] Jung would regard as delusional the idea that everything that issues from the unconscious is goodness and light.

But Jung would see some value in today's naive receptivity to the unconscious, recognising that what a learned person might dismiss as abhorrent or loathsome, as dangerous or bizarre, may have something of enduring value and worth, not only for the individual but for society. Jung wrote:

> In view of the present widespread interest in all sorts of psychic phenomena, an interest such as the world has not experienced since the last half of the seventeenth century, it does not seem beyond the range of possibility to believe that we stand on the threshold of a new spiritual epoch; and that from the depths of man's own psychic life new spiritual forms will be born.[27]

In an interview shortly before his death, Jung said:

> What comes next? Aquarius, the Waterpourer, the falling of water from one place to another. And the little fish receiving the water from the pitcher of the Waterpourer ... But there is danger in the water, on the banks.[28]

Jung understood that the water of spirit would become plentiful in the near future, that there would be a 'falling of water from one place to another', as expressed in the symbol of Aquarius. Yet he recognised 'danger in the water'. After the drought of reason and the desiccating heat of logos, we now face the opposite danger of spiritual flooding. T.S. Eliot wrote in 'Death by Water':

> A current under sea
> Picked his bones in whispers. As he rose and fell
> He past the stages of his age and youth
> Entering the whirlpool.[29]

This dangerous regression is now possible for civilisation as a whole, which may be returned to 'the stages of [its] age and youth'. There are signs already that we are going back to the infancy of civilisation in a bid to recover the sacred awareness that we lost when we decided we were too clever to believe in the gods. Religious fundamentalism is a foreboding sign of our cultural regression.

LACK OF CONTAINMENT

Spiritual water becomes dangerous when we have no containers to hold it, and no symbols to transform it. 'Spirituality', that is the careful and reflective art of developing a relationship with the sacred, cannot find its mature expression unless the water of spirit can be contained and transformed. 'Man today hungers and thirsts for a *safe* relationship to the psychic forces within himself.'[30] The safe containers of the spirit are the religious symbols, and until such time as we recover a shared, public spirituality, many of us will feel 'at sea' in the spiritual realm.

There is no guarantee that spiritual water will work towards the good, or lead to the benefit of the community. These waters can be unruly and disintegrative, especially when they well up from great depths and have been contaminated by repression. The waters of spirit need guidance and direction, to ensure that they work towards wholeness, rather than disintegration. If uncontained, such water can sweep through people's lives with uncanny force, leading to irrational behaviour.

Various kinds of fascism have expressed 'spiritual' movements, that is social myths of revival and renewal. They have employed spiritual language and used mystical ideas about blood, soil, race, and fatherland or motherland. Fascism, and others kinds of fanatical behaviour, including religious fundamentalism, racism and cults, are to be expected if spiritual energy is not transformed by culture, or guided into humane forms by tradition. If not recognised by culture, it will be taken by dangerous 'subcultures', who will exploit the spiritual vitality for power, corruption and domination. When the official culture loses its capacity to attract and hold spirit, the forces of evil and power appropriate the rising spirit and all hell breaks loose. Thus the response to the upwelling of spirit determines whether or not it will be a force for good.

SOCIAL VISION AND PUBLIC MORALITY

Spiritual energy can set society alight with enthusiasm, but such energy needs to be directed towards the good and history has shown that this is by no means automatic. Popular idealisation of spirit can mean a refusal to see danger, an inability to discern good spirits from bad, inundation from renewal, or safe from unsafe engagement with the spiritual world.

We are as naive and gullible about spirit today as we have been in the past about liberation ideologies and political programs. This is because we have transferred our idealism, hopes and dreams from one to the other. Now spirit, rather than politics, will bring liberation and deliver us from evil. Politics has failed, so we turn to spirit with the same innocent enthusiasm. We have a need to elevate an ideal beyond criticism. When spirit enjoys good press and public endorsement, it is almost impossible to say anything critical or discerning about it.

When spirit 'visits' us but we do not recognise what it is, we have a tendency to appropriate it for our own needs without due reverence for its origin or goal. Without a recognition of the sacred source from whence this energy comes, we inflate our own significance beyond normal boundaries. When this occurs, we do not become 'spiritual', but we become demonic and maniacal, that is, less rather than more human. The history of fascisms, cults and fanaticisms show the tragic results of outbreaks of spiritual energy that lacked a mature goal. We are candidates for such evil transformations today. We have plenty of spiritual water at our disposal but few ideas about what to do with it, contain it, transform it or use it for the benefit of others.

Our responsibility is to find a new social language for this spirituality, as well as to define community outlets, goals, objectives and possibilities for this energy. The responsibility lies with the educated, the informed and the tolerant to show leadership in this field, and to grasp the meaning and opportunity of spirituality in our time. New languages, understandings and practices need to be sought, so that 'spirituality' does not become another word for narcissism, fanaticism, or self-aggrandisement. When there is a rise in spiritual water, there must be a corresponding rise in public morality, social meaning and responsibility, otherwise we might remain the victims of a flooding rather than the emissaries of life-giving renewal. We urgently require spiritual knowledge, education and culture so that we develop a creative relationship with spirit rather than become possessed by it.

CHAPTER 2

Spirit without form

Every day people are straying away from the church and going back to God.

Lenny Bruce[31]

A statement often heard these days, particularly from young people but by no means confined to them, is, 'I am not a very religious person, but I am interested in spirituality'.

I have heard this said throughout Australia, Britain and Europe, and Sandra Schneiders reports that the same remark, reflecting 'intense interest in spirituality and alienation from religion' is 'often expressed' in North America.[32] It would have seemed puzzling a couple of generations ago, when much of Western society was embraced by religious tradition, and when the distinction between religion and spirituality would not have been understood in this way.

In the past, spirituality was felt to be the living, emotional core of religion, and those who were 'very' religious were often said to be 'spiritual'. Today, those who are '*not* very' religious are claiming to be spiritual. What has happened in society and culture to bring about this radical split? Why have religion and spirituality, or religious practice and religious feeling, parted company, and what is lost and gained by this splitting?

SPIRIT AGAINST FORM

In philosophical terms, we are reporting on a cultural crisis in which 'spirit' has been divorced from its traditional 'form'. Spirit without form is free and spontaneous, but it is also invisible, and of ambiguous social value since it is difficult to harness something invisible for the common good. We live in a time in which form is discounted and spirit is highly valued. Form, we often hear, merely hides or disguises spirit. We have to tear away the form and allow spirit to be set free.

But form is not just a hindrance or encumbrance, it allows the spirit to be shaped, expressed and experienced. Without form, spirit wanders shapeless and without coherent expression. It turns occult, invisible, and has to be hinted at or inferred by abstract concepts. Form is not just an added extra, or a hollow presence or mask, but an organ of the spirit. It is how spirit shapes, contains and reveals itself.

Our time undervalues form because there is a perceived rift between religious forms and the intuited reality of spirit. At least, this is the impression I have received over years of discussions with students, and in books dealing with this subject. Spirit is felt to be spontaneous, freely available and democratically structured, whereas religion is perceived to be doctrinal, regulated and authoritarian. Spirit is felt to be holistic and urging us towards wholeness and completion, whereas religion is perceived to be promoting perfection, one-sidedness and imbalance. There are numerous other rifts and divisions which I will explore in a moment. But my point here is that when form no longer expresses 'spirit' as intuited by the age, it is mercilessly discarded, and its sacred status is forgotten or even repressed. There is little regard for the fact that spirit once took up residence in this form, and little feeling extended to, in T.S. Eliot's words, the 'heap of broken images'[33] in the contemporary junkyard of symbolic forms.

THE MAGIC CIRCLE OF RELIGION AND THE INNER CORE OF SPIRITUALITY

In stable cultural times, spirit is successfully contained by symbolic forms, and spirit is 'at home' in religious tradition. In unstable times, the symbolic forms are experienced as constraining, limiting or anachronistic, and spirit struggles to break free from tradition. Ours is a critical and unstable period, in which spirit frequently reverts to informal or non-religious expressions, and it is therefore hard to see, discern or measure. When spirituality is no longer 'religious', sociologists declare the times to be secular,[34] but psychologists and therapists report a great deal of religious feeling often 'buried' in the inner lives of individuals.[35]

In stable societies, religion is like a magic circle that surrounds and nurtures our lives, binding us into indissoluble community and protecting us from potentially harmful incursions of the living spirit. In such times, we do not choose to belong to our religious tradition. We are simply 'born into' the religion of our parents and grandparents, are ritually inducted as an infant, and life moves ahead in its rhythms and cycles in an almost automatic, unconscious way. Our natal faith tradition relates to us like a cosmic parent, caring for our spiritual well-being and providing spiritual nourishment and support at every major life transition, including baptism, confirmation, marriage, the birth of children and death.

To question or doubt the validity of such all-inclusive religiousness is to risk one's place in the extended and immediate family, and to face the possibility of social ostracism, isolation and rejection. Religion is the very basis of our human identity, and our task is to keep the faith at all costs, to pray fervently, to maintain a devotional attitude to the creeds, and to support the spiritual authority of ministers or priests. If we do this well, and with perseverance and conviction, our souls will be cared for by religious tradition, and we need not have to risk a personal encounter with the spirit nor a 'fall into the hands of the living God' (Hebrews 10:31).

In stable times, spirituality is the personal and lived experience of the revealed mystery celebrated in religious services, prayers, liturgies and sacraments. Spirituality in this context is a unique, exclusive activity and a rare achievement. The majority of people are expected to lead normal lives in conformity with religious doctrine and guidelines, and are not encouraged to discover a personal relationship with God. But there are always some individuals who aspire to a higher life in communion with the spirit. This elite group generally aspire to a state of spiritual perfection in the lived experience of the spirit. As Sandra Schneiders writes, by the 19th century the term 'spirituality' referred to 'the practice of the interior life by those oriented to the life of perfection', and spirituality was radically distinguished from 'the ordinary life of faith'.[36]

TENSIONS BETWEEN CREATIVITY AND DEVOTION

We know that individual appropriations of the faith were regarded by the churches as a mixed blessing. In one sense, such personal experiences had the capacity to revivify and renew the tradition, and to give new direction and impulse to faith. But from an institutional point of view, individual experiences of the spirit could lead to variation and diversity that the churches might deem heretical or dangerous. For example, mystics like Meister Eckhart or Francis of Assisi were strongly criticised by authorities in their time, as they were felt to be departing from tradition. If spirituality led to new interpretations of faith that contrasted with or contradicted the dogmas of the church, they would be seen as a threat to the authority of the institution. Consequently, as Schneiders explained:

> The term 'spirituality' often carried pejorative connotations; it came to be associated with questionable enthusiasm or even heretical forms of spiritual practice in contrast to 'devotion', which placed a proper emphasis on sobriety and human effort.[37]

Devotion does not ask questions or raise doubts, but places the individual in a subordinate position to a mystery that the faith institutions seek to control. Spirituality might give new vitality and direction to the spirit, but if it comes at too high a price for the institution, spirituality is banned or even persecuted, leading to a perverse situation in which the church seeks to destroy the very thing that could bring it new life. Thus there is, even in relatively stable times, an essential and underlying tension between the spiritual core and the religious periphery and its over-arching tradition. The creative spirit is a headache for religious authorities, since it is sometimes iconoclastic, original and radical.

FORM AGAINST SPIRIT

In a creative culture, form and spirit are in constant dialogue with each other, and this conversation ensures the stability of religion and society alike. But when religious form stops having dialogue with the spirit, it becomes frozen, petrified and does not feel alive. Religions might shut out the spirit in a bid to bolster their own forms and give them eternal validity, but this attempt to eradicate change and to place form above the movements of the spirit has disastrous consequences. When religion sees itself as eternal and beyond change, this can lead to idolatry and bigotry, rather than to creative religiousness. For while God may be eternal, religion, as a cultural response to God, is necessarily subject to time and place, and cannot escape these realities.

God may be eternal in 'heaven', but 'on earth' God moves through the spirit and enters into the rhythms and cycles of nature and ever-changing creation. Spirit manifests as 'the spirit of place' and as 'the spirit of the time', that is as the mood, essence or dynamic of a particular period. A religion that seeks to emulate eternity, and to view itself as eternal, is a religion that cuts itself off from the changing moods and dynamics of its historical period. Most human institutions, such as law, science, medicine and education recognise the need to undergo revision in order to stay in touch with the historical process, but religion often sees itself as exempt. It sees its function as the imitation of the past, and tradition is sometimes understood as the endless repetition of past patterns. In this way, religion unwittingly makes itself 'irrelevant' to the time, because it deliberately chooses to ignore the rhythms and cycles that it views as dangerous and unsettling.

The living core of the spirit could revitalise religion and keep its forms supple and full of life, as the heart delivers oxygen and blood to the limbs and organs of the body. Religion resists this heart, and defends itself against it by developing defensive structures so that a thick wall is built around the creative spiritual core to prevent it from disrupting religious life. This wall consists mainly of a series of refusals: a refusal to listen to the spirit of the time, a refusal to engage the insights of poets, artists, visionaries and prophets, a refusal to change its moral attitudes and spiritual assumptions.

In isolating itself from the living core of spirit, religion eventually becomes lifeless and petrified, and no longer appears 'relevant' to contemporary culture. Jung wrote that 'Eternal truth needs a human language that alters with the spirit of the times'.[38] He also said, 'All the true things must change and only that which changes remains true'.[39] Religion acts unwisely if it moves against nature and considers itself above the laws of change. Eventually, it inhabits a kind of time-warp, and it clings to this state with some self-righteousness, believing it is upholding and representing the will of God.

In this posture, religion commits a sin of hubris and, like anything inflated, can be punctured or humbled by the realities of time and history. Creative theologians can identify the problem and even call for change, as does Paul Tillich: 'We must pray for the prophetic spirit which has been dead for so long in the churches'.[40] But the creative minds are marginalised, along with the prophetic spirit for which they hope and pray.

THE EXPLODING CORE OF SPIRIT

Formal religion can repress certain realities for a time, but eventually the walled-in city of the spirit begins to hit back, and a kind of civil war breaks out in the human psyche and in the social experience of meaning. Religion and the spirit of the time, which in creative cultures are complementary, turn against each other and warfare begins. The thing that 'eternal' religion rejects, namely time and history, begins to attack it, and in this predicament, as W.B. Yeats wrote:

> Things fall apart; the centre cannot hold;
> Mere anarchy is loosed upon the world.[41]

When religion has repeatedly refused to respond to changing times, the spiritual centre of civilisation becomes active and volatile. The centre 'cannot hold' and begins to explode its former boundaries. Disruptive spiritual energy seeks outlet and expression at various points of weakness or vulnerability in the religious culture. Such energy searches the formerly settled and stable surface of society with great interest, hoping to expose its errors and limitations to bring about its demise. Today, secular newspapers and journalists are constantly looking for the points of vulnerability and weakness in the religious formal edifice, always seeking a chance of destabilisation.

These volcanic eruptions are naturally viewed as hostile by religion, which represents them as undermining the churches and destructive to society. But to progressives and revolutionaries, these disruptions are seen as blows for freedom and as advances of the human spirit. When the centre cannot hold, it typically accuses religion of being 'man-made' rather than instituted by God. Religious dogmas, ideas, assumptions and attitudes are seen as artificial and socially constructed, as vehicles of social ideology rather than of divine revelation. The new wine accuses the old wineskins of being inadequate, repressive and restricting.

Here are some of the strongest and most fundamental criticisms that the present age has of the dogmatic structures of religion.

- Religion is patriarchal and masculinist; it appears to be made by men to further their own power. It oppresses women and undermines their authority; represses the feminine element in men, and excludes the feminine dimension of the divine.
- Religion is based on a pre-modern cosmology and an archaic vision of reality that can no longer be believed. Its God is externalist and interventionist, inhabiting a distant metaphysical space and performing actions that are no more credible to us today than the thunderbolt temper-tantrums of Zeus or Jupiter upon Mt Olympus.
- Religion is based on a conception of spirit that is supernatural. Spirit is conceived as an outside agency that works miracles and wonders with a 'kingdom' in another reality. It seems wholly implausible and unattractive to modern understanding.
- Religion is otherworldly and transcendentalist. It does not have enough to say about the experience of the sacred in creation. It does not teach us how to live harmoniously with nature but to have power and 'dominion' over the earth. In our time of ecological crisis, what can a human-centred religion contribute to the survival of the planet?
- Religion seeks perfection as its goal, but the contemporary era has found perfection to be unrealistic, dangerously one-sided and even anti-life. Instead, our time seeks 'wholeness' as its goal, an altogether more complex and paradoxical conception, but one which seems to be in accord with our most basic and spiritual impulses.
- Religion is dualistic and instructs the spirit to triumph over the body and its vital desires, but new spirituality seeks to bring spirit and body, sacredness and sexuality, together in a redemptive experience of the totality and mystery of life.
- Religion is hierarchical and elitist. It rules from above, and excludes the voice of the people and democratic understanding. Religion belongs to a former era in which spiritual authority was invested in authority figures, priests, bishops, clergy, and people freely gave authority to such figures. Now we want to own such

authority for ourselves, and for two reasons: the inner authority of conscience and spirit is compelling, and people no longer trust old authority figures.

- Religion is dogmatic and external to our lives. It imposes laws and rules upon us, without enquiring into the nature of the self that it is transforming. It does not offer a psychology or pathway by which the individual can be transformed, but simply demands that the person conform to devotional practices.

- Religion imposes the 'big story' of theology upon our experience, without exploring the 'little stories' of our individual biographies, which might give theology a foothold in our lives. Religion is rejected not because a person does not believe, but because he or she is not believed. If religion expanded its horizons to include the spirituality of individuals, it might be renewed by such expansion, and individuals would not feel excluded, pushed out or irrelevant.

- Religion is fused with the social establishment and too identified with business, government and commercial enterprise to be able to offer a critique of this world. It does not allow for the true radicality of the spirit, which is always 'at odds' with worldliness. Religion does not provide enough challenge to society, but simply reinforces and supports its basic values and, as such, it cannot represent the life of the spirit.

These criticisms wound and puncture the body of religion, and arise from the volcanic core that religion has sought to repress. The criticisms have more vitality and energy-potential than religion has reserves or defences to withstand these attacks. The attacks are therefore fatal to religion, which loses credibility and integrity as each criticism makes its 'reasonable' protest and interrogation.

In this revolutionary crisis, religion and spirituality change places, and 'spirituality', as defined by the mood of the time, becomes the new higher authority and the arbiter of social identity and human interaction. But the new spirituality is not organised by any institution, and therefore its actions and developments often have a chaotic, random or haphazard character. Indeed, it appears to the former, highly organised religious culture that 'mere anarchy is loosed upon the world'. But the spirit of the time, although instinctual and unplanned, is not irrational, but follows an inner logic of its own.

A NEW PARADIGM: ALL-INCLUSIVE SPIRITUALITY

In the new cultural paradigm, which has been taking shape for some time, 'spirituality' bursts free from its former confinement, and becomes a much larger field of human activity. 'Spirituality' is the new, broad, umbrella term, and the understanding of the term 'religion' shrinks and is more narrowly defined. The term today is equated with formal religious practice or church attendance. It has lost its more general meaning, referring to the larger context of our relations with the divine and the community.

'Spirituality' now refers to our relationship with the sacredness of life, nature, and the universe, and this relationship is no longer felt to be confined to formal devotional practice or to institutional places of worship. As time moves on, we find we are able to define spirituality less and less, because it includes more and more, becoming a veritable baggy monster containing a multitude of activities and expectations.

Spirituality has become diverse, plural, manifold, and seems to have countless forms of expression, many of which are highly individualistic and personal. Spirituality is now for everyone, and almost everyone seems to be involved, but in radically different ways. It is an inclusive term, covering all pathways that lead to meaning and purpose. It is concerned with connectedness and relatedness to other realities and existences, including other people, society, the world, the stars, the universe and the holy. It is typically intensely inward, and most often involves an exploration of the so-called inner or true self, in which divinity is felt to reside.

Significantly, the new spirituality is democratic and non-hierarchical, which is alien to the traditional forms of religious life. If a parent/child model governed the old religion, together with an authoritarianism underpinning this top-down style, the new paradigm is ruled by a sibling model of brotherhood or sisterhood, in which every person is felt to be equal in the eyes of the holy. Our spiritual lives are no longer ruled by bishops and clergy, but by our own inward conscience, by insights gleaned from self-reflection, reading, meditation, and talks with friends and spiritual counsellors. This is the new style of spiritual culture, and is exemplified clearly in the experiences of youth, as discussed later.

Spirituality in this new context is a form of personal religion that has gone through various social revolutions—democratic, governmental, political, racial, sexual and intellectual. Many people had hoped that communal religion would pass through these social revolutions, and they waited anxiously for a faith tradition to catch up with the times so that they could link their own faith with the tradition. But because religion has not gone through these revolutions, people have acted independently and created a new revolutionary religious concept, a kind of people's religion called spirituality. Although willed into existence by a collective aspiration, new spirituality is not collective, but is a personal experience. This is both its triumph and, of course, its severe limitation.

EMPTY CHURCHES, CROWDED PATHWAYS

While only a tiny minority of people continue to practise formal religion in the developed nations of the world, huge numbers are keenly pursuing spirituality and individual pathways to sacred meaning. Creative theologians and religious thinkers such as Sandra Schneiders are obviously alert to the spiritual revolution that has taken place, and seek to describe its changing contents and contours:

> The term 'spirituality' no longer refers exclusively or even primarily to prayer and spiritual exercises, much less to an elite state or superior practice of Christianity. Rather, from its original reference to the 'interior life' of the person, usually a cleric or religious, who was 'striving for perfection', for a life of prayer and virtue that exceeded in scope and intensity that of the 'ordinary' believer, the term has broadened to connote the whole of the life of faith and even the life of the person as a whole, including its bodily, psychological, social and political dimensions.[42]

Theologian John Heagle has similarly attempted to define the new cultural paradigm, and to summarise the major differences between old and new concepts of spirituality. The old spirituality, at the core of formal religion, 'was theoretical, elitist, otherworldly, ahistorical, anti-secular, individualistic, concentrated on the interior life and perfection'. By contrast, Heagle argues:

> the emerging spirituality of our age is intensely personal
> without being private. It is visionary without being theoretical.
> It is prophetic without being partisan, and it is incarnational
> without becoming worldly. It emphasises personal response and
> interior commitment but it radically changes the context within
> which this response takes place.[43]

Many theological commentators point to the major characteristics of the new spirituality: the new is creation-centred without being pagan, sexually alert without being pornographic, holistic without being sentimental, and personal without being private.

We are concerned with a radically new and surprising experience of spirit, and yet it is a version that is close to the original conception of spirituality. It is only 'new' because religious tradition lost touch with the unitary experience of spirit-and-life at some point in its historical development. The curse, 'May you live in interesting times' is relevant to our time, in which the churches are emptying and yet the pathways of spiritual discovery are crowded and full of activity. The time is rife with spiritual opportunities and challenges, and anyone with understanding or insight is in great public demand. Speakers who address spirituality with integrity and depth find themselves flooded with invitations in today's needy climate.

Whether the new spirituality is a result of people power or commercial power is a question worth posing, especially in light of the proliferation of New Age industries and marketing networks. Such commercial industries thrive on the appearance of individualistic, do-it-yourself, free-floating spirituality, and see the demise of collective faith as a business opportunity. Many people feel that they have liberated themselves from the control of the churches, but some have placed themselves in the hands of the commercial interests that patrol the new spiritual waters like sharks in the sea. Our free-floating and formless spiritual hunger can be ruthlessly exploited and manipulated by those who see the crisis as an opportunity to make money and win prestige. There are more false prophets than true prophets in today's world, and most people who claim to be prophets are almost by definition not. The title of prophet is best awarded by others, rather than claimed by oneself.

GAINS AND LOSSES

We have experienced a revolution of the spirit, in which spiritual authority has been placed in the hands of the individual person and his or her conscience. Many celebrate the new dispensation, but we have brought upon our heads many serious problems, some of which are ignored or repressed in a bid to emphasise the positives.

To some extent we have merely exchanged the authority of the churches for the dubious authority of New Age industries. But there are more subtle levels of entrapment and despair. The spirituality revolution assumes that the individual knows best, and that to gain personal control of our spiritual lives is the desired outcome. This attitude is a product of individualism, an ideology that keeps us wedded to the idea of the individual who is independent of culture and apart from tradition. This ideology promises 'freedom' from tradition, but when this freedom is attained, we do not feel liberated, only alienated.

Individualism leads to isolation and loneliness because it encourages us to think of ourselves as self-sufficient and self-enclosed, whereas we are deeply communal creatures who need the support and communality of others. Freud, Jung, and especially Adler felt that a person could only achieve full potential and individuation in creative relationship with others.

Moreover, the idea that 'spirit' is some kind of personal possession or inward endeavour is a curious myth of our time. Poetry and philosophy indicate that spirit is universal and collective: it is a shared experience, and cannot be confined to the narrow limits of the personal self. To go deeply into spirit is to be led into universality, away from subjectivity towards the world and the objective life of the spirit.

We are wrongly assuming that because spirit is experienced 'within' ourselves, spirit is somehow intrinsically introspective and even subjective. The inward journey, if followed with commitment and courage, leads us through and beyond our subjective lives, because the spirit 'within' us is the same spirit that is found in everything else. To encounter the spirit within the psyche is to encounter a reality that longs for involvement with others, and this spirit is not truly satisfied unless it has found communion with the world and exchange with other people. Therefore, the idea of a 'private' spirituality is somehow fraudulent and deceptive. It is a powerful modern myth, linked to ideas of egoic liberation, but the personal domain is experienced by the spirit as a solitary confinement.

This is where *form* proves to be more central to the experience of spirit than we had realised, and more important than contemporary fashion would suggest. Without form, spirit does not know how to reach out to others, nor how to express itself in communal or social activities. In walking away from religious tradition, the modern seeker turns his or her back on the symbolic forms that provide or contain shared meaning, memory and the experience of belonging to a sacramental community. These are great assets of the spirit and a high price to pay if we renounce form and go in search of a new spirit. Some people manage to create or invent new spiritual communities, and to provide a different or alternative sense of memory by attaching themselves to unconventional, non-Western, esoteric or psychological and therapeutic traditions. But the new attempts at belonging, however courageous or well intended, are mostly fragile, transient and easily destroyed by egotism, power play and personal differences, because they are not grounded in the earth of one's own society. New attempts at community, based on spiritual precepts, start off with high hopes but frequently end in tragedy when the all-too-human side appears.

The contemporary experience of the spirit is built upon shifting sands and constant change, because it is unsupported by forms that afford containment and security. Such experience can be savage and wild, and yet I continue to meet people, especially young people, who deny that this is so, and who emphasise the freedom and fun of the new situation. Perhaps it is exciting as long as the good times roll on, but when tragedy strikes or the adventuring spirit is depleted, the rawness and lack of containment will be sorely felt. Eventually, the modern seeker is forced to discover peace within the self, because everything outside is whirling and chaotic. The self, and its deep recesses of quiet wisdom, is often the only refuge we have against the howling storms of spiritual movement and social alienation. This is why meditation, retreat and autobiographical reflection have become important features of the postmodern landscape. We have to protect peace of mind and sanity in the face of our own spiritual anarchy.

RELIGIONS AS SUBSETS OF THE SPIRITUAL

In the new cultural paradigm, religion is no longer singular but plural. 'Religions', Western and Eastern, modern and ancient, have been downgraded to subsets of the broader category of spirituality. They are no longer *a priori* givens, but are options or choices that one makes as one advances along the spiritual journey. At the core of the new paradigm are clusters of religions, and these are 'used' for personal insight or for deepening the spiritual pursuit. Society does not regard any one religion as better or greater than another, and Christianity, which for centuries had believed itself to be the greatest of all, has been dealt an almost fatal blow to its pride. Christianity has had to embark on a massive attempt to reposition itself in the new, plural world of many faiths and competing truths. Its fundamentalism and absolutism will always be in question from now on and subject to rigorous scrutiny and opposition from within, by its best and most creative theologians, and from without, by its most vigorous critics.

People no longer feel obliged to remain loyal to one religious tradition or denomination, but tend to roam widely across the spectrum. Schneiders writes:

> Whatever else can be said, it is no longer the case in the first
> world that most people are initiated from childhood into a
> family religious affiliation and remain within it for a lifetime,
> never seriously questioning its validity and, in turn, passing it on
> to their own offspring.[44]

Instead of the uniform stability of the past, we find a sense of continuous movement across traditions, as people replace loyalty to their natal faith with a new kind of loyalty to their inner striving or personal spiritual quest.

One is no longer born into a particular faith, remaining true to that tradition. Rather, if one enters a religious path at all, it is because one chooses to be inducted. St Paul originally 'put on' Christ, but we no longer 'put on' religion, we 'try it on' for size and taste. If we are not satisfied we become detached and critical or move out and onwards. If the inner striving seems to require contact with a new religious community, we move on according to these promptings. Or people choose a ritual or liturgy from one tradition, and a sacred text or scriptural source from another, supplementing, as it were, their fund of spiritual intuition with a selection of insights and images.

THE CULTURE OF PICK AND MIX

Plurality, diversity and choice continues to be denounced by religious traditions as fickleness, faithlessness and promiscuity. If you pick and mix, the traditions say, you will end up with a confusing array of conflicting ideas and views. This is found not only in the hostility to ecumenicalism in many traditions but also in their intolerance toward young people's experimentation with spiritual paths and views. The old religions still view 'loyalty' in its external or institutional sense, meaning loyalty to a single tradition. The fact that people might be 'loyal' to an inner spiritual process or quest is not recognised or, if seen, not sufficiently respected.

The era of diversity is upon us, no matter how distasteful it may appear to tradition. While I understand this jaundiced response, it is also true that syncretism, plurality and choice are not going to diminish now that people have broken free from old religious constraints. It is no use lamenting the postmodern condition now that it has become the norm. People see themselves as inhabiting a complex, fragmented world, in which they have to gradually 'piece together' the puzzle of their lives and sacred reality. The very breadth and scope of the newly defined sense of spirit gives people the support and moral backing to move across a wide spectrum of religious and historical possibilities. Since spirit is 'in everything', it can be 'found everywhere'. The sacred is no longer experienced in one's own little corner of the world.

To call for 'purity' in a racial context, or in a social and ethnic matter, is greeted with suspicion and scorn. There is usually another agenda behind the call, a desire to impose order or old-world values upon the new. A closer look can reveal a disenfranchised political hierarchy longing for power in a society that has slipped out of its control. The religious opposition to spiritual diversity can be seen in this light, as a final attempt by disenfranchised authorities to bring the people back into the fold. This is tactfully disguised as moral instruction about what is 'good' for our spiritual health, and what we ought to do to live more fulfilling lives. But unless our own experiences teach us otherwise, it is better for the time being to regard such calls for purity and loyalty with some suspicion, as the remnant cries of an imperial religion trying to bolster itself with moral defences.

The traditional sense of belonging to one specific interpretation of the world not only runs counter to the new experience of diversity and social plurality, but is also contrary to the modern experience of education, based as it is on the scientific method. Educated people have been taught by science to observe the world, to develop a hypothesis, to test the hypothesis against reality, and to draw conclusions. It is hardly surprising if many of us begin to live our spiritual lives according to this same pattern, by looking at our own needs and the various world religions in terms of what makes sense to us and what can be concluded by our experimentation. We 'test' the claims of religion against reality as we see it, and against our emotional and intuitive responses, and we draw conclusions based on these observations. We also recognise that this process and our conclusions may change in time as our needs and inner demands change.

What is berated by religious conservatives as 'pick and mix' could be the logical and necessary application of the scientific method to our spiritual experiences. Rather than seeing this behaviour as disloyalty or faithlessness, it could be reconfigured through the lens of science in a radically different way; as a sign that people are taking their spiritual lives seriously, and applying the best criteria they know to the lived experience of the spiritual life. The point of being outside the magic circle of religion, and in a new world governed by different values, is that one has to use one's own conscience as guide.

RELATIVITY AND RELATIVISM

The great danger of plurality is not the claim that we are sure to lose the 'purity' of a single tradition, but that we might end up sliding into a radical relativism in which no religious forms or differences are upheld, and where nothing matters because every revelation is 'as good as' any other. Here we need to make a distinction between relativity and relativism. Relativity shows us that the sacred is greater and more mysterious than any one religious revelation or cultural manifestation. Relativity indicates that all religious systems are to some extent 'productions' of time, place and history, and that when we enter into any religious system we are necessarily participating in the historical and social influences of that system. Relativity, however, does not deny that the sacred is present in the religious system, nor that if we dig deeply into any authentic tradition we are sure to reach the reality of the holy.

Relativism, on the other hand, tends to deny the presence of the sacred in all religious systems, and sees them all as mere products of society, culture, politics, power and 'functionality'. In this style of reductionism, the sacred is nowhere to be found, because religions are human constructs designed to make sense of a basically meaningless world. Relativism is the dangerous product of a lazy mind and a lack of imagination. It is the revenge of 'common sense' against the reality and presence of the sacred. Relativism is notoriously attractive to those who find themselves confused by the plethora of religious manifestations and their competing claims—in one sweep of a partially educated mind, all is declared to be human construction. Relativism does not look for, and therefore does not see, the ways in which the sacred has broken into all authentic meaning systems, giving them elements of truth and affording them glimpses of divine reality. It is not a spiritual response to plurality, but an imposition of an old-world reductive materialism upon the reality of a plural world.

PART 2

Youth

spirituality

CHAPTER 3

Going to the underground stream

The highest good is like water.
Water gives life . . . and does not strive.
It flows in places men reject
And so it is like the Tao.

Tao Te Ching

Noticing the existence of youth spirituality is one of the most precious and unexpected gifts of my academic career as a university teacher in the humanities. It is like discovering an underground stream beneath the often dry and sometimes barren academic landscape, and if we have eyes to see and ears to hear we can go to this underground stream and be replenished by it.

I teach in a literature department at La Trobe University in Melbourne, but I have been actively involved in interdisciplinary areas, and have taught courses in the psychology of culture and consciousness. I began to notice signs of spirituality in my students about fifteen years ago. These were vague and indistinct at first, and included hearing the word 'spirituality' used occasionally in tutorials and discussions. These signs seemed remarkable in the context of my secular university setting, and were doubly incongruent because most students using this language were not religious and had not been brought up by religious families.

The appearance of a partly submerged spiritual current in some of my students had a catalytic effect on my own imagination. I began to reflect: What if I set up a new course called 'Spirituality' and made it widely available to undergraduates from a broad range of disciplines? Who would come? What would happen? What would we study? How would we manage the balancing act between academic knowledge and emotional and affective awareness? Spirituality is not just a cerebral activity, but involves feeling, intuition, and emotional areas of human experience. At this point in my career, I was looking for something different, for a sense of challenge, and my intellectual life was dry and in need of moistening.

In 1999, I drew up proposals for a new course which would be called 'Spirituality and Rites of Passage'. This course is available to first year students in the Bachelor of Arts degree, and it operates in the literature program of the Faculty of Humanities. In a recent development, the course has also been added to the subject list of a new Bachelor of Pastoral Care, which is taught in the School of Public Health in the Faculty of Health Sciences. I have long felt that spirituality should be seen as a public health issue, and so this recent development has pleased me.

In the course I teach various kinds of spirituality, but deliberately steer away from the mainstream religions because 'religion' is not my direct concern. Rather, I seek to access and uncover something which is prior to religion. I teach Celtic, Aboriginal, Feminist, Romantic and secular spiritualities, using a number of literary and cultural texts as well as drawing on the experiences and intuitions of my students. For Celtic spirituality, the key work is *Anam Cara* by the contemporary Irish writer John O'Donohue.[45] For Aboriginal spirituality, the main reference is *Yorro, Yorro: Everything Standing Up Alive*, by the Aboriginal philosopher and lawman, David Mowaljarlai.[46] I explore the possibilities of a feminist spirituality in the visionary classic, *Surfacing* by the Canadian novelist Margaret Atwood.[47]

The loss and recovery of spiritual vision is studied in the Australian novel, *Tirra Lirra by the River* by Jessica Anderson.[48] Spiritual insights are gleaned from English Romantic poetry (using Wordsworth and Blake), and from other kinds of English poetry which explore spiritual themes in secular, non-religious or even atheist contexts (using Matthew Arnold, Thomas Hardy and Philip Larkin). I am also interested in the role of spirit in age-related transitions of human experience, and so the search for the sacred becomes an important theme in the context of rites of passage and transitional stages (using Mircea Eliade).[49]

This course attracted 70 students in its first year, 90 in its second, and 120 in its third. Each time I teach it, the course proves to be full of surprises and it takes unexpected twists and turns. The course has afforded me with many opportunities for insight and reflection on youth spirituality. Drawing on these experiences, I reflect in Chapter 4 on some of the problems that arise when youth spirituality meets the secular education system, and in Chapter 5 I look at the essential differences between youth spirituality and formal religion, and the tensions between them. In Chapter 6 I provide a serious but also humorous account of my own work as a spiritual educator, and in Chapter 7 I review typical experiences of young adults in their encounter with spirit.

But in this brief introductory chapter, I want to reflect poetically and philosophically on the meaning of youth spirituality, before tackling the problems that it poses for society and its institutions.

IN PLACES MEN REJECT

Youth spirituality is like an underground stream beneath our ordinary world, and yet this stream is rarely noticed. It keeps on flowing, but the life-giving waters are not utilised, tapped or directed into the dry places of our culture. Adult society marches ahead with a business-as-usual attitude, while the large volumes of spiritual water surge forwards silently, beneath notice, towards some unknown destination. As the Irish writer John O'Donohue says:

> Society functions in an external way, its collective eye does not
> know interiority, it sees only through the lens of image,
> impression and function.[50]

The eighth chapter of the *Tao Te Ching* opens with the passage quoted at the head of this chapter. It compares the Tao, or the Way, with life-giving water. Water, like the spirit, 'does not strive' but 'flows'. This is useful and cogent imagery, and helps us to contrast the spirit with the human ego and the power drive. The human ego 'strives' for its achievements, and striving, toil and labour define its character. However, to contact the spirit one has to let go of this striving ego and reduce our attachment to ordinary desires. The saying, 'Let go and let God' captures the essence of this process, but the art of letting go and of 'flowing' is not to be confused with mere passivity or inertia, as was often the case in 1960s spirituality. The art of attending to the spirit is a process requiring considerable concentration. Spiritual exercises such as prayer, meditation and contemplation are needed to pry us away from ordinary desires and connect us with a deeper will and purpose.

The *Tao Te Ching* warns that spiritual water flows 'in places men reject'. We do not understand the logic or meaning of this deeper reality, and are apparently unable to appreciate the extent to which our lives are dependent on the invisible currents that flow beneath our lives, and between ourselves and other lives. We are largely ignorant of the role of spirit in sustaining and nurturing us, and wisdom, scripture and prophecy are needed to remind us of this vital reality. A secular society is less able to respect the sacred currents in life than a religious one, and so today we need all the help we can get, from wisdom, literature, psychology, mysticism and philosophy, to remind us of the value and importance of turning to the spirit to be renewed.

YOUTH LIVING IN TWO WORLDS

The youth of any time or culture have a particular interest in the 'places men reject'. Their desire to rebel against the social establishment is often expressed as a natural interest in the tabooed or repressed areas of the spirit. But there are not many signposts or guides to facilitate their journey. Often young people have to 'feel' their own way, and rely on hunches, intuitions or unusual experiences to lead them in the direction of spirit. Dreams can also be an important guide, since dreams throw up buried or repressed areas of social experience, and in secular society our dreams are often intensely spiritual in nature.

Adults are rarely admitted to the half-secret world of youth spirituality, because this world is protected by a great many defences and barricades, lest the coldly rational light of adult consciousness destroys what is regarded by youth as incredibly important and too sensitive to be exposed to ridicule or disrespect. Adults seem to confuse spirituality with fantasy and escapism, not understanding the difference between a spiritual imagination that reveals more of reality, and a fantasy life that cloaks or disguises reality.

For the most part, youth have grown to accept that their interior spirituality and their outer lives are quite separate. In order to adjust to society and become successful in its terms, the inner life of the spirit often has to be bracketed out, forgotten or left undeveloped. Youth, like adults, learn to leave their underground stream in order to participate in life at the surface. Our society does not encourage them to divert their spiritual water to the surface, but instructs them to leave such mysteries to the depths and darkness of the underworld. Spirit is feared and shut out because it cannot readily be controlled or manipulated, nor can it be seen by the profane eye.

Hence, in modern society, we are encouraged to be divided, torn, to lead two lives, to forget the spirit and live entirely at the surface. Spirit is regarded as maladaptive in social terms, because it relates to a range of invisible forces and meanings that complicates the *normal* social experience. The spirituality revolution has to find a new 'normal'. The present concept is repressive of much human and emotional reality, and we can no longer place so much emphasis on 'fitting in' or 'adjusting' to norms when we realise that those norms are inadequate and need to be replaced.

FALLING OUT OF SOCIAL MEANING

Living on the social surface and denying the depths is only possible when the surface culture is able to sustain and nourish us. Society moves along fairly smoothly, if somewhat monotonously, while there are officially sanctioned myths, ideas, stories and ideologies that keep us bound securely to the social order. These myths and ideologies give us the impression or taste of meaning, even if the primal experience of the spirit and its power to renew our lives lies elsewhere. But when social myths and ideologies become hollow, or no longer sustain our interest or support, then the surface culture is radically weakened and undermined.

When 'social progress' is exposed as a fraud, or 'liberal capitalism' is seen as a euphemism for social exploitation, or 'the advancement of science' is seen as a sinister motto of drug and petrol companies, then people are no longer able to believe in the surface culture. Young people are especially able to see through the official myths and stories of society, and to debunk them as baseless and without credibility. It is precisely this lack of belief in the surface that acts as a catalyst to the spirituality revolution. The poet Margaret Montague put this well, when she wrote:

If the world be shut without, I'll sail the hidden seas within.[51]

Montague was thinking about the disenfranchisement of women in patriarchal society, and their 'turning inward' in response to the absence of social or political engagement. But what feminists have written about the disempowerment of women is increasingly experienced as a state of disenchantment by all people, whether male or female, and especially by youth. Many youth feel 'locked out', even though the world pretends to invite them in. Some youth have options to enter the social world and reject them as unattractive; others feel that such entry is denied them, and that the discourse that suggests otherwise is fraudulent.

Whatever its cause, social alienation is a reality and keenly experienced today. To fall out of society and into the dark unknown can be extremely disorienting and unpleasant. One feels strangely unsupported by life, apart from social norms and customs, and uncertain of the way forwards. Such slips and falls can give rise to mental illness and disturbance, to fatigue and exhaustion, to depression and maladjustment. These problems can be the prelude to various kinds of escapism, addictions and risk-taking behaviours, which are designed to reduce the pain of dislocation and loss. But the fall out of social identification can also be a *felix culpa*, a fortunate fall, if the individual is able to find his or her way to the underground stream that brings renewal and healing.

The way is precarious and the path is dark and uncertain, but an encounter with the spirit brings new vitality. Paradoxically, the spirit thrusts the wandering soul back into life and returns him or her to the surface, with renewed enthusiasm and commitment for the work that has to be done. True spirit will not drag down and destroy, because its passion is to revitalise life and transform the ordinary world by its extraordinary power. Thus, the fortunate fall can lead to reversals, conversions and prophetic commitment to a new sense of destiny or purpose. Down and out one minute, the individual can suddenly find him or herself hurled back into life and serving a greater will with considerable verve and gusto.

CYNICISM VERSUS HOPE

In our postmodern era, these experiences seem to be more common than before. The surface layer of socially constructed meaning is wearing very thin, and appears unconvincing even to the youngest observer. The myths and stories that formerly propped up our rational universe, such as belief in social progress, humanism and liberal democracy, have been exposed as fake or phony, and no longer compel commitment or belief. The idea that social evils will be overcome by new developments in science, technology and medicine is no longer a convincing or compelling idea. The youth of today, the generations x, y or z, are simply not won over by the old myths that used to bind the social compact into a viable whole. They have seen through much of our social pretence at order and meaning and they do not like what they see.

The new generations are not just cynical or despairing, however, and to represent them as such is to miss the point. Side by side with this social disillusionment is a search for a new kind of vision or enchantment. They are hungry for an enchantment given, not by society and its institutions, but by the spirit and its promise of new life. On the other side of postmodern malaise and disappointment is the gradual recovery of hope and the capacity to dream. Most youth do not see such hope and vision arising from the institutions of faith, as there is a sense in which they are like other institutions, humanly constructed, artificial and in need of spiritual renewal.

SPIRITUALITY AND LITERATURE

Literature departments in universities throughout the world are well-known for their secular and materialistic approach to literature, and yet there are two anomalies in this appraisal. One is that most great literature, especially traditional literature and good poetry (contemporary and traditional), is written from a spiritual perspective, and is very often a celebration of the spirit in life, society and experience. The other is that many students are drawn to literature for its spiritual content, and for its inspirational and elevating potential. As Simone Weil, the contemporary French mystic, writes:

> **A poem is beautiful to the precise degree in which the attention whilst it was being composed has been turned towards the inexpressible.**[52]

Like many students, I was first drawn to literary study because of the presence of spirit and soul in the literature that interested me. During my school days in Alice Springs, in central Australia, I had grown fond of literature, especially poetry, for its capacity to reveal the difficult, obscure and often invisible life of the spirit. I experienced delight in seeing poets and writers give vivid expression to interior states and spiritual intuitions that were not readily accessed in any other way. I found literature more expressive of the creative spirit than religion. It seemed to encase the radical spirit in dogma, myth and ritual, thus making something wild seem very tame, while literature knew no such limitations and seemed to speak more directly to my existential situation.

For the first two decades in various universities, I tried to adhere to the official paths of secular approaches to the subject. In order to 'fit in' to my discipline, I had to divide myself into two people: an inner, private person who experienced literature through a spiritual lens and who read literature for spiritual reasons, and an outer, public person who taught literature as a secular subject for historical, cultural or sociological reasons. I knew that spirituality would not benefit my career, a career based on a literary culture defined by materialist assumptions about life. But after achieving some academic success, and after my university position seemed secure, I began to allow my private, inward self to break out of its hiding place and invade the public realm of my teaching and research.

At this same time, as synchronicity would have it, I began to notice and listen to the references to spirituality in student discussions. It is hard to know which came first: the suggestive influence of my students on my thinking, or my own inner development that compelled me towards certain spiritual recognitions. Colleagues tended to trivialise the student interest in spirituality as a cultural fashion from America, or as the influence of popular culture, which I suppose amounts to the same thing. But I was interested in the talk about spirit in an environment that was officially opposed to such thinking. The fact that these students were not talking about formal religion made it clear to me that we were in the grip of a new social movement, a nascent spirituality revolution.

As I began to discuss spiritual issues in the classroom, I observed a considerable, and largely unfulfilled, spiritual hunger in my students, which then led me to the construction of my course on spirituality.

SPIRITUAL ARTISTS AND SECULAR THINKING

At this same time, I began to realise why so many creative artists, writers and poets develop distaste for academia and resentment towards university teachers. By imposing secular perspectives on literature, academic study has the effect of repressing and even destroying the spiritual life of literary materials, which is especially hurtful to artists for whom spiritual content is important. Is it surprising that creative artists such as Patrick White, Judith Wright and Les Murray, to name three contemporary writers known to me, have despised academics? These spiritual writers can see clearly that the academics who speak for their work, and teach it in mass educational institutions, are depriving their work of its spiritual force, and imposing their secular assumptions on their writing.

But now I understand why students can become bored and frustrated when we teach literature in a strictly secular and unimaginative way. Who can blame them, when our own teaching fails to 'lift their spirits' or to induct them into the living spiritual reality that underpins their lives? Spirituality is not only about the deep, the meaningful and the serious, but it also connects to the very wellsprings of human vitality, and when it is omitted or repressed we unwittingly repress a great deal of human energy. It is not accidental that the word 'enthusiasm' literally means 'the God within' (*en-theos*), and when we cut ourselves off from the sacred we are depriving our students and society alike of a very real source of libido and motivation.

This argument needs to be developed: the consideration of spirituality from a socio-economic and outcomes perspective in order to counter the standard perception that it is irrelevant to society and the economy. If research can show that spiritual vitality and aliveness can offer significant benefits, for instance a reduction in disorientation or alienation, a more secure sense of personal identity, or a compelling love of life that makes us less likely to succumb to depression, alcoholism or drug addiction, then pragmatic societies may turn towards spirituality with renewed interest. Perhaps, finally, we only acknowledge the underground stream of the spirit when life at the surface has become impossibly difficult, unbearably dull or despairing, so that we willingly lay aside our socially constructed ideologies and turn to the primal waters for renewal and healing.

CHAPTER 4

Student spirituality and educational authority

There is another world, but it is in this one.

Paul Eluard[53]

The rise of interest in spirituality in school, college and university students has placed the state educational authority (with its 'free, secular and compulsory' system) in a difficult and curious situation. I address the situation as I see it in Australia, but I will assume there are parallels in other Western-style democracies. I teach in a faculty of humanities and social sciences, where spirituality gets short shrift and students espousing interests in this area are cautioned and encouraged to return to the secular pursuit of knowledge. The contemporary humanities and social sciences have no intellectual understanding of spirit, even though the term might be used in casual expressions or various discursive contexts, such as spirit of place, spirit of the time, or the spirit of a group, society or sporting club. Mostly, spirit in these contexts refers to the human spirit or to a generalised feeling generated by human activities, but spirit in a sacred context, with reference to a universal or cosmic power, is too religious or theological for the secular academy to deal with. Yet it is in this sacred context that many students are talking about spirit today.

Moreover, students in my subjects report wanting to 'develop' their spirituality, which suggests that they want to go on some kind of journey into hidden depths and self-knowledge. This raises another problem for intellectual authority. Not only is this interest sacred rather than secular, but it is transformational rather than informational. The secular university has constructed itself as a place where knowledge is imparted and information shared, and if lives are changed in the process, so much the better. But it does not seek to change lives in the sense of directing or guiding human experience into spiritual depths. The job of the university is to inform its students, but the students increasingly ask for something more. They wish to be transformed, not only informed.

The whole concept of the university is put at risk here, as it will claim that its task is educational, not therapeutic or theological. It is happy to confine itself to the pursuit of knowledge and to leave the search for wisdom to the institutions of faith. But the concept of education comes from the Latin *educare*, meaning 'to lead out', in the sense of drawing out what is within. If students are reporting that what is 'within' is a spiritual reality that needs to be 'led out', this poses problems for the secular institution. If spirit is present in students, our institutions are not fulfilling the promise that is inherent in the word 'education' itself. There is more human reality to be 'led out' than the institutions are comfortable with. Education is not able to deliver what it promises, much less is it able to claim that it is satisfying the needs of its clientele.

LIBERATION DISCOURSES

The contemporary university prides itself on being a place where students discover various kinds of liberation discourses. Since the radical 1960s, numerous ideologies and systems of thought have been promoted by staff under the banner of liberation and freedom. Mostly, these discourses have been social, political and external to the inner self. There has never been any focus on interior or spiritual liberation, which would be interpreted as narcissistic or indulgent by most of the established liberation discourses.

However, the 'spiritual' student experiences these radical discourses as oppressive, to the extent that they overlook, ignore or rule out the realm of the spirit. Often the lecturer schooled in Marxist, feminist, psychoanalytic or postmodern thought is advocating a style of liberation that the spiritual student experiences as incomplete because there is no spiritual dimension in it. By 'spiritual' we refer to an encounter with a source of mystery that transforms us as we come into contact with it.[54] Marxist, feminist, psychoanalytic or postmodern thinkers are facing a student population that increasingly rejects their liberation discourses as old-fashioned, out of touch, or lacking in breadth of vision. In this postmodern era, the liberation theorist has to think more deeply about human liberation, lest his or her system of liberation is experienced as tyrannical by the rising generation and its different needs.

This is quite a challenge, as many academics refuse to entertain the realm of the spirit, which they tend to see, following Freud[55] and Marx, as fanciful or illusory. Students and teachers sometimes criticise each other for being out of touch or behind the times. Some teachers make these criticisms because they associate spirit with antiquity and the premodern, and therefore students advocating a spiritual dimension are viewed as oddly eccentric, New Age or premodern. Some students view staff as out of touch because students experience spirit as contemporary and postmodern. I have observed teachers tolerating spirit just to humour students and to keep them on side during the educational process, but students want to see their lecturers take the spirit seriously and not regard it as a premodern chimera. Often this undermining is not direct, but occurs through subtle put-downs.

THE PROJECT OF A POSTMODERN SPIRITUALITY

What we need to discover, I believe, is a genuinely postmodern spirituality. It is true that some student interest in the spirit is atavistic and regressive, but the spirit simply needs a new language and a new imagining[56] to make it part of the postmodern intellectual landscape. This is a task or quest that can be developed by students and staff alike. Students will bring their intuitions and experiences to this conversation, and staff should be able to introduce historical and cultural perspectives that place those experiences in a meaningful social context. The key to this new development is conversation and listening. Rather than just imparting information to students, staff need to listen more carefully and sensitively to the students' often startling and insightful revelations of the spirit. Listening to the other, and allowing a dominant discourse to be interrupted by the other, is the theoretical core of the postmodern enterprise, and we can employ this enterprise in the service of a postmodern spirituality.

Contemporary knowledge and education have made the transition into the postmodern paradigm in several important ways. A great many of our 'modern' assumptions and 'absolute' conceptions have been transformed by postmodern fluidity and uncertainty, and by a new exposure to process and mystery. But precisely because modern academic thought is so profoundly secular and resistant to religion, we find that spirituality and religion have not undergone significant transformation in our intellectual understanding. They are still treated as incredulous claims or unfounded propositions that have no basis in reality. Within professional theology and its teaching institutes, religion has been deconstructed and reimagined for a new era of faith and understanding.[57] But the deconstruction of religion in theology has not, or not yet, had much impact on how religion and spirituality are viewed in the disciplines of sociology, history, philosophy, literature or cultural studies.

In these disciplines, spirituality is still viewed as implausible, incredulous and vague. Modernist prejudices have not been shifted by the transition into postmodern thought. The university's leap into the postmodern has been selective and partial, because it is not in the secular university's interests to reconsider religion or spirituality in a positive light. Although Derrida, Vattimo and other postmodern philosophers have recently turned towards religion with a new and sympathetic gaze, the secular university will not follow their lead if it imagines that such consideration might prove to be subversive to the secular project of knowledge. A serious postmodern revaluation of spirit might upset the assumptions of too many people.

Many of the highly educated in our community have been coerced into a godless view of the world, and throughout the modern era education has almost been synonymous with loss of belief, loss of spiritual orientation, and the banishment of myths, symbols and images that gave our forebears spiritual nourishment and meaning. The postmodern philosopher Eugenio Trias writes:

> It is in the struggle against religion that reason has sought to secure its own legitimacy. Religion has been judged and controlled by the use of the word *superstition*. Religion [has been] brought before the tribunal of science, of reason, to be examined, interrogated, tested and placed under enquiry. The common point of departure [for advocates of reason] is the

rationalist-Enlightenment premise that religion is, as such, illusion, ideology, an inadequate concept, sickness, false consciousness.[58]

Those of us who have been educated in the paradigm of knowledge that derives from the Enlightenment have participated in a rationalist conspiracy against spirituality and sacred meaning. We have believed that intellectual enlightenment would lead to the death of religion and the decline of the mythological world. All the spiritual arts, such as cosmology, mysticism, symbolism and religious poetry would eventually be eclipsed and replaced by science, technology, prose and secular descriptions of experience.

In his recent essay, 'Faith and Knowledge', Derrida speaks of 'the return of the religious', of 'its interminable and ineluctable return'.[59] Religion, he says, is that impulse which forces us to 'give ourselves back, and up, to the other. To every other and to the utterly other'.[60] Religion means 'bringing together in order to return and begin again'.[61] Ironically, most followers of Derridean deconstruction in universities are people who employ deconstructive techniques in the service of reductive analyses of culture. They appear to have little idea that Derrida himself has moved on from the stand point of suspicion that governed his early approach to religion and its 'master narratives'. This new turn in Derrida's work will, of course, not be made popular or advocated throughout the university system, because that system does not want to change its core assumptions or values. Like any institution, it suffers from defensive inertia and a horrified response to change, especially where the pursuit of rationality is concerned.

Derrida is still highly critical of religion and suspicious of the power-play that operates under its name, but there is a real change of attitude and vision in the later work of this important philosopher. He seems to have become more influenced by, and sympathetic to, the moral-theological speculations of Emmanuel Levinas, Martin Heidegger and Kevin Hart. It is as if the spiritual claims of religion have begun to be separated from its political or hegemonic claims, thus exposing Derridean thought to the possibility of mysticism and even to religious conversion. As his Italian colleague and co-editor, Gianni Vattimo writes:

> In religion, something that we had thought irrevocably forgotten is made present again, a dormant trace is reawakened, a wound

re-opened, the repressed returns and what we took to be an overcoming is no more than a long convalescence.[62]

The spiritual has not been eradicated from modern knowledge, but has been in a state of sleep or 'long convalescence'. Vattimo expresses well the sense of surprise, dismay and even disorientation that the return of the religious impulse in the West brings to the postmodern situation. What we 'had thought irrevocably forgotten is made present again'.

THE PROFESSIONAL PUT-DOWN: SPIRITUALITY AS FROTH AND BUBBLE

The modernist agenda was heavily shaped by the cultural materialism of Marx, Freud, Nietzsche, and the French and American schools of anthropology and social theory. Spirituality was 'opium for the masses', and its status in culture was illusory and therefore held in great suspicion. During my student days, we were newly exposed to French theory and reading Roland Barthes, who writes, in his famous 1957 essay on 'Soap-powders and detergents':

Foam can even be the sign of a certain spirituality, inasmuch as the spirit has the reputation of being able to make something out of nothing, a large surface of effects out of a small volume of causes; creams have a very different psychoanalytical meaning, of a soothing kind: they suppress wrinkles, pain, smarting, etc.[63]

The emphasis of modern thought has been to reduce the great to the small, to reduce spirituality to foam in a bath, and high culture and religion to a series of power-relations in society. This destructive attack on religious culture can only be regarded from a postmodern perspective as a modernist disease, which swept through education and culture with devastating results. But we have all been affected by this tendency to destroy the great by reducing it to the small, the neurotic, or the absurd, an 'enlightenment' that William James correctly diagnosed in his 1902 Gifford Lectures as false intellectualism.[64]

In modern universities controlled by cultural materialism, spirituality in our students has been largely dismissed as froth and bubble. Since at least the 1980s we have had the handy term 'New Age' to help us to beat spirituality over the head and undermine spiritual stirrings in our students. When students venture into spiritual territory, we employ this term to protect us against the irrational, and to facilitate our learned conspiracy against the spirit. Use of this term silences students in their tracks, in the same way that the term 'superstition', as Eugenio Trias said, had 'judged and controlled' the world of religion by the close of the 19th century. I believe the intelligentsia has grotesquely over-used the term 'New Age' as a defence mechanism against the spiritual, and as an excuse for not taking student interests seriously. The opposite of these defensive manoeuvres is the creation of a 'climate of validity' in the classroom. In creating such a climate for students one has to grapple with one's own neurotic defences, including the classification of all spiritual interest as air-headed fantasy.

William James aptly pointed out that it is easy to discredit the spiritual interests of others by using reductive interpretations based on misplaced sexual fantasy, or displaced hysterical symptoms, but we begin to realise the incredible destructiveness of these strategies whenever they are turned against ourselves:

> We are surely all familiar in a general way with this method of discrediting states of mind for which we have an antipathy. We all use it to some degree in criticising persons whose states of mind we regard as overstrained. But when other people criticise our own more exalted soul-flights by calling them 'nothing but' expressions of our organic disposition, we feel outraged and hurt, for we know that, whatever be our organism's peculiarities, our mental states have their substantive value as revelations of the living truth; and we wish that all this medical materialism could be made to hold its tongue.[65]

I recall feeling the force of this statement when an 18-year-old student burst into tears in my office, because she said she was mortified by the way in which her educated Marxist-feminist father continually dismissed her spiritual interests as 'New Age' fantasy. In this scenario, I was being called upon to play the role of the good father who cared for the spirituality of the student. She could not tolerate her father's emotional abuse of a sensitive area of her experience, and felt impelled to move away from home and live with students in an inner-city apartment. Apparently the father could not see the irony of being a 'feminist' while perpetrating the cycle of male abuse in a new way. The intellectual tyranny that has taken place in the modern era under the cloak of cleverness is part of the untold history of oppression.

I will return to the problem of the New Age in a moment. But the point I am trying to make here is that the expression is largely a cliché of our academic invention, a derogatory category into which we place everything that appears not to fit our secular paradigm of knowledge. This leads to anomalies and even absurdities of classification, such as referring to believing Catholic or enthusiastic Buddhist students as 'New Age' simply because staff cannot cope with their religious enthusiasm, and seek ways to undermine or discredit their experience.

ENGAGED SPIRITUALITY: COUNTERING THE CHARGE OF ESCAPISM

While it is true that some youth spirituality is guilty as charged, namely that it appears flaky, vague and waffly, I believe that a great deal of it is much more substantial than is recognised. A typical put-down of youth spirituality by academic staff involves the discrediting of their spirituality as escapist, dreamy or otherworldly. University education likes to believe that it is eminently this-worldly, that it is about real problems and dilemmas facing society, culture, human suffering and the struggle for liberation. There is so much to sort out and understand about this world, academics often declare, that they have not the time, patience or endurance to focus on the next world, or on some imagined or invented other world.

Here, I think, the problem we face is largely one of terminology and prejudice. For many academics the term 'spiritual' connotes otherworldliness and esotericism. But students are very often not referring to otherworldly matters when they speak of spirituality. They are not using this term in a way that signifies a quest for perfection through piety and devotion. Again, it could be that academics are deliberately misconstruing the meaning to avoid having to deal with a problematic area.

For many of our youth spirituality is the search for guiding visions and values within this world, for the deep currents of spiritual impulse and reality that give life meaning and direction. Even if they sometimes dabble in esoterica and occult philosophies that seem remotely connected with history or philosophy as the university conceives them, this search is in order to know our human experience more fully. What academics perceive to be a flight from the real is often a quest for the heart of the real.

If we care to listen to what youth are saying, they are indicating that their spirituality is *engaged* spirituality, concerned with the welfare of the world and the sacredness of endangered nature. They see spirituality as the basis for a new or renewed sense of human responsibility and social justice. It is worldly and pragmatic. Spirituality is advocated as a cure for racism, an essential ingredient of the new ecological awareness, an antidote to domestic violence and civil unrest, and a remedy for religious sectarianism and holy wars. It has acquired a public conscience, and has very little of the anti-social, pleasure-seeking flavour that it had for the university students of my own generation.

Although spirituality suggests internal and personal experiences, it is clearly not seen as *private* or shut away from reality. The point of this new spirituality is that we touch a level of unitary reality that binds us to the universe. Through genuine spiritual experience, we are released from the burden of ego, and discharged into a larger world that enables us to focus less on our ego and more on our larger cosmic identity. This shift of focus gives us the space and opportunity to reduce our egoic tension and to shed hostilities associated with being a victim or an alienated self. In other words, it allows us to love rather than to hate. Spirituality is about personal empowerment, but it is not 'private' because from this transformation will flow political and social transformations.

My students often argue that if one can learn to relate to the universe as an extension of oneself, as a field animated with life and meaning along the lines of the Gaia hypothesis, then one will relate to the world and to other beings with profound sensitivity and concern. A kind of cosmic religious awareness, similar in some ways to the environmental morality offered by Buddhism, Sufism or Christian mysticism, becomes synonymous with the ecological revolution. This is not romantic escapism, but eco-politics. In the same way that feminism taught university students to know that 'the personal is political', so youth today are engaged in a further revolution whose slogan might be 'the spiritual is political'.

One of my own students wrote this in an essay on spirituality:

By refusing to develop ourselves spiritually we are restricting
our human potential and our capacity to transform the world. If
we could focus more on spiritual realities, greed would no
longer control us. Without greed, I think we could achieve
greater happiness and peace of mind. Spiritual awakening could
have a powerful effect on stopping the downfall of society.

(Scott, 19, 2001)

It is because of the new link with broad public issues, such as land-use, race relations, and environmentalism, that youth spirituality deserves to be taken seriously. It is not about navel-gazing but about establishing a moral basis in an increasingly amoral or immoral world. The old secular view that spirituality is a pleasure-seeking ego-trip into otherworlds no longer appears to be relevant, and academics who attack youth spirituality on political grounds are obviously failing to see that spirituality has become central to political life for young people.

In some ways, we have to revise our sense of what 'internal' means. It no longer refers to what is private and tucked away, but 'interiority' refers to a depth or resonance in all parts of reality. Spirituality is not just about my subjectivity, but about the deep subjectivity of all things and the world. This is what Thomas Berry the ecological philosopher[66] meant when he said that we have to reconfigure the world, not as a collection of objects, but as a communion of subjects.

This is new to us, although hardly surprising to the indigenous peoples of the world. Spirituality allows us to feel and experience the 'soul of the world', or what Platonists referred to as *anima mundi* and many indigenous people refer to as the 'spirits' in things. Young people are seeking to rediscover the inner side of everything, and this surely is not navel-gazing, but a philosophical attempt to rebuild the world from the inside, after the collapse of meaning that has taken place through modernity and the death of God. Their spirituality is internal and external, personal and public, at the same time. A lot of our typical dualities and boundaries are being collapsed.

REGRESSIVE ELEMENTS: THE POOR SYMBOLS OF THE NEW AGE

Postmodern elements of youth spirituality undoubtedly include the worldliness of their spiritual expression, the refusal of authoritarian styles of religion, and the breakdown of conventional dualities such as internal/external, heavenly/earthly, and spirit/matter. The dualism between spirit and body is constantly being challenged, which is why sexuality is so often viewed as part of, rather than opposed to, the human experience of a spiritual reality.

But I believe we have to make a real distinction between the *style* of youth spirituality and its *content*. Its style strikes me as postmodern, while its content often seems premodern, ancient and archaic. I frequently meet students who have a passionate interest in such areas as shamanism, animism, supernaturalism and witchcraft. They also appear to be fascinated by the ancient divinatory systems, including astrology, runes, tarot and I Ching. In some ways, their motto appears to be 'the older the better'. The content of youth spirituality is what adults and teachers most often notice, if they notice anything at all, and it appears to be regressive, archaic and atavistic.

Teachers and parents should not be so easily repelled. To some extent, the archaism is metaphorical rather than literal. That is to say, like archaeologists of the soul, young people are trying to 'dig down' to our spiritual and animistic roots, in a bid to find a solid basis of spirit and cosmology from which the contemporary world might be re-enchanted and reimagined. They are fascinated by what is oldest and most ancient, because these are the elements, they believe, from which a new spiritual orientation will come. Jung was alert to this tendency of our time to look back to develop a spiritual future. He said, 'Everything old in our unconscious hints at something coming'.[67] This appears to be true for youth today, who often distrust the modern because it seems to be too human, manufactured or artificial. They turn back in a bid to discover what is prior to the human, and to the merely human or man-made.

This New Age dimension of youth experience is also a result of the New Age industries and enterprises, which are expert in producing ancient esoteric cosmologies and divinatory systems. I would point out that our religious and educational institutions are partly responsible for the 'regressive' nature of popular spiritual interest. The spiritual curiosity of youth is not fully engaged by the materials that our institutions offer them. They turn to the animistic systems of the ancient past because these systems are freely available, and because so many others, old and young, are talking about these systems off campus. If education provided new ways of approaching the spiritual world, then these offerings would be taken seriously. Students are not introduced to recent developments in postmodern theology or religion, which are conducted for and by professional insiders. We cannot blame them for being ignorant, but must blame society for keeping them in ignorance. Here we do well to heed the statement of William James:

> Religious language clothes itself in such poor symbols as our life affords.[68]

The New Age interests are indeed a series of 'poor symbols', and bespeak a cultural impoverishment that education should correct. This realisation made me see the New Age in a different light and caused me to study it in depth.[69] It is a vulgar series of spiritual technologies that exist because there is nothing better on offer. It is because the institutions fail to generate a sense of spiritual wonder and delight that our young people are attracted to these vulgar representations in the first place.

Jung's response to the theosophical movement in his day gave me the clue about how to respond to the New Age movement in ours. Jung wrote that the educated and sophisticated minds of his time snarled at theosophy and at Madame Blavatsky. The educated mind, he said, recoiled at theosophy's appropriations of exotic, Asiatic, indigenous and esoteric mysteries. This movement was condemned as anti-intellectual, 'superstitious', 'wholly irrelevant and fortuitous', and 'a regrettable aberration'.[70] Intellectuals 'prophesy an early and inglorious end to these movements'. But such hostile attacks, he writes:

> overlook the fact that such movements derive their force from the fascination of the psyche, and that it will express itself in these forms until they are replaced by something better. They are transitional or embryonic stages from which new and riper forms will emerge.[71]

The same can be said of the New Age interests of today, which are a contemporary extension of the theosophical movement.[72] They are to be regarded as 'transitional or embryonic stages'. The value of these phenomena lies in what they point to in the future. Only if we take our cue from Jung and James, and realise that spirit must 'clothe itself in such poor symbols as our life affords', only then can we be patient and tolerant of New Age passions, in the hope that they shed their nascent forms and give rise to something new. We are stuck with these expressions 'until they are replaced by something better'.

We must not criticise our students too harshly, for their interests are often a prelude to a deeper and more mature kind of spiritual awareness. The influential philosopher Hegel put this argument succinctly in 1807:

> The false, however immature and distorted, must reveal itself as a prefiguration of something to come, without which its very deformity could not exist, but within which the negative aspect of that deformity is transmuted into a positive function of a larger whole.[73]

This is a philosophical or 'Hegelian' way of repeating the truth that the stone rejected by the builders could become the cornerstone of a new vision. We must be careful how we respond to the New Age, because it could hold within itself the seeds of the genuinely prophetic.

THE REVOLUTIONARY PROTEST: MARX, HEGEL AND SPIRIT

The fact that youth and university students are defining their search for spirituality as a search for 'connectedness' should interest the Marx-inspired lecturers who are teaching them, because Marxism is at once a theory of social alienation, that is of disconnection, and a practical philosophical attempt to heal that disconnection through political and social means. It is therefore ironic that intellectual Marxists fail to recognise their own deepest yearnings in the popular discourses of spirituality, which is a grassroots attempt to further the revolutionary force and potential that was the inspirational source of Marxism. It could be argued that youth spirituality has its historical antecedent in Marxism. Both strive for liberation, seek to identify and attack the sources of alienation, and look to a revolutionary program. But these philosophies are working on different levels. Youth spirituality is seeking a primordial level of experience upon which the battle against alienation can be waged and won. It is a postmodern, post-utopian political movement, but it is political in an entirely new sense.

Marxism articulated an age-old cry of the human spirit for liberation and freedom, and gave this cry a political interpretation and an ideological resolution. Marxism was the 'modern' cure for our alienation, a cure that dramatically failed, although the glow of its original revolutionary impetus continues to inspire academics, historians and intellectuals in the West. Youth today are revolutionary but in a completely new way. The climate of protest and revolt is still present, but it is no longer directed into utopian politics. Marxism has collapsed and youth do not seem to believe in the ability of the political process to bring about their dreams and hopes. There is a 'reversion' to the primal source of revolutionary dreams in the spiritual life. The fight against alienation moves ahead, although ideological Marxists would not necessarily be able to recognise it as such.

If we move one step back from Marx, to the speculative idealism of Hegel's philosophy from which Karl Marx drew, we might understand more clearly the links between the youth spirituality of today, and the Marxist idealism of revolutionary students and young people a generation ago. The difference between them is slight, involving a shift in category and a change of emphasis. Instead of politics we talk of spirituality, and instead of revolution we speak of liberation. But apart from a change of proper nouns, the discourse is similar, presenting a desire to shift present unhappiness into future happiness. Marx and Lenin, and also Kierkegaard and Sartre, were profoundly influenced by Hegel's portrayal of the 'Unhappy consciousness', and the cure of this state, for Hegel, was spiritual or metaphysical.

Marxists seem to forget or repress the spiritual sources of Marxian dialectics, although some Marxists are beginning to recover these numinous roots, for example Joel Kovel in his work *History and Spirit* (1991). Marx borrowed heavily from Hegel's system, especially from the dialectic of 'Lordship and Bondage' and the concept of alienation (*entfremdung*). But he stripped Hegel of his metaphysics, and gutted the Hegelian model of its spiritual idealism. According to Hegel, alienation is above all a spiritual affliction, and we feel alienated from ourselves, society and nature because we are fallen creatures who have become alienated from God. Our persistent feeling of alienation, Hegel argues, is a simple if painful consequence of our coming-into-consciousness, which is a coming into separateness and aloneness. The spirit in us, he says:

is alienated and divided, but only so as to be able thus to find itself and return to itself. Only in this manner does spirit attain its freedom.[74]

Here Hegel sounds like the German mystics who informed his early thought, and his philosophical antecedents are Platonic philosophy and Christianity. The whole point of existence, for Hegel, is that the divine spirit seeks to 'return to itself out of this estranged state'. Human existence 'is Spirit estranged from itself'.[75] Just about every student interested in spirituality would agree.

They would also agree with Hegel that the premodern condition of human civilisation, with its emphasis on spirit and its sights set on heaven, is becoming more attractive to us as we grow weary from the world and its burden upon our souls. The premodern sensibility was misrepresented by the modern era as otherworldly and concerned with 'another life' after death. In actual fact it was focused on a spiritual reality within this world, or with a 'present that lies beyond':

> Time was when man had a heaven, decked and fitted out with
> endless wealth of thoughts and pictures. The significance of all
> that lay in the thread of light by which it was attached to
> heaven; instead of dwelling in the present as it is here and now,
> the eye glanced away over the present to the Divine, away, so to
> say, to a present that lies beyond.
>
> The mind's gaze had to be directed under compulsion to
> what is earthly, and kept fixed there; and it has needed a long
> time to introduce that clearness, which only celestial realities
> had, into the crassness and confusion shrouding the sense of
> things earthly, and to make attention to the immediate present
> of interest and of value.[76]

Students know about 'the crassness and confusion shrouding the sense of things earthly', and they feel, like Hegel, the new appeal of heaven and spirit, which appears as a possibility beneath or behind the crassness of the mundane. But it would be wrong to say that they spurn the mundane, just as it is wrong to say that they are otherworldly and non-political. Rather, they are interested in bringing the depth of life to the foreground of experience. Like Hegel, they see the 'non-divine secularity of things' as an optical illusion, a way of perceiving the world that blocks out the spirit at the core of our experience. With Hegel, they affirm the paradox that 'each and every secular thing is God'.[77]

REVOLUTION IN EDUCATION

I have been discussing the situation of young adults in the secular university system, but there are obvious parallels to be drawn with children in primary and secondary schools. Since my professional field is not education as such but cultural studies and the history of ideas, I have not had any professional exposure to secondary or primary schooling, although as a parent and guest speaker at schools I have often tried to bridge the gap between my tertiary experience and the other levels of education. The struggle at primary and secondary levels of education are similar, although it could be the case that teachers at tertiary level are far more judgemental and critical of spiritual inclinations in students, as such inclinations might be regarded as regressive or indicative of a childhood romance that should be abandoned as young adults make their transition into the real world of adult values. It may be the case that spirituality is tolerated more at earlier levels because it is associated with imagination, artistic inclinations and childlike concerns. The university environment functions almost as if such childhood fascinations should have been sacrificed in the rite of passage into social reality.

University students do not appear to want a values-free induction into 'adult' or disenchanted social reality. The social norms of the past are no longer adequate, and we clearly need a new understanding of 'normal' living. The impulses that gave rise to neutral educational policies belong to a former era that was reacting against the hegemony and power of the churches. Secular education was associated with freedom, free-thinking and liberation from ecclesiastical authorities. The free-thinkers could think their own thoughts without having to conform to official religious views. But now secular education bestows a new kind of baleful authoritarianism, in which the soul and spirit are imprisoned and never allowed to take flight. Our deepest spiritual impulses are repressed and denied by secular education. As the cycle of history turns, we discover that the freedom of one era is the oppression and tyranny of another. Students now view our academic liberation discourses with the same doubtful eye that early modern intellectuals turned towards religion and the faith institutions.

Young adults want spirituality back on the public agenda and this will force leaders in secular society to rethink education and, more challengingly, to rethink their own personal connection to spirituality. Youth spirituality forces adults out of their protective cocoons of neutrality and liberal education, urging us to arrive at a personal position on whether or not the world is mysterious.

CHAPTER 5

Mind the gap: youth spirituality and religion

God is certainly not dead; people are simply experiencing God in new ways and seeing God differently.

(Beth, 19, 2001)

'Mind the gap' warns the public announcement at underground tube stations in London. The gap to mind is that between the platform and the rail carriage, which is wider at certain inner city stations than at others. But as I teach and conduct research on youth spirituality, I am often reminded of this warning about the 'gap', especially when asked to comment on the relationship between youth spirituality and formal religion. Religious educators and faith leaders are often keen to have my observations on youth spirituality, once they know that I teach university courses on spirituality, and that youth are attracted to these courses in large numbers.

I can certainly report to religious enquirers that youth spirituality is alive and well, growing in strength and full of diversity. Youth spirituality is a vast potential resource of spiritual vitality, and holds tremendous promise for the religious, moral and environmental renewal of society. But as far as religion is concerned there is a tremendous lack of fit between youth spirituality and religion, and the gaps are more significant than those encountered on railway platforms.

SPIRITUAL EDUCATION: AWAKENING THE SPIRIT

I am conscious of many gaps in our fragmented world, and I should speak first about the gap between myself and religious educators. I am a spiritual educator, not a religious educator. My task is to educate the spirit in the person, by enabling students to see and recognise the spirit in culture, literature, art and their experience of life. The spiritual, as I understand it, is the primary ground of the religious, but it is, as it were, prior to formal religion as such (here I follow William James). My role is to educate the spirit so that it begins to recognise itself. I encourage students to explore the spirit in poetry, art and inspirational writings (culture), in nature and landscape (creation), and in personal reflections, intuitions and feelings (experience). Culture, creation and experience are the three fields I explore, and I have never yet met any student who fails to be moved or engaged by one or more of these areas.

Religious education often works at a different, perhaps higher level. It begins, not with experience, but with scripture, tradition, history, liturgy and worship. Generally it is not psychological, creation-based or grounded in the imagination. Having said that, I am aware that there are 'progressive' teachers in religious studies who recognise that in order to best mobilise student interest they must begin with experience, and thus adopt a practical approach to the subject. These teachers are already developing spiritual education under the umbrella of religious education, and such teachers will not find anything radically new in what I am proposing, although I hope that they find some of my ideas and formulations helpful. My concern is to define spiritual education as a discrete field of its own, whether it arises out of religious studies or, as in my own case, as a new area within cultural and literary studies.

INSIDE OUT: BEGINNING WITH THE GROUND OF EXPERIENCE

In my teaching, I deliberately work behind religious lines. I till the soil of soul and spirit, attempt to develop an appreciation of these realities, and that is all I do. I do not plant the seeds of religion in the soil because that is not my role. I lecture to radically diverse groups of students, many of whom are secular, agnostic or atheist. Some are

Buddhist, Islamic, Hindu and Jewish students, and my task is not to convert them, offend or insult their beliefs, nor impose my own sense of religion upon them. Some evangelical people see my work as vague or ill-defined, but my role is not to promote any religion, but to develop a religious attitude and to express the spiritual ground of our lives. This ground, I believe, is universal and can be seen and felt in everyone, regardless of whether they are from religious or non-religious backgrounds or whether they designate themselves as believers, atheists or agnostics.

Actually, I am not very interested in the labels we use to describe ourselves, because these labels are often misleading and reveal little about who we are. I have set up my course on spirituality deliberately to attract broad and diverse kinds of people, because I want to study the spirit in its various manifestations. Some students deny the existence of spirit, others have quite developed intuitions of the spirit in their lives and in culture, but my interest is primarily to explore the condition of the spirit in a secular society. If I were to call my course 'religion', I would probably have a dozen or so students turn up, but calling it 'spirituality' brings in large numbers of students, because that is the term that enjoys current favour.

In a secular society, religion is not understood very well, if at all. Responses to the idea of religion among students range from fanatical loyalty to fanatical opposition, with a great many positions in between. Spirituality activates a completely different dynamic in a large group, and can be used to explore points of similarity, rather than discordant differences, between ethnically, religiously and philosophically diverse students. I should say that when the spirit is activated and recognised, the student tends to develop or rediscover (as the case may be) a natural interest in religion, because religion offers the spirit a complex language, a sense of tradition and cultural memory.

But an interest in religion that proceeds from a spiritual awakening is essentially different from more conventional or extrinsic appropriations of religious positions. The inward or spiritual approach to religion is deeper, based on personal experience, tolerant towards difference, compassionate towards those who make different life-choices, and relatively free of ideological fanaticism. This is all the more reason why religious educators should seek to explore the spiritual approach to religious mystery, rather than continue exclusively with extrinsic approaches. If religion is imposed on young lives before they have had an inkling or intuition of their own spirit, they tend to reject religion, regarding it as alien and external to the self. It is an intruder, perhaps even an enemy. Spiritual education should become a priority for religion, if it wants to contact and engage the lives that it seeks to form and transform in the religious enterprise.

The idea of spiritual experience must not be exaggerated or distorted by religious educators in order to make such experiences seem doctrinally correct or theologically sound. Nor should they be inflated or distorted by non-believers and the anti-religious, who may seek to sensationalise such experiences to make them seem otherworldly and less credible. We are not talking about direct or unmitigated experiences of a supernatural realm, personal communications with God, or first-hand sightings of angelic beings. Actually, I am not thinking about anything metaphysical or magical at all, but something quite ordinary and existential. By spiritual experience I mean a deeper and more profound apprehension of our ordinary lives. I am not imagining anything 'added on' to our lives from above, but rather a new dimension revealed to our understanding from below. This dimension is revealed to our sight when we 'see through' the mundane encasement of our lives to the mystery beneath, within and around us.

By spiritual awakening I am not talking about a miraculous zap from heaven, a thunderbolt of divine origin, but simply of a dawning awareness, a growing hunch or intuition of a deeper mystery. The term 'religious experience' is probably too grand for what I have in mind. T. S. Eliot describes what I am imagining in *Murder in the Cathedral*:

I have had a tremor of bliss, a wink of heaven, a whisper.[78]

In the realm of the spirit, a great deal can be based on something that is relatively small and humble. Lives can be turned around by simple adjustments to our perception, and spirituality as I conceive it is, in this sense, the art of the small.

A PARADIGM GAP: TOWARDS A CREATION SPIRITUALITY

With regard to the gap between youth spirituality and formal religion, we are not simply talking about a generation gap that will be healed in time and with attention to the different needs and demands of the young and the old. Rather, in the conflict between youth spirituality and formal religion we are dealing with a 'lack of fit' between different models or paradigms of the sacred. In the emerging vision of youth spirituality, we see a new model in which the sacred is intimate and close, a felt resonance within the self, and a deep and radiant presence in the natural world. If the old sacredness was distant, aloof and a standard of moral perfection against which we judged ourselves to be unworthy, the new sacredness is embodied in our physicality and vital lives, an incarnational presence that asks us not to be perfect but to strive for wholeness and integration.

These models are based on different theologies and give rise to different kinds of moral or ethical awareness, but they are not necessarily different 'religions'. Some religious critics of youth spirituality often claim that it is a variant of paganism or gnosticism. This is simple to say, and rolls off the pursed lips of disapproving conservatives rather easily. But such categorisations convey enormous prejudice and bias against the new expressions of the spirit. A former dualism is being questioned and challenged by youth spirituality, which is not so much paganism or gnosticism as it is the re-emergence of the lost tradition of immanence or the mystical tradition. In the collision of the old and the new we are witnessing the clash between transcendentalist and immanental streams of the same experience of the divine reality.

With Christian religious educators in mind particularly, let me say this—youth spirituality may not be very churchy, but that does not make it non-religious or anti-Christian. I think we have to look at youth spirituality for what is potentially good about it, rather than just cast a blanket negative judgement upon it. We should be more alert to finding God in the strange and the unfamiliar. This, surely, is what the Christian gospel teaches, especially the story about the road to Emmaus, where the travellers are unaware that the stranger who has joined them on the road is none other than the Risen Christ. Today we must look for the Risen Christ where we least expect to find him. The stone rejected by the builders of religion may become the cornerstone of a new spiritual awareness. Obviously, religious educators cannot completely silence their theological criticisms of youth experience, and there should not be a blanket approval of everything that youth think or feel. But instead of imposing adult religious prejudices on the young, we have to learn to listen to them for what the spirit is revealing of its new reality and experience in today's world.

ASSUMPTIONS OF YOUTH SPIRITUALITY: HOLISTIC, INFORMAL, INDIVIDUAL

In youth spirituality and religion we discover divergent experiences of the sacred that are separated by time, space, core assumptions and expectations. There is sometimes hostility and crossfire between these different paradigms, an hostility that is fueled by prejudices on both sides. Many of the assumptions held by formal religion are not held by youth spirituality, which is why communication between them is difficult and fraught. It is true that what youth culture deems to be sacred, namely ecology, nature and the physical world, or the stars, planets and stellar cosmology, or the search for the inner or true self, or the quest for mystical experiences, appears to be at odds with what traditional religion has deemed to be sacred, namely scripture, rituals, dogmas and ecclesiastical faith.

It is clear that most young people neither understand nor appreciate traditional religious ideas about the need to aspire to moral perfection, respect institutional authority and perform regular communal rites in order to be reunited with God. Youth spirituality is not interested in moral perfection, but only in a search for wholeness, which is a different kind of moral ideal, one that is often at odds with the pursuit of perfection.

Youth spirituality is more interested in listening to the inward conscience than in obeying the external dictates of religious authority. Young people seem to believe that conscience, not an outside authority or tradition, is the true moral guide. This reliance on conscience is a product of modernity and the democratic principles inherent in contemporary society. Part of the 'gap' between youth culture and religion is the gap that separates religion from secular society. Youth are more influenced by secular society than they are by religious culture, and this is true for youth in religious schools as much as it is for youth in government or state schools. Their attitudes and assumptions bear the marks of secular society, and their spirituality is modern and secular, not religious or traditional.

SACREDNESS IN ORDINARY AND NATURAL CONTEXTS

For youth today, being holy is not synonymous with attending traditional religious services, but with an attitude of mind and heart that allows the sacred to enter their lives and experiences at all times.

Ironically, youth spirituality, seemingly wayward or wild, is sometimes more intently spiritual than much religiousness in adults, insofar as some adult religiousness can be described as routine attendance on automatic pilot. When young people are open to the sacred dimension they are rarely on automatic pilot, but are usually closely focused on the spiritual possibilities of their experience. They often report 'peak experiences' during trips to rural districts or while on excursions or nature camps, whether these are held in parks, deserts, mountains or beside the sea. In my university course on spirituality, I often receive beautiful essays written by students about their peak experiences in nature, and about how these experiences have changed their lives and revised their thinking on their identity, on life, social justice and everything else. Such experiences are pivotal, and come very close to the traditional religious understanding of *metanoia* or conversion.

Compared to the intensity of these lived mystical experiences in nature, much adult religiousness pales in comparison, and therefore what right have adults to say that youth today are not religious? We have to qualify this remark, and say that youth are not conventionally religious, but we cannot deny the religious element in their experience. There is a sense in youth culture that life is lived under a sacred canopy. All places, not just places designated as such by religious organisations, and all times are potentially holy depending upon how they are experienced.

Many people seem content to allow youth spirituality and formal religion to go their separate ways. The differences are radical and revolutionary, and it is easy to fall into the gap when it is so wide. But my interest is to call them into relationship and conversation. My view is that such splits in the contemporary experience of sacred meaning call out for healing and reconciliation, and that these splits, if left unattended, can have a debilitating effect on the community and on the psyche of the individual.

Formal religion could be enriched and renewed by the mystical experiences of young adults, and a greater understanding of the important relationship between the sacred and the natural world, which appears to be clearer to youth than to many adults, could develop. Moreover, youth could realise that their mystical experiences in nature are not just random events or arbitrary happenings, but have a great and long tradition with many saints, mystics and visionaries. Their mystical experiences are part of an evolving sacred tradition, and are not simply random New Age encounters with the cosmos. I maintain that youth need to feel connected to tradition and not alienated from it. After all, 'connectedness' is their popular definition of spirituality, so they should be encouraged to feel connected to scriptural and sacred tradition, as well as to the rocks, trees, skies and seas, that mean so much to them. They should not be made to feel alienated by a formal religion that has lost its sense of the immediacy of the sacred, and that seems oblivious to the experience of transcendence that can be afforded by the natural world.

MYSTICAL EMPHASIS ON THE GOD WITHIN

Youth appear convinced that something deep within the human person needs to be encountered and nourished, and this is what they refer to as the 'true self'. Within the true self, God is to be discovered and engaged, and while this idea is familiar in mysticism and the mystical truths found in numerous religions and cultures, it is challenging and new to formal religion, since the self has been typically devalued to emphasise the separate and entirely objective or external reality of the sacred. Youth appear convinced that the way to God is through the self, not beyond the self or through pious disregard of the self. What appears axiomatic to youth culture is highly contentious and debatable to religious culture, which can be seen to construct the self as an obstacle to God rather than as an instrument of God. The development of the inner life is generally frowned upon as an indulgence of our psycho-therapeutic age.

Religion often claims that such inward activity is negative, wasteful, indulgent and navel-gazing. This would be so if the human self were as old religion imagines it, namely a self that is distant from God and therefore circumscribed by sin. But in terms of the new creation spirituality, which imagines the world to be graced by the presence of God, our most immediate experience of God is within the depths of the self. Today, the young, and large numbers of adults, are engaged in self-exploration, not just to indulge the personal but to move beyond the personal into the transpersonal and the numinous. The self can be a legitimate doorway into the sacred, so long as the investigator moves deeply and far enough into the self so that he or she moves beyond the subjective into an inward objectivity. The guide to this dimension of the self is not Freud or academic psychology, but Jung and the 'spiritual psychology' that recognises something eternal at the core of the personality. Religion has its own resources—mysticism, meditation and the tradition of spiritual discernment—and need not necessarily become dependent on depth psychology, a form of psychology that takes into account the workings of the unconscious mind. These resources, however, have been overlaid by centuries of emphasis on extrinsic or external religion, and so have to be uncovered, reclaimed and made relevant to a new social climate.

In the conventional religious view, the self and creation can be seen to be characterised by sinfulness and evil, and so the exploration of self or interiority is not viewed with much enthusiasm. There is always the possibility of grace, but in traditional religion grace comes only through the agency of God, through ritual activity and external authority. The self, by contrast, is viewed as a maze of indulgence, a pitfall for the unwary, and as a narcissistic pond of illusion. But this language and belief system is out of date. The repression of self leads to neurosis and emptiness, rather than to spiritual illumination. In employing the old puritan ethic and its abnegation of self, people can become angry, shallow and resentful, rather than genuinely religious. The old talk about the 'indulgence' of self-reflection has become untenable, and if Western religion wants to renew itself it would do well to help people embark on interiority and internal exploration, rather than devalue this activity as bad or wasteful.

The old pattern of repressing the self no longer appeals to modern taste. What does appeal is dropping the ego and following the true self, in which truth may reside. This may seem like a minor adjustment, but it actually makes a world of difference. The old pattern leaves the believer without psychological resources, and the psyche or soul. When the self is ignored in the name of religion, we are left without internal development or foundation, making us all the more dependent on outside authority for guidance and support; which is why a controlling church once favoured this dispensation. But people understandably no longer want to hand over their authority to external forces that may be unreliable or misguided. They do not want to make 'leaps of faith' into the blind unknown, because they want to see what they are doing.

The hunger for internal, person-based spiritual experience is greater than ever before, and this can be read not as a weakening of religion, but an intensification of religion as intimate personal experience. To drop the ego and explore the self is a spiritual discipline that actually comes close to Buddhism and Eastern religions, which appear to show more psychological sophistication than our Western religions. But the flight to the East is not entirely necessary. We already have highly developed mystical traditions involving interiority and the exploration of the God within. What we have to do is draw these traditions from their historical obscurity and into the light of the present. Conventional religiosity based on devotional practice and the 'leap of faith' is coming to an end, but a mysticism based on interiority and care of the soul is likely to flourish and develop well into the future.

GOOD AND EVIL IN A NEW CONTEXT

Youth culture's quest is for a mystical and creation-centred theology, and this clashes with Western religion's fall-and-redemption theology. This theology has typically emphasised evil and sin, a critical separation from the body, negative attitudes towards sexuality, and a suspicion of nature as the arena of paganism and the devil. Youth spirituality appears as a 'natural' expression of religiousness, that is a spontaneous response to the presence of the sacred in creation, and it does not always appreciate the metaphysics of a religion that appears to be unworldly and dualistic. The Western dualities such as those between spirit and earth, spirit and body, spirit and nature, spirit and sexuality, are typically dishonoured by youth spirituality, which often sees no irreconcilable differences between this world and the other world.

Religion is often dumbfounded and astonished by this assumption that the world is good, and that creation is graced by the presence of the divine. Because youth see the world as essentially good and creation as graced, they often do not recognise the moral or spiritual urgency at the heart of Judeo-Christianity, namely the need to be saved from the world by a redeemer or messiah who grapples with evil and triumphs over it in life, death and resurrection. From my own experience, youth generally have nothing against Jesus, for example, but they see him more as a prophet or philosopher, rather than as a messiah or redeemer. Perhaps the gap in these assumptions arises from the fact that youth have not experienced enough evil or moral darkness in their own lives to recognise it as a palpable force in themselves or the world, and hence as something from which they need to be delivered. But they are not generally thrilled by the pronouncement that the world is flawed or evil, and that we need to forge a relationship with a redeemer to be released from the world.

My own view is that both parties are right. Western religion is correct in its conviction that evil is a reality and we need to be redeemed from it. Youth spirituality is also correct in its perception that the world is charged with the grandeur of God, and that we need to align ourselves more fully with the divinity that can be found within it. Both religion and youth spirituality are possessed of valuable truths, and each can learn something important from the other.

Religion can learn how to relax into a deeper sense of the sacredness inherent in creation. Its traditional focus can be one-sided and transcendentalist, so that the 'immanence' of the divine is often overlooked, causing a loss of value in nature, creation, the body and the instincts. Religion's focus has been narrowly confined to the vertical connection between people and heaven, and not enough attention has been paid to our horizontal connection with the realm of creation. Ecological awareness indicates that humanity can no longer be regarded as a special case apart from the natural world. Ecology shows that unless humanity can learn to revere the whole of creation, and not just the human part, the entire world, including our own species, is in danger of extinction.

Popular spirituality is also one-sided with its tendency to celebrate the good and ignore evil or sin. Its spiritual optimism and romantic attitude need to be complimented by religious 'realism' and a deeper understanding of the conflict between good and evil. Religion is so alert to this moral conflict that it can become unduly pessimistic and burdened by its awareness of the reality of evil, often to the detriment of a receptivity to the immediacy of the divine and the presence of the good. Youth spirituality is so receptive to this immediacy that it often fails to appreciate the obstacles that separate us from the divine, and fails to respect the immediacy of evil, with its cunning and wily ways and capacity to infiltrate society. Youth judges religion to be paranoid about evil, whereas religion deems youth to be naive, escapist and fanciful.

If both sides can stop calling each other names, they can learn a great deal from each other, and arrive at a deeper understanding of sacred reality. It is not an adequate response for religion to insist that it has the final truth and that youth are dabbling in heretical or wrongful activities, which are often referred to as New Age mysticism. Instead, it seems that we are dealing with a clash of cultural paradigms, a traditional paradigm in which religious truth is fixed and certain, and a new paradigm in which everything religious and spiritual is fluid and changing. In youth spirituality we see the 'spirit of the time' pushing towards a more incarnational and creation-friendly religion, one which understands more fully the meaning of the sacred in creation, and the way in which an awareness of this presence dramatically affects our relations with the world, the body, other people and the physical environment.

BREAKING 'RELIGION' TO RELEASE SPIRIT

Youth are not inventing a new religion or going back to paganism, as conservative voices often claim. Rather, youth spirituality is revealing an aspect of formal religion that was present in the beginning but got lost. This lost aspect is the primal vision of a holy spirit that makes whole. This is not a spirit that shies away from the body and matter, but a spirit that longs deeply and fully for the incarnation of spirit in life and embodiment. Youth seem to feel justified in the difficult task of hacking away the present dull forms of formal religion in an attempt to liberate the spirit that they discern within or beneath it.

Religious conservatives see this hacking and deconstructing as a dangerous attack on the body of the sacred, but to many young people it is a work of serious liberation. Typically, students write statements such as these:

> Perhaps religion has to be broken apart before spirituality can be born. Perhaps the demise of religion is necessary before we see a new development in spiritual awareness.
>
> (Beth, 19, 2001)

> In this age of 'new spirituality' we cast religion aside on the scrap heap as an out-of-date, paternalistic and corrupt system controlled by out of touch, narrow-minded men. Thank God! Throughout this time of transition, I do not think that many of

us have lost our faith in the idea of some kind of God. Rather, I think it is probably more that we have wanted to redefine what God is, and what it means to us as individuals. The task of the new spirituality is to fashion this new image of God.

(Matthew, 22, 2001)

Young people make it clear that this hacking away and breaking down is not conducted to destroy religion, but to arrive at the integral core of religion, which is spirituality:

Spirituality is after all the origin of all religions, and in reaching back to the source of all religions we are hoping to discover the primal ground from which life springs. When religion is dead and stagnant, our only option is to reach beyond religion to the spiritual core.

(Wendy, 18, 2001)

It is subtle but evident that an inner yearning is rising within the younger generation to go back to their roots, back to the beginning, and this is what the new spirituality is about.

(Marie, 18, 2001)

The present, established religious form is usurped by something that it sees as an arrogant new growth lacking in roots or foundations, but the new, insofar as it represents a genuine outbreak of the spirit, lays claim to a tradition which is far older than the one it is usurping. In a breathtaking reversal, the new denounces the old as sophisticated, artificial and recent, and it lays claim to a more distant and primal past, from which it draws its present authority. In the same way, new Christianity said to old Judaism, 'Before Abraham was, I am'.

Sometimes, the more passionately religious students are the bitterest critics of religion, because they sense what religion really is, or could be.

I aspire to be a religionless Christian. I want to get back to the essence of Christianity. For me, 'religion' gets in the way of Christianity. I want us to return to the simple message of the Gospel.

(Danny, 18, 2001)

> The most destructive force against Christianity has been
> Christians and the complacency of the Church. Churchianity
> has virtually destroyed a good religion.
>
> (Simon, 19, 2001)

The profundity of what students say always baffles and astonishes me. But what alarms and stresses me is that the beauty and importance of what they say is not being tracked by any of our institutions. Religious leaders and educators may dislike the current promiscuous and vague use of the term 'spirituality', but I see it as a return to the radical, original and primitive uses of the word 'spirit' in the days of the early Christian church. For St Paul and the first Christians, spirit was a term of protest and affirmation. It was a protest against the religious establishment of the day, which was felt to be degenerate and empty, and it was a protest against the worldly authority of ancient Rome, which imposed upon its colonies a hegemonic and imperial rule.

Youth often see the situation today as similar to that of Christ's time:

> Traditional churches are now in a state very similar to the state
> of the church when Jesus was alive: elitist, devoid of the Holy
> Spirit, hierarchical.
>
> (Danny, 18, 2001)

For the first Christians, 'spirit' and the 'spiritual man' (*pneumatikos*) was an affirmation of a truth beyond decaying religious structures or corrupt political institutions, a truth that belongs to a higher order of reality and to a future and greater manifestation of spirit. Authentic spirit is always prophetic and forward-looking, pointing ahead to an as-yet unrealised Coming Age. We must not forget that primitive Christianity must have looked very much like a New Age cult to the Pharisees, scribes and religious authorities of the day, even though that 'New Age' cult eventually gave rise to the high cultures of Byzantium and Christendom.

Youth are placed in a situation similar to the difficult lot of Hamlet, who sees that something is out of joint in the world, and he has to set about to correct it. For youth today, not Denmark, but 'religion' is out of joint, and youth feel called by fate or destiny to do something about it. 'O cursed spite', declares Hamlet, 'that ever I was born to set it right!' Youth do not necessarily want to enter into a fight with religion, but they feel impelled to do so by the spirit of the time. They have something very important to offer, but religion is rarely in the mood to be preached to by young people who show little experience of life and often little or no understanding of theology. What chance do they have to make a difference, if religion continues with this kind of patronising attitude? Youth clearly must be listened to, and listening to them could give religion the key to its own future. The stone rejected by the builders could become the cornerstone of the new church, if we are prepared to sit down and become involved in earnest negotiation and true conversation.

THE CHALLENGE OF NEGOTIATION

I am hoping that religion will eventually see its role not as a superego which condemns youth spirituality as wrong or bad, but rather as a sympathetic listener that offers discernment and gentle criticism to what is unfamiliar, strange or challenging. It is clear that bridges of communication need to be built across the gaps that separate 'civilised' religion and the 'natural' experience of the spirit. To enter into conversation will be challenging and difficult for both parties but, if the conversation is creative, neither side will remain unchanged, nor remain oblivious to the needs and views of the other. The act of conversation is itself a prelude to deeper spiritual experience, insofar as it sensitises us to the authenticity and difference of the sacred other.

Dialogue and conversation brings healing, but it also has the effect of making us more aware of our woundedness, and of the sharp differences between warring elements. An emphasis on differences can be painful, and yet there can be no healing without embarking on a pilgrimage to our pain, and allowing ourselves to feel its intensity. Sometimes religious organisations think that I present too much pain and harsh reality; perhaps more than they can comfortably assimilate. If my portrait of youth spirituality is too stark or graphic, if it varies too greatly from the norms and expectations of religion, there can be a desire on the part of religious organisations to shoot the messenger of this bad news, or to argue that I am being unduly difficult. But again, I try to do justice to youth spirituality, and do not intend to smooth over the differences simply to allow any organisation to feel better about itself.

It has to be admitted that this exercise in bridge-building or conversation is generally of more interest to religious adults than it is to the majority of youth. Sometimes young people are resistant to dialogue with formal religion, because their spirituality is styled as a personal protest against the authority of the institutions of faith. The very word 'spirituality', as it is used by young people today, often signals a protest against formal religion, which may be perceived by them as oppressive, heavy or burdensome. Their magic word 'spirituality' announces that they are free to establish a personal relationship with the sacred outside church and without its guidance or support. So, for some young people, bridge-building would be vehemently resisted, and where it is attempted it could be viewed as a way of imposing 'establishment' views upon their own spiritual expression.

But for religious adults, especially those who are engaged with youth on a regular basis, bridge-building is vitally important, and without it not much can be achieved. Teachers and principals in religious schools, religious educators, counsellors, health and community workers, and chaplains in schools and universities must attempt to reach out across the gap that separates formal religion and youth experience. If there is no attempt to cross this gap, there is no contact made with students, and hence religious education or spiritual formation does not really take place. Educators can go through the motions of conveying religious values and formations, but if they have not caught the interest or passion of youth, if they have failed to engage their experience or capture their imagination, not a lot can be achieved.

THE SPIRIT AND MAKING NEW

Religious adults who have little or no contact with youth may protest that religion is perfectly good as it stands, and see no need to make any accommodations to contemporary experience. But religious adults who are closer to the grassroots of society recognise the ever-present need of religion to reinterpret itself for the rising generations, lest it lose its efficacy and meaning. This work of renewal and reinterpretation is inspired by the spirit, in whom everything is made new and in whom the eternal word is made accessible to the contemporary generations.

Religion that is resistant to the life of the spirit never sees the need to change its direction or accent, and clings tightly to the forms of the past, seeking to reproduce those forms in the present. Only receptivity to the spirit gives us the courage to be creative in religious tradition, and only the spirit makes us look forward to the future rather than defer constantly to the past. Through the spirit, we understand that tradition is not simply about repetition of the past, but about growing into new and deeper forms of the source that nourishes us. This daring understanding of tradition, which invites rather than discourages change, can only be understood by educators, parents and adults when we give ourselves over to a mystery that is greater than ourselves. Working with young people in the arena of spirituality can only be effective if we are prepared to look to the future and be guided by its creative spirit. When that spirit is contacted, we can then reach out to youth with love and compassion, rather than seek to control or punish them with adult authority.

CHAPTER 6

Spiritual education:
a difficult kind of bliss

Religion appears to create a lot of trouble, not only in recent times but throughout history. Perhaps spirituality is the only neutral platform we have available to us, a platform for unity and peace.

Natasha, 18, 2001

The term 'spiritual education' has a great ring to it, but perhaps the term sounds exalted or even grandiose to those who hear it for the first time. Spiritual education expresses the ideal or hope that education can, even today, move the heart and quicken the spirit. It best describes what I try to do in my courses at university, so I am happy to have my teaching activities described by this term. I first heard the term mentioned in the United Kingdom, and in Australia I am developing my own version. I am not exactly sure that what I am doing under this term is related to what is happening elsewhere, but I like to imagine that I am part of an international network of researchers who have a broadly similar idea about this kind of endeavour.

THE IDEA AND PLACE OF SPIRITUAL EDUCATION

My work in spiritual education operates in two contexts: it is in tertiary education, and it is in a secular, multicultural environment. Most of the work going on internationally appears to be focused on secondary and primary levels of education, that is on children and adolescents in schools. I think there is a huge need to develop spiritual education with young adults at the tertiary level, but at that level, of course, we face considerable problems about where such activity belongs in the university structure. Should it be in religious studies, theology, education theory, literature, psychology, philosophy, sociology or public health? The current compartmentalisation of knowledge in the university means that a subject such as spiritual education, which insists on a holistic approach to mind, body and spirit, has no obvious home or location.

Perhaps the introduction of spiritual education in the schools will mean that teachers in training should have the option of studying spiritual education in their preparatory degrees. But I would like to see the field moving beyond departments of teacher training to include such areas as psychology, philosophy and public health. It will be important not to 'ghettoise' spiritual education in one discipline, or its holistic potentials and broader cultural implications will be stymied and reduced. Spirituality is not just a new style of teaching but a new style of consciousness, and as such it needs to be made available to a broad range of students in a variety of training.

In the same vein, while it is important to introduce spiritual education in religious schools, it is just as important to introduce it in state or secular schools, and not to confine it to an experiential side of religious instruction. The spirit is a universal aspect of human character, and it needs to be developed and educated in every educational setting. So far, my own consultations with schools have been confined to religious secondary schools. This is rewarding in its own way, because spiritual education represents a new challenge to religious schools, urging them to step back from formal religion and make contact with the inner life of the student, which is where spiritual education begins. As yet, I have not had the opportunity to work with state or secular schools, partly because such schools wonder what 'spirit' has to do with them. But I am looking forward to such openings and discussions, because my own academic experience in spiritual education has been in the secular domain.

Since Western societies are primarily secular, we have to view the secular, and not just the religious, as a major site for the return of spirit in the world. I like the challenge of spirit arising in secular contexts that have no formal religious understanding of the spirit. This appeals to my desire to work with human basics and fundamentals. The spirit appears like a thief in the night, and in the dark night of our secular culture we see many signs of spirit appearing in people's lives, and moving them to new and radical constructions of reality.

INTRODUCING SPIRIT IN NEW CONTEXTS

The first thing to note about spiritual education is that it is a new area and, as such, it meets with resistance of various kinds. I often refer to my own experience in spiritual education as a 'difficult kind of bliss', noting the irony that although spirituality is about peace, connectedness and equanimity it often produces enmity, alienation and discord, at least in the early stages and in a professional setting. Spirituality is a kind of wild space that civilisation looks upon with some degree of suspicion and doubt. Religious education sometimes wants to know why spiritual education is desirable or needed, and whether it promotes the causes and purposes of religion, or whether it subverts those causes by appealing to a more primal ground of experience, outside the purview and control of religion as such.

Secular education has the opposite kind of resistance. Spiritual education is resisted precisely because it looks too religious, and secular authorities worry that their own authority is going to be undermined by the return of a religious sensibility that secular education thought it had eradicated long ago. Is spiritual education just religious passion with a new name, with religious fanaticism just around the corner? Is spirituality the thin end of a wedge that will drive tolerance and compassion out of society, to be replaced by religious intolerance and oppression? Is the teacher who suddenly sets up shop as a spiritual educator, and who feels 'called' to spiritual education an inspired educator, or just some lost soul who is trying to create a one-person cult because he or she does not fit into any established church?

These and other questions appear in the minds of secular and humanist colleagues when spiritual education is identified as a possible area of development in secular institutions. I think these questions are very important. It is vital that we protect the hard-won values of secular education, including openness, free-thinking and liberal attitudes to knowledge and compassionate attitudes to students from any fanaticisms that might be encouraged by religious passions. From an historical point of view, it is the responsibility of any culture or group to police its own boundaries and to insist on border control. Since secular education arose partly in opposition to religious convictions, we might expect that secular institutes are never going to give way to spiritual education without some kind of enquiry into the nature of the new enterprise. Exactly what is this spirit that seeks to be introduced? How can we know it or define it, and how can we guard against its excesses?

Certainly we should engage in discussions about what we are doing and what education is about. However, I feel it is just a matter of time before the secular bubble of education is burst, and its resistances are overcome by a new interest in things spiritual and mystical. Part of the postmodern imperative is to overcome the modernist resistance towards the sacred, and to defeat the modernist assertion that God is dead. Such certainty can no longer be maintained, and it now becomes important to break out of the confines of purely rational and reductive thought. A new paradigm of knowledge is already in the making, and it will invite us out of the iron-cage of rationality into broader categories of thought, in which poetry, mystery and symbolic thinking are reaffirmed and experienced anew. Models of knowledge are changing. But before change becomes possible, the old secular model, sensing its imminent demise, can become agitated in its bid to regain the control to which it has become accustomed.

Intellectually, the word 'spirit' raises the alarm bells in the halls of academe. The problem is that many academics and scholars have no concept of 'spirit' apart from its pre-modern and ancient expressions. They regard any talk about spirit as backward-looking and regressive, a return to the dark ages. This makes the need for contemporary expressions of spirit even more urgent, so that models can be established that do not imply or necessitate returning to the past.

THE WINGS OF INSPIRATION

I say that I 'teach' a course on spirituality but this is hardly the right word if by 'teach' we mean the usual hard grind that attends to the process of imparting knowledge to students who are half-hearted, often unprepared, and not always sufficiently committed to the task at hand. This subject is a peculiar phenomenon. It appears to teach itself, and the usual problem of trying to win student attention does not seem to exist. The level of student interest and motivation is unusually high because they have decided that this subject is speaking to them in their own kind of language. The course matters to them, and it evokes an internal commitment or personal response often expressed by the fact that the set texts have been read before the formal commencement of the semester. Discussions in tutorials are animated, and conversations frequently spill over the formal times into after-hours or lunch times.

I sometimes get the sense that all I have to do is put up a sail, and the wind or *pneuma* of the spirit catches it and carries the subject forwards. If I am ill, the classes often meet without me and discuss the reading of the week. It is an uncanny experience for me as a teacher for I have never met this level of commitment before. The reason it works so well is because the ideas are emotional, and have existential purchase on the students' minds and hearts. The ideas have effect and arouse affections. It is the only subject I have ever taught where the numbers do not decline after a few weeks. In fact enrolments often increase because students tell their friends about the excitement they are experiencing.

The first stages of the course are often idyllic. Students are excited by the prospect of a university course seeking to engage their spiritual lives, and this is a novelty that keeps the ship afloat in smooth sailing, under a dreamy full moon. When I first raised the idea of this course with colleagues, some were worried by the possible outcomes. One said that the course would act as a magnet to all the New Age disciples on campus, and I would spend a great deal of my energy battling with New Age rigidity, dogmatism and fundamentalism. The witches, wizards, fortune-tellers and wisdom hippies would be present in their full regalia, with fixed views on the spirit and entrenched ideologies about the sacred. This prospect worried me so much that, as the course approached, I became increasingly alarmed and panicky.

I was pleasantly surprised to find that these morbid fears were unfounded, and a typical example of academic resistance, within my colleague and myself. The spirituality of youth looks at first like an unattractive pool of irrationality. Do we look into that pool and see reflected back the ugly face of our own unattended spiritual life? Yes, there are always some New Age students in the class; a variety of witches, wizards, druids, pagans, gothics, eco-warriors and occultists. But they are not aggressively pushy about their interests, and sometimes I find I can hardly get them to talk about their personal spiritual commitments, because they are quite protective of an inner life that means a great deal to them. They are not in the course to parade and push their New Age wares, but are enormously interested in the range of course materials that I am presenting to them.

THE PROJECT OF RE-ENCHANTMENT

The expressed goal of the subject is to develop the contours and directions of a postmodern spirituality. This is the common goal we are all focused on, and the subject moves steadily towards this objective. We begin the course with a consideration of the non-religious condition of modernity, with the state of disenchantment and the absence of sacred cosmology characteristic of the secular era, using Max Weber[79] and Nietzsche[80] as our points of reference. The task is to move from the condition of disenchantment to re-enchantment, exploring various mythic sources and primordial elements that can lift us out of the spiritual wasteland into a soulful and vital sense of reality.

The subject makes it clear that there are many elements to a postmodern spirituality. Almost by definition it has to use, and value, diversity and plurality. This means, in principle, that the pagans, witches and astrologers can feel validated and included, even though their ideological interests are not featured in the course. This emphasis on diversity means that they can see themselves as participants in the new spiritual landscape. I suspect this is all they really want and, because they feel included, they are not pushy in the way that my colleague had anticipated.

THE SPIRITUALITY WARS

Perhaps predictably, my only real source of disturbance and complaint is not from New Age rebels but from old-style Christian fundamentalists. Generally, they are not happy about the emphasis on plurality and diversity in the new spiritual dispensation. It is the religious fundamentalists who break the blissful beginning, and who terminate the honeymoon period by complaints about relativism, fragmentation and disrespect for objective truth and revelation. When I taught this subject for the first time, I thought I was steering wonderfully through the hazardous path by emphasising plurality and variety, thinking this would make everyone feel included. I was not sufficiently aware that there were traditionalists in the group who were seething with resentment at this direction. For them, there was only one genuine spiritual pathway, and only one spiritual redeemer. For most students, the subject is a rite of passage into the postmodern condition of plurality, and into the new spiritual tolerance that must be part of this condition. But for a few this attitude is regarded as blasphemy and strongly protested.

So the course commences with a blissful feeling of spiritual fellowship, but after a couple of weeks this is over and the 'spirituality wars' begin. Shots are fired as religious students announce in tutorials or in the lecture room that they are shocked to find that their secular peers have appropriated spirituality for themselves. The religious students, who are always the minority, seem to have come from a different world, to have stepped out of a cultural bubble. They often seem utterly astonished by the postmodern landscape. They claim not to have realised that so many secular people have appropriated spirituality, and had no idea that spirituality had become so popular.

At first they are astonished, but later they can express a degree of anger and indignation. How come, they announce, there is all this casual, do-it-yourself spirituality, when we felt that in order to be spiritual you had to be religious as well? It is quite common for verbal battles to break out at this time. The more stridently religious students sometimes tell the secular students that they are deluding themselves. They say there can be no spirituality without religion, and certainly none without due reverence towards sacred tradition. They find their secular peers to be irreverent and unduly critical towards religion, and they sometimes advise their peers to join a faith community and to find spiritual life in the context of a tradition of faith.

In response to this, the more outspoken and extraverted secular students will reply that spirituality and religion are entirely different, and even opposite things. They are strangers or perhaps rivals at 'the banquet of transcendence'.[81] Secular students might announce that it is the religious students who are fooling or deluding themselves, because there is no true or living spirituality in religion. 'Just go to my local church and see for yourself', blurted out one secular student in class, as others laughed in agreement. He had tried religion, he said, and found only routine devotion, dull worship and blind belief. There was no spirituality, which he said is a living personal relationship with the sacred.

After this interjection, someone else said we cannot trust the clergy with our spiritual lives, because some of them are paedophiles and sexual monsters who should be regarded as criminals and put behind bars, not treated as spiritual guides or holy men. This young man disagreed vehemently with the young religious woman who said that students should find spirituality in religion. The woman then invited him to come along to her church to see for himself. Secular students often say there is more social conditioning and cultural engineering in religion than there is contact with the sacredness of life. A common attack is for secular students to say 'There is plenty of God talk, but no God presence in religion'.

BREAKING UP TACKLES IN THE SPIRITUALITY WARS

Feminist students will often describe Christianity as a patriarchal invention and this offends the Christians in class. Self-described pagan or wicca students will say that religion is partly responsible for the desecration of the earth and the destruction of the environment, and this leaves the religious students in a mild rage. Esoteric and occult students will say that Christianity lost its spirituality hundreds of years ago, and the only way to recover spirituality today is to get out of religion and into nature, or rediscover the ancient esoteric traditions and divinatory systems of antiquity. This kind of talk creates heated argument and passionate disagreement. A Christian revivalist student once stood up in the class and announced that the only way to achieve spiritual life was to take Jesus into our hearts right now. At this, the secular students rolled their eyes in disbelief, and some fell about laughing and offered noisy ridicule.

When it comes to argument and battle, Christianity is usually at the front line and eager to prove itself as a worthy opponent to alien points of view. This means that, several weeks into the course, Christianity is at the heart of every fight and at the core of much public discussion. Here I often have to intervene and to introduce wider perspectives. Jewish, Islamic and secular students have complained to me about Christian domination in the classroom. When Christianity becomes stridently assertive, a formidable opposition is arraigned against it, including those who are either secular, agnostic, atheist, wicca, pagan, feminist, Jewish, Islamic, Hindu or Buddhist. This diverse group might seem to be composed of strange bedfellows, but such a broad alliance is formed when outspoken Christians dominate in the classroom.

Often my role in the battles that rage in tutorials and seminars is to play the role of umpire or referee. Sometimes my job is to engage in conflict resolution. I break up tackles and hose down the heated remarks. If necessary I urge one person to apologise to another, and generally try to insist on civilised and humane conduct. I have to get the Christian student to apologise to the wicca student for calling their religion 'crap'. When I first offered courses in spirituality, I did not realise I would be walking into this kind of battlefield. Would I do it all again if I knew then what I know now? Yes, because these are the debates and battles that society has to have. We are only having spirituality wars because we are not having spirituality talks. I live in the hope that through conversation and dialogue we can sort out some of the differences and bring competing sides into a clearer sense of understanding. Perhaps some enemies may develop regard for each other simply by understanding what the other person represents and what he or she believes.

I have discovered that the best way to resolve religious disputes is to try to shift the discussion away from religion to spirituality again. Drawing the attention of the group back to the living spirit in our experience seems to unite the group in a common human bond, and to alleviate the tension that arises from religious or traditional affiliations. Shifting the focus from the larger religious claims to the personal encounter with spirit seems to act as a balm that smoothes over troubled waters. Squabbles are defused as soon as one suggests that the sacred is 'at hand', as soon as one indicates that the divine is close and available to all. The potential that spirituality presents for world peace and the resolution of religious or sectarian conflict seems to be enormous, and yet such potentials remain essentially unexplored. Religious organisations will not explore them because their province is religion not spirituality. Secular organisations will not explore them because their province is secularism and not spirituality. Commenting in a seminar on this topic, one of my students wrote, 'spirituality unites and religion divides'.

THE RELIGIOUS POSITION OF THE SPIRITUAL EDUCATOR

It has to be admitted that this return of focus to universal spirituality does not please the fundamentalist minority. They do not like my basic assumption that everyone can enjoy the spiritual life, whether or not we are part of a religious tradition or institution of faith. The fundamentalists frequently demand to know what my own religious orientation is, and when I point out that I am a mystical Christian, they want to know why I am letting the side down and not engaging in the practice of evangelisation. They tend to assume that I am being weak and, like Peter, denying my Lord. These students will then discuss my attitudes with fundamentalist chaplains on campus, and try in vain to figure out what is going on. I have had several fundamentalist students formally withdrawing from the subject, and writing letters to me about why this course does not satisfy them, and why it lacks the courage of its convictions. It is, wrote one complaining student, the 'religious course we have when we are not being religious'. I just have to weather these storms, and realise that they are part of the total experience of exploring such sensitive and delicate areas of human experience.

My declared religiousness at this point makes the fundamentalist students more angered and excited, and the secular students more suspicious. To the secular majority, I seemed at the outset to be reasonable and postmodern, and now I spoil this by indicating my commitment to a faith tradition. A group of secular students once invited me to the university bar for a drink, to talk me out of my connection with Christianity. One student said, 'We want you to be like us, to make spirituality your religion'. I am in a different state of mind to many of my students, and the age difference means that I am at a very different stage in my journey of spirit. Usually the secular students are happy for me to be religious and spiritual at the same time, so long as I do not seek to impose my views on them or to cramp their style. In a university cafe, I overheard one student say to another, 'He's Christian, but he's good though'. I took this as a compliment. 'Good though' is shorthand for saying he does not impose his beliefs on us. The secular students are generally far more tolerant of difference than the religious students, and that includes being tolerant of differences between themselves and their teacher. But as one religious student said to me, 'They are tolerant towards differences because they do not care enough about religious belief to really oppose it'.

THE DISAPPEARANCE OF OLD BATTLELINES

Caring enough to be passionate and quarrelsome makes me reflect on earlier religious conflicts. When I was a boy, the old battlelines between Catholic and Protestant used to be charged with energy and a real source of potential personal and social conflict. But this old battleline seems to have receded into the dim past. Indeed, I cannot recall that it has been raised as an issue in any of my classes in recent years. Students today seem to belong to a different world, so that old-world conflicts between Catholic and Protestant, still important in old-world countries such as Ireland, are of no concern at all to Australian students. A student of mine was born in Belfast, but migrated with her parents to Australia when she was 12-years-old. She recently visited her native Ireland, and various people there seemed to want to know if she was Catholic or Protestant. 'Oh no,' she told one enquirer, 'I'm Australian'. The primary designation in a secular society is with place and nationality, not with religion or denomination.

Students do not seem to care whether you belong to this or that denomination. They do not worry about Catholic or Protestant, and this is true for the religious students as much as for the secular ones. To them, the issue of natal faith or family faith tradition seems almost incidental to what one believes now. Hardly anyone assumes that young adults remain loyal to their natal traditions, and even the more fanatical fundamentalists have generally converted to revivalist movements from a different religious background. The new battlelines are not denominational, but existential and urgent. Is there a God or not? Is there a spiritual world, or is it illusory? Are we related to something eternal or not? These spiritual questions are existential and pre-theological, which is why denominationalism has faded as a reality. Most students have no idea what transubstantiation is, let alone see it as a cause for social dispute and personal enmity.

IS THERE VALUE IN WITCHCRAFT AND WICCA?

The spiritual educator learns much from the students about the area of spirit. Although entering my courses with conventional Christian prejudices against wicca and paganism, the course has actually taught me a new respect for the wicca point of view. Wicca students can be far more interesting than teachers anticipate. They often write beautiful essays about their quest for sacredness and truth in nature. They have an important contribution to make, and this is partly to demonstrate to official and mainstream religions that the West has lost contact with nature and needs to relocate God in the world, and not merely focus on God in a distant transcendental heaven. In fact, after some fascinating discussions with self-described witches and wizards, I have begun to see that these students are compensating for the transcendental one-sidedness of Western religious culture.

Such students are offering an invaluable critique of what could be called the ideology of 'heavenism' in Christianity, and are demonstrating in extreme form the very elements that Christianity needs to re-integrate into itself. Of course, calling themselves witches and wizards is bound to incite anger in mainstream Christians, and that is partly why they designate themselves in this way. But beneath the anger, the splitting and the conflict we may discern a more important message for our time: the realm of nature must be rediscovered as a major site for sacred celebration and religious worship. If Christianity learnt the lessons that St Francis of Assisi, Teilhard de Chardin and Thomas Berry were preaching, perhaps students would not feel so obliged to act out the repressed content of our religion in such split-off, adversarial ways.

THE RELIGIOUSNESS OF SPIRITUALITY

If we are to reach people today, to make contact with their spiritual and emotional lives, we have to engage in what some theologians call pre-evangelisation. That is to say, we have to ask basic and core questions about life, outside the security of dogma and theology, because that is where most of us are, beyond such boundaries. If we want to reach young people, we have to meet them where they are. Thus, during the whole process of spiritual education, it is wise to make clear distinctions between religion and spirituality.

But sometimes the distinctions I make for practical purposes become dualisms that hamper my vision of what is actually taking place. For various public, professional and pedagogical reasons, I tend to exaggerate the differences between religion and spirituality, thereby losing touch with the religious dimension of spiritual education. I am often reminded of this dimension when students ask me to recommend a religious path. The spirituality course often awakens in them a new interest in religion, and they sometimes choose to re-explore the faith of their childhood or, if they had no natal faith, new channels for their religious interest. I have been forced to recognise that, despite my defensive separation of religion and spirituality, the education of the spiritual impulse leads directly to new or renewed interest in religion. I have been told many times by students, after they have finished the course, that they now intend to consider religion in a new light.

The new light can be stated in this way: religion need not be considered an obstacle to spirituality, but a resource for spiritual wisdom and insight. Students realise that if the dogma and doctrine are peeled away, religion can be an aid to spiritual journeying, and not just an external or extrinsic system of empty signifiers. I am very reluctant to give students advice about their choice of a religious path. I am ambivalent about religion. It does provide history, memory and substance, but religion in our time is so poorly presented and spiritually undeveloped that anyone with a specific interest in spirituality is going to find religion problematical at the very least. Anyway, my role as spiritual educator is not to make suggestions to students about which religion to adopt. The students need to make up their own minds about religious direction, and I will be interested in whatever path they choose to explore.

HOLISTIC EDUCATION AND INTELLECTUAL RIGOUR

Spiritual education, as I understand it, seeks to educate the whole person. It is not just cerebral or intellectual, but is also imaginative, affective and creative. It tries to fire up both left and right hemispheres of the brain, and it does not seek to develop the rational capacities at the expense of the imaginative or intuitive aspects. Spiritual education encourages, and sometimes even initiates, the development of an inner life, and to this extent it can appear subversive to the kind of education that insists on the externality of knowledge and intellectual enquiry.

But the emphasis on the intuitive and the creative can raise the spectre of intellectual softness and vagueness. As we relax the iron grip of the rational intellect, do we open the door to a certain laxity or loss of intellectual standards? This is a fear that many educators have, and I have felt this fear myself. When the spiritual life is activated, is there a corresponding suspension of the critical faculty? The answer to this question is yes and no. If the head and the heart are deeply divided, then we tend to shift from the one to the other in dramatic and radical ways. The Western psyche in particular seems to be deeply divided along the lines of reason and faith, or intellect and feeling. As the philosopher Paul Ricoeur[82] has argued, we are faced with a choice between an 'hermeneutics of suspicion' (reason), and an 'hermeneutics of affirmation' (faith), and often it is difficult to have the two hermeneutical responses at one and the same time.

But we must struggle towards a wholeness of response, because intellect and heart need each other, and we should not use the new interest in spirituality as an excuse to shift from one extremism to another. It is possibly this fear that prevents many educators from shifting into the spiritual mode of teaching and learning. It is perhaps felt that critical education must be preserved at all costs, and that as soon as we set foot in the spiritual domain we degenerate into responses that are warm, fuzzy and irrational. While this is a real danger, I think the fear mostly arises from ignorance of the spiritual domain. I am assuming that those of us who are interested in spiritual education proceed from the assumption that we are interested in educating the whole person, and not merely wallowing in the non-rational.[83] We gain enormous inner or psychological support in this task, because it seems to me that the spiritual function inherently longs to become united with the intellectual function. Spirituality seeks reason to free it from the burden of the irrational.

Here Hegel is illuminating, although his language is not always helpful. 'Spirit which knows itself to be Spirit is science'. Hegel said that although spirit is often 'intuited rather than thought', we must not 'fall back on intuition and set it above reflective thought'. 'This is a mistake', he said, 'for one cannot philosophise out of intuition. What is intuited must also be thought, the isolated parts must be brought back by thought to simple universality; into ... an immanent self-moving unity which contains the specific differences'.[84] In Jung's language, not quite as difficult as Hegel's, an impulse towards wholeness arises from the very core of the inner self, and unless we meddle with or abuse the component parts of the psyche, the parts of the mind seek union with the whole.

Certainly in my teaching I have found this to be the case more often than not. To release the spiritual side of the student is not to release only warm and fuzzy feelings that seek ecstasy and quietude (meditation, relaxation), but to release deep sources of inspiration that quicken the mind and restore excitement and personal motivation to learning. To teach through the spirit is to bring to life the inner core of the person and to relate that core to the intellectual material that is being discussed.

CHAPTER 7

Losing my religion, recovering the sacred

Modern non-religious man forms himself by a series of denials and refusals, but he continues to be haunted by the realities he has refused and denied.

Mircea Eliade[85]

Among the students I teach, it is fairly common to hear stories about the abandonment of a former religious affiliation, or the loss of one's natal faith, and the subsequent adoption of a non-religious spirituality. Many reasons are put forward by those who are now without religion about why they have divested themselves of its trappings. As Sandra Schneiders writes:

> Religion is in trouble, spirituality is in the ascendancy [and everywhere we hear] justification among those who have traded the religion of their past for the spirituality of their present.[86]

THE FIVE-FOLD PATH

The pattern I discern in many of these cases has a five-fold structure:

1 NATAL FAITH

'I was born into a religious family, and inducted into its faith traditions and institutions.'

2 ADOLESCENT SEPARATION

'I began to ask questions about faith in teenage life, questions for which I did not receive satisfactory or adequate answers.'

3 SECULAR IDENTIFICATION

'I gradually lost contact with my natal faith, and renounced my institutional affiliation. I may even have begun to denounce my faith tradition, referring to myself as secular, humanist, agnostic or atheist. Meanwhile, Mum and Dad had loosened their ties to religion; they still felt it was important, but did not necessarily practise it themselves, and they felt I could make up my own mind about religious matters.'

4 SECULAR DISILLUSIONMENT

'I made the transition to the secular society, but still did not feel satisfied. The secular world said I was free, but I did not really feel free. I began to feel something was missing; there was a God-shaped hole in my life. The secular world says I need to consume more goods, take more holidays, or seek more entertainment, but somehow this seems unfulfilling.'

5 ADULT 'SECULAR' SPIRITUALITY

'I eventually developed my own "secular" spirituality, free from religious influence, outside the church, temple or synagogue, and part of the "resurgence" of spiritual feeling in today's society.'

This pattern is so typical we might almost refer to it as 'archetypal', a universally recurring pattern of contemporary experience. It is the story of 'Losing my religion and discovering my spirituality'. It is a story often told with enthusiasm and optimism, as if telling of a movement from bondage to freedom, from darkness to light. This is a fascinating sociological narrative, but it always raises in my mind some suspicion and critical awareness. I would like to know what this narrative is really saying about the person and his or her lived experience of religion and society. In particular, what is this narrative omitting, leaving out or hiding? The fact that it is so pervasive could lead us to suspect that we are in the grips of a new social myth.

THE TYRANNY OF THE SECULAR

One thing this story leaves out, as I have discovered in numerous conversations, is that one's early belonging to a faith tradition could have been a positive rather than a negative experience. It is only given a negative spin because this story is now told from a secular or so-called 'enlightened' position, in which religion is now associated with childhood darkness, and secular humanism with the bright light of reason and rationality. The memory that natal faith could have been essentially positive is repressed by this schematised and sketchy reconstruction of one's personal past. A new secular consciousness re-reads the personal past in a different way, and a 'false' memory is substituted in which religion is seen as basically negative or oppressive, and movement away from it is constructed as a journey from bondage to light.

The secular world constantly tells us that 'religion' is about indoctrination, conditioning and coercion, and therefore must be bad. What it does not tell us is that secularism itself is a potent form of indoctrination, all the more potent for not being detected as such. Secularism is driven by rationality and 'common' sense, and it has long attempted to view religion through a distorting lens, making it seem unpleasant, corrupted or unattractive. This is not to deny the fact that some individuals have had disturbing or negative experiences of the faith institutions and their authority figures, leaders or representatives. I do not want to suggest that everyone who complains about religious authority is making things up, or fabricating stories that are then used to condemn the church concerned. But I am suggesting that the abusive and harmful aspects of formal religion have been inflated by our secular culture, and in particular by the media, which is fearful of religion, unable to understand it, and threatened by its continued existence. Young people who tell the familiar story of dropping their religion are unaware of the secular myth in which they are held, and are unconscious of the new kind of conditioning that passes for personal liberation.

The loss of religion in adolescence is not always the result of a loss of faith as such, but the product of an overwhelming desire to belong to mainstream society. In other words, religion and religious identity become casualties of socialisation. Students often report not so much a turning away from God and religion, as a turning towards society and 'life' as it is defined in secular terms. God and religion are placed 'on hold', as some students write, and secular values are embraced to further this identification with society and their connectedness with peers and friendship circles.

The individual who is born into a religious faith often finds him- or herself in the situation of being coerced into a secular identity, in which a feeling of embarrassment attaches to the memory of their background and family tradition, and religion is discarded as quickly and fully as possible to accommodate the smooth transition into an adult social reality. Students in this situation are often unaware of what they are leaving behind, and unable to articulate their sense of loss and bereavement, since they are subscribing to a new myth that says their needs and desires will be fulfilled in the secular domain.

NATAL FAITH AS A PRESENCE IN THE SOUL

Secular identity does not deliver the hoped-for panacea of freedom and enlightenment. Young adults are freed from religious and parental authority, but inwardly they do not feel liberated, since the life of the spirit has merely been cut off and disconnected. The outward freedom is welcomed, but inwardly they feel more unfree and unhappy. A deep part of their human nature is neither fulfilled nor supported by secular identity, and so typically the lapsed Catholic, Anglican or Jew, goes in search of a new kind of enchantment, in which the longings of the spirit can be engaged.

Such people are not always aware of the continuing presence of their natal faith in their reconstituted and post-religious spirituality. The announcement that they are 'not very religious' is meant to emphasise their present secular state, and to assure their friends and peers that they are free from the burden of religion. But 'religion' is not merely an external formal practice, much as secularism might like to pretend that it is. Religion is also internalised by the person, and has gained some existential presence in the soul. At least some of its values and attitudes are discovered in the inner recesses of the personality and, I would argue, form the basis for much of the 'non-religious' spirituality that emerges in later life.

If there were positive experiences of faith as a child, and if some of the faith values were internalised, these elements remain as features of the personality, even if they are overlaid, suppressed or stifled by subsequent adaptation. Beneath the secular persona, there are vague but real resonances, memories and echoes of religious life, which may serve as the basis for a renewal of faith and spiritual identity at a later stage. As the individual enters maturity, he or she becomes aware of a lost heritage or memory, which continues to resound in the mind and heart even though a different path has been taken. In 'Four Quartets' Eliot writes:

> Footfalls echo in the memory
> Down the passage which we did not take
> Towards the door we never opened.[87]

These footfalls, echoes and resonances cannot be underestimated, and may form the basis of a renewed commitment to faith when the individual is no longer pressured by society or friends to conform to standard expectations. I often hear young adults boasting that they have left religion behind, and then a few moments later they are wistful and even nostalgic about the path that was not taken. The secular adaptation is not as successful as our first contact with many young people would lead us to suppose.

WHEN RELIGION IS ERASED FROM MEMORY

If the early religious affiliation was primarily negative, or experienced as destructive by the child, a different scenario develops. Such people experience the defeat of religion as a personal triumph, and there are no lingering footfalls or echoes of the path not taken. I have observed this pattern in a number of my students, and there is a sense that something fundamental has gone wrong, and that negative attitudes towards religion will have a persistently retarding influence, effectively preventing the person from ever approaching the mysterious door of the in-dwelling spirit.

A negative experience of religion does not necessarily mean that religious authorities have acted towards the child in harmful, emotionally injurious, sexually abusive, or otherwise threatening ways. From my experience with students, there need be no malevolent intent or activity at all for religion to leave an indelibly negative impression on the mind. Religion need only be perceived by the child as coldly external, as having no claims on their personal affections or interests, for it to be lost irrevocably in their minds and hearts. The transgression of religion is often not that it has impacted too strongly on the person, but that it has left no lasting impression at all. It has not moved, touched or opened the soul; in other words, it has not been experienced as having any spiritual content, so that nothing resonates lovingly in the human soul.

The failure of religion to move the soul can, however, also result from the opposite process. If religion strives too hard to make an impression on the child, the child can experience it as invasive, destructive and anti-life. In this case the child withdraws defensively and closes off from the claims of religion. An authoritarian, insensitive or heavy-handed approach can result in a siege mentality in the psyche, where the child withdraws behind barriers of protection from religious and moral instruction. This has the same result of making the child feel that religion is entirely external to his or her life, having no purchase on the soul. The art of religion is an art of relationship, and just as interpersonal relationships go wrong and become bungled in life, so our relationship to religion is complex and can easily go wrong.

If religion has made no lasting impression on the soul, or has been experienced as invasive and dangerous, an attitude results that we can call 'indifferentism'. The individual shrugs his or her shoulders and decides that the enterprise of religion is not for them. Here the matter rests, at least until such time as a life crisis ensues, and the ultimate questions have to be faced again. Those with negative experiences or memories are most likely to find their spiritual meaning, if they search for it at all, in exotic, alien or non-Western traditions. Buddhism may be flourishing in the West precisely because there are no footfalls or echoes that are able to lead people back to where they began, and to know their inherited faith for the first time. Here, of course, I am paraphrasing T.S. Eliot, who writes:

We shall not cease from exploration
And the end of all our exploring
Will be to arrive where we started
And know the place for the first time.[88]

RELIGION AS STARTING POINT

Life compels us to deeper engagement with spiritual meaning, and I suspect that hardly anyone can remain in the secular condition for long, for we are by nature religious beings who have deep longings that must be attended. When young or mature adults go in search of spiritual meaning, it is then that the lost inheritance of early childhood often comes to the fore, but often unconsciously, because by now the individual is so thoroughly secularised that he or she has literally forgotten the religion of early childhood.

A student of mine wrote the following in an undergraduate essay on spirituality:

> **Secular people are looking for spiritual renewal but don't know where to look. I think that people who have been given the opportunity to grow up with some connection with a faith have more of a starting point to explore their own spiritual beliefs.**
>
> (Beth, 18, 2000)

This is an important perspective on the contemporary spiritual quest, and it is all the more fascinating because it puts a relatively unfashionable point of view. The popular view asserts that religion and spirituality are opposed, and student spirituality often views itself as autonomous and independent of religion. It believes it does not need religion because it is self-sufficient and self-directing. However, this student has hit upon the insight that religion can act as a vital resource for spirituality, and the two need not be opposed. She suggests that those who grow up with 'some connection with a faith' may have 'more of a starting point' to explore their own spirituality.

The spiritual journey may bring the individual back into the broad religious fold, so that the inward reflection revivifies and reawakens the tradition from the inside. Many individuals today are on a personal path outside formal religion. They do not attend church or profess membership of any denomination, but are nonetheless 'religious' in a broad sense, and often draw on traditional religious ideas, scriptures, practices and beliefs in their spiritual lives.

Once again Sandra Schneiders is illuminating:

The justification of intense interest in spirituality and alienation from religion is often expressed in a statement such as, 'I am a spiritual person, but I am not very religious'. Interestingly enough, and especially among the young, this religionless spirituality often freely avails itself of the accoutrements of religion. Invocation of angels, practices such as meditation or fasting, personal and communal rituals, the use of symbols and sacramentals from various traditions ... are common. Indeed, even the most secular types of spirituality seem bound to borrow some of their resources from the religious traditions they repudiate.[89]

Such spiritual paths, as Schneiders affirmed, are broadly religious, but the people walking these paths claim not to be religious. Nor does formal religion view such people as members of its flock, because they remain invisible to the organisational life of institutions, which judge 'religiousness' according to conventional criteria. This large and increasing segment of the population are exiles from institutionalised church, but are nevertheless walking the path of a broad-band religious faith. People who have had some early foundational experience of faith and community are often deeply supported from within by these foundations.

THE ATTRACTIONS OF THE SECULAR

A 19-year-old student, whom I will call 'Elizabeth', wrote an autobiographical essay about her struggle with religious belief and her secular identity in my course on spirituality. Elizabeth indicated that she had come from a very religious family, and that her early experience of religion had been essentially positive. Elizabeth wrote that she had been born into the Catholic faith, and she had followed the faith of her family in childhood. But by the arrival of adolescence, she had adopted a 'secular' identity as a way of distancing herself from the family, and as a way of staking out her own relationship to the world:

I suppose I was attracted to things outside the church and outside my religious family. New interests and experimentations led me to put religion on hold and to live a secular kind of life, along with most of my friends. Despite having a strong religious presence in my early life, I entered adulthood as a non-Christian, although I don't think I ever lost the sense that there was a God.

(Elizabeth, 19, 2000)

Elizabeth is in the typical situation of being a 'modern' person who is reacting against the religiousness of her upbringing. In her story, we discover the meaning of the term 'secular', which is to struggle against a firmly established religious tradition, with a view to shrugging off the demands and attitudes of the tradition. The idea of 'inheriting' a faith did not interest her, as she wanted to trust her own experience and follow wherever it would lead. She was not against God or explicitly anti-religious, but simply wanted to place these elements 'on hold' while she got on with the business of living.

RELIGION VERSUS LIFE AND SEX

Elizabeth indicated in her essay that she had pushed religion aside for a variety of reasons. First there was the desire to be like her friends who, despite attending a religious school, had formed their identity around the secular society. Religion was 'there', but it seemed largely irrelevant. Religion to her and her friends seemed distant, improbable, worn and out of touch. It was easily set aside.

'Sexuality was an obstacle to my faith', she indicated in the essay. This is a recurring theme of young people who have felt alienated from religion. The sexuality question looms large, and is frequently surrounded by misunderstanding and unresolved feelings. It is especially important to young people around the age of twelve or thirteen, who stand at the brink of sexual awakening, and who understandably want their religious faith to help them come to terms with sexuality and to integrate it into the big picture of life.

To the young Elizabeth who was maturing into a woman, religion appeared to be saying 'no' to sexuality, while the secular world, the media, pop culture, music, and television appeared to be saying 'yes'. The churches often imagine that young people are asking them to sanction their lust and promiscuity, but this is not what a 'yes' to sexuality means. A 'yes' to sexuality means that sexuality is integrated into the whole of life, and not left on the margins as an embarrassing added extra that we strive to repress or ignore. Young people want to have their developing sexuality accepted and affirmed by the sacred world, and not told that it is evil or sinful. As a result, countless teenagers in our society abandon religion because they regard it as something which sits in judgement on their sexuality. If it comes to a showdown between sexuality and God during these sensitive years of development, in most cases sexuality wins the day. If God represents a blanket 'no' to sexuality, then God is rejected as a stultifying force, and religion and its moralism is pushed away.

Religion has placed itself in an invidious position by representing God as an antagonist to the bodily vitalities, and in styling the creator as a stern judge who disproves of our instincts. The fact that God, as creator, gave us these instincts and impulses to begin with seems to confound the thinking of moralistic religion. Religion has failed to produce a fair, balanced and reasoned account of sin and evil in the human world, and by placing the burden of sin upon sexuality and the body it has weakened its own credibility. This is especially ironic for a religion such as Christianity, which is based on the idea of the incarnation, and of the divine becoming human (and therefore sexual) in the person of Christ.

If God took on human form and assumed bodily reality, then God could hardly be squeamish about the body and its functions, because God must know those functions intimately and must celebrate the capacity of the body for expressing the longings of the spirit. The God who created the body, who saw that it was good, who took on bodily form, and who asked us to live life to the full, is absent from a religion that has tended to represent the creator as a persecutory superego. 'I have come that they may have life and have it to the full' (John 10:10), but few teenagers feel this message of affirmation and joy. If religion is to survive in the future, it must deconstruct this dualism of God versus Life that destroys its own vitality.

THE FRAGMENTATION OF PERSONALITY

When we throw out religion, we throw out the language of the soul and spirit. We not only toss out what seems 'irrelevant' and 'out of touch', we not only get rid of cultural 'baggage', but we also throw out the baby Jesus with the bathwater. Therefore, I never recommend to any student a wholesale rejection of their natal faith, but rather a patient and critical analysis, and a close study of both good and bad features. The secular world encourages us to be impatient and reckless. If at first glance religion makes no sense, or is contrary to feeling good, then the secular world and the media encourage us to chuck it out. This is the truly destructive aspect of secularism. It allows anger, hurt, woundedness, inadequacy and misunderstanding to determine our relationship to the sacred. The secular world does not encourage people to discernment and study, but to narcissistic rage against a religious system that appears to threaten our physical vitality.

The secular person often pretends to be happy and adjusted, but inwardly, if he or she dares to look, there is a deep unhappiness and a lack of fulfilment. The heart is broken and the psyche is at war with itself. When religion is rejected, it does not mean that the spirit and soul go away or disappear. They are simply repressed into the unconscious, where they become factors of disturbance and causes of psychic suffering. In particular, the person feels a sense of incompletion or self-division, because the deeper parts of the self are denied expression and are not allowed to live. An internal war ensues, because the self that is in control is at odds with the self that 'remembers' that its task is to serve a sacred purpose.

In the case of Elizabeth, who was inducted early into religious understanding, there continues within her the 'memory' of what life is about. This memory is suppressed as much as possible, but it simmers away beneath the secular persona and causes a fragmentation of personality, which can develop into a full-blown neurosis or even a psychosis if left unattended:

> From the age of eleven to the present day (nineteen), I have
> been divided. I have been a different person to different people,
> never quite knowing who I really am nor what I really believe. I
> adopted a position of almost total ignorance towards the sacred.
> This position is almost entirely viable in our materialistic society.
> But hidden within the recesses of my life was another life, that I
> secretly wanted to be connected to, but was scared to
> acknowledge very often, if at all.

In 'normal' conditions, the secular person has to stage-manage and control this inner fragmentation, and make the best of it. If the ego is resilient, the individual may even convince him- or herself that nothing is wrong, that there is nothing missing in life, and no need for a relationship with a sacred other. But if the ego is sensitive to the demands of the spirit, then it will not be able to maintain the charade for very long, and a new personal reckoning will take place.

Jung argued that this reorientation takes place at the mid-life crisis, after the ego has established itself in the world and is ready to be displaced by the inner life. However, I think this part of Jung's theory is out of date, because what he describes as a crisis at the middle of life is today happening to teenagers and young adults in a 'quarter-life crisis', almost as if the process of spiritual development has been accelerated, due to the circumstances of our time. Life can no longer support a soul-less ego structure for half a lifetime, but makes its demands for transformation and development much earlier.

THE HUMAN FEAR OF THE SACRED

The 19-year-old Elizabeth is conscious of 'another life' within her life, and acknowledges that she wants to be connected to this hidden reality, but finds it difficult. She goes on to say in her essay:

> I was scared to acknowledge the sacred in case it meant the ultimate death of the subtle underlying apathy that protected myself, and all of us, from the shocking reality of the presence of mystery in our lives.

This made me sit up and take notice, because I could sense she had discovered an important existential truth at the core of the rejection of religion. The modern mind rejects religion not simply because it fails to square with commonsense, but because our mind is terrified of the existence of a reality greater than itself. The modern person likes to imagine that he or she is the master of his or her world, and although we may be miserable masters of the universe, that illusion is self-protective, sentimental and comforting. The reality of the sacred shatters, as she says, the 'subtle underlying apathy' that protects us from the admission that there is something other.

In his work *The Idea of the Holy*, Rudolf Otto[90] declares that spirituality is paradoxical and double-sided. On the one hand we are 'fascinated' by its mystery; on the other hand we live in 'dread' and may even be 'appalled' at the reality of the sacred. The darker, more foreboding aspect he called the *mysterium tremendum*, that is an awesome awareness of a sacredness that overrides and envelops our lives, an overwhelming aspect that can be associated with death and the fear of dying. With spirituality becoming more popular and fashionable, the foreboding or shocking aspect of the sacred is frequently repressed, or is projected outside us.

To her considerable credit, Elizabeth has refused to split off and project elsewhere her experience of the 'dreadful' aspect of the sacred, which makes me all the more encouraged by her project, since it has the feeling of authentic spiritual experience. Spirituality is not just 'good' or 'cool', as students often say, but carries within it our fear of death, our resistance to being turned around by unseen forces, our dread of the unknown, and our rage against our own impotence in the face of destiny and forces beyond the self. This dreadful aspect of spirituality is not the public face of this popular phenomenon, but it can sometimes be discovered in genuine cases of authentic self-discovery.

INCOMPLETION DRIVES US ON

Elizabeth has the emotional maturity to realise that it is partly the emptiness of the secular life that has driven her to seek out a more profound reality beneath her personal existence. She is impelled to a sense of the sacred not because she is looking for fun or excitement, but out of the sense of imperfection in her existence. She is driven to a deeper realisation by an admission of poverty and loss, by an acknowledgement of the incompletion of the secular life:

> Why did my life feel so empty? Perhaps, for me, spirituality is an essence noticed more easily in the absence. Was this absence a holy thing? I mean, was the absence a prelude to a deeper sense of presence? Realising your own emptiness, and thinking about its possible meaning, is scary and hard. I had to confront this unknown quality, let it change my life, and this is pretty scary, pretty hard.

I was arrested by the honesty and integrity of this self-disclosure. Elizabeth is approaching the spiritual life because she has the courage to recognise the emptiness inside, and not to run away from it. It is our openness to our emptiness that allows the sense of presence to be felt in our experience. As a Buddhist will say, it is only the empty glass that can be filled by the nectar of enlightenment. This facing of our own emptiness is not easy work, and most of us will do anything to avoid it. As Elizabeth has discovered, this inner work is scary and hard, but if we are able to endure it, it will change our lives.

THE DEMANDS OF A REALISED FAITH

Elizabeth took stock of her situation, and reflects on the life-changing implications of what she has just revealed about herself:

> In these sentences I have revealed something which is extremely difficult and confronting to admit. I realise I do believe in an Other, in a sacred other. If I analyse my feelings thoroughly, I would probably conclude that it was God. The reason I put God on hold was because it is easier to live in the distractions of the secular without commitment or responsibility towards the sacred. To make that conscious choice is to admit my own weaknesses and frailty as a human being amid other human beings like me. It is to admit my dependence on a mystery and a beauty greater than myself.

The term 'sacred other' was introduced in my lectures and I often use it as an umbrella term, inviting students to use a more specific term where appropriate. Elizabeth is able to lift her self-imposed bans on the idea of God and the reality of a sacred presence. It is almost as if the idea of the sacred other was a necessary middle term or transitional idea, which acted as a bridge between her secularism and her new position of recovered faith.

Importantly, we notice that the achievement of faith is not simply a blind leap into the dark, but a position involving personal 'commitment' and a 'responsibility towards the sacred'. The religious awareness is *relational*, an admission that we live our lives in relationship with a mystery that is greater than ourselves. The secular life blocks out this relationality, and assumes that we live as free agents. The secular life appeals to our egocentricity, but such selfishness is strangely unrewarding and the self is not fulfilled by it. Elizabeth reflected on these problems in personal and philosophical terms:

> It seems desirable to believe in 'modern' man and his secular utopia without the gods. But when you think about this at some length, and realise the beauty and mystery around us, you realise how ridiculous this secular belief is. We have to let go of this idea of our autonomy from the sacred other. It is easier to delude oneself, to be false, than it is to face the truth. Easy, but without satisfaction.

She considered the possibility of adopting a 'secular' spirituality, like so many of her fellow students, but she rejected this option in these terms:

> The problem of 'secular' spirituality is that it is full of holes. We want it all. We want the conviction that we are masters of our own destiny, and we want a sense of mystery without God and without ethical responsibility.

For her, secular spirituality is having the cake and eating it too; or wanting the satisfaction of a sense of mystery without the embarrassment of God. It is, she argues, an easy option, where we benefit from the sense that the world is enchanted, but we are not answerable to a greater moral force because we are godless. This is tough reasoning, and she realises the isolating implications of what she is saying. Her new position of theistic reverence will alienate her from the other students in the class who say they are 'spiritual but not religious'.

But Elizabeth no longer wants to arrive at a philosophical position merely with a view to pleasing others or fitting into a prevailing ethos. She wants to take possession of herself and her experience, and she hopes that this new self-possession will unify her identity and protect her from the fragmentation that has plagued her teenage years:

> I don't want to be all these different people any more. I want to be the same person to everyone. To be *real*. And so the struggle begins to keep your soul. To have soul is to dedicate your life to others, and to pursue the straight and narrow, while all those around you live in 'blessed' ignorance, and feel no sense of responsibility either to God or to fellow humans.

She senses the possibility of a real breakthrough, and if she has the courage of her convictions she could experience great joy and celebration:

> But my sense is that if I take a step further along this path, after what I have seen and revealed, there is the potential for great joy, wholeness, purpose and worth.

The problem of identity

Although Elizabeth achieved this breakthrough, and these considerable insights, there was still the problem of how she is to present herself to others. Who or what is she now? How is she to present herself to her family, her brothers and her secular friends. Is she a born-again Christian? Is she a 'normal' Catholic with a personally realised faith?

In some sense, she has been 'born again' by her new recognitions, but she does not wish to announce this in any strident or assertive way. She does not wish to boast about her new wholeness, for she knows only too well how it feels to be broken and incomplete. The process she has experienced has been arduous and difficult, and she does not want to cheapen her experience by converting it into slogans or clichés, nor does she intend to jeopardise her sense of wholeness by espousing a position that will please some and alienate others.

In a passage of remarkable maturity, Elizabeth recognised that to be truly spiritual is to accept struggle and suffering as part of the spiritual journey. Her problems with identity and self-description will most likely remain for some time, but she looks forward to the future with an attitude of hope and good heart:

> In Eastern and Western spiritual traditions, it is made clear that to be spiritual is a struggle, and to be in contact with the sacred other you need to work hard on being aware, being careful about the way you live and the way you treat others and the earth. I want to open up the possibility of a spirituality which is not alienating to the people I love, that could possibly unite them, and in doing so, unite me too, body, soul, spirit, as one person to everyone. I have to take the leap. I still don't know in what direction to jump. But I feel I'll actually come to something, find what I'm looking for.

She recognises she will face difficulties of a different kind in her new situation, but there is a quiet confidence now because she is moving into the future as a more unified person. Her openness to the sacred has given her a sense of openness to other people, and her acceptance of her spiritual life gives her the capacity to accept others in their difference and to seek unity and love. When our internal wounds and divisions are healed, we gain the capacity and the courage to seek healing and wholeness in the world, and to act with mindfulness and sensitivity towards our internal and external environments. To recover one's 'vertical' connection with the sacred other is at the same time to restore and renew our 'horizontal' connections with self, others and the world. This, from a theological point of view, is the Cross of completion.

WHO IS RELIGIOUS, WHO SECULAR?

Elizabeth indicated in a conversation that she did not intend to go back to church. She may well have gone through a journey of reconciliation, so that she is back in relationship with the spirit, but her church, she said, has not gone through a similar journey. It still remains 'out of touch' with the world, with sexuality, and with the living spirit. This places her identity in a puzzling situation, but one which is typically postmodern. She is religious, but does not 'practise' religion in any conventional way. Despite having returned to the spiritual attitude of her childhood, she would probably still be regarded as secular by a religious survey that only recognised 'religiousness' in those who attended church on a regular basis.

But her friends will no doubt classify her as 'religious' when they next take up a conversation with her. What we discover in the postmodern experience of the sacred is the extreme poverty and imprecision of our terms and language. What does 'religious' mean today, and what does 'secular' mean in this context? These words are monolithic and heavy, and they fail to grasp the subtlety of individual spiritual experience.

Today we have to ask ourselves a great many questions. How secular are secular people? How religious are church-going people? How spiritual are the religious organisations? Almost everything is uncertain, difficult, complex. But it does seem that secularism is a kind of transitional state, not a true human condition. The secular person is the one who has not yet achieved a personal relationship with the sacred. The secular person often wants to form such a relationship, but for various reasons does not know how to go about it. Secularism is a mask or pose which hides our longing for the sacred. Secularism is bolstered by society, and by 'common' sense, but it is eroded as soon as the longing of the heart is contacted and made accessible to reason. Secularism lasts only as long as we are alienated from our true natures.

Elizabeth has journeyed beyond secularism to the mystical experience of the presence of the divine which is the positive option that awaits the secular world. It is a terrible irony if this climactic experience of religious life is not recognised as such by religion. Who or what can celebrate Elizabeth's personal triumph? The secular university might see her as 'too religious', and yet religious organisations might see her as 'too secular'. These assessments reveal the inadequacy of our institutions and their inability to see the wood for the trees. Institutions deal in generalisations and in imprecise and totalising categories. We need an entirely new lexicon and language to deal with the complexity of postmodern experience of the sacred, and we will have to turn to mysticism, philosophy, anthropology and depth psychology to find the appropriate terms and categories.

The task today is to explore the state of consciousness that represses the sacred, and to understand the new kind of consciousness that opens the door to the sacred and expands to a new communion with the world. It was a personal relief for Elizabeth to put her faith on hold at the age of eleven, but now it is an even greater relief to take on a position of faith at nineteen. Loss of faith gives way to the recovery of faith, the circle turns, and a process in her journey has been completed. She arrives at where she started, but she knows that place for the first time.

PART 3

Discernment

CHAPTER 8

Post-religion: the return
to beginnings

*When we speak, we Europeans, so ordinarily and so confusedly
today about a 'return of the religious', what do we thereby
name? To what do we refer?*

Jacques Derrida[91]

Contemporary society is in a dilemma. It appears to 'need' religion as a
container of spirit, but does not want it or, for various historical
reasons, cannot accept it in its traditional form. Post-Marxist Eastern
Europe exemplifies the condition of the present era. After the collapse
of utopian politics and the pseudo-religion of state-sponsored atheism,
what comes next?

Is it back to religion as it was practised before modernism,
existentialism, psychoanalysis, feminism, and the revolutions of
sex, race and gender politics? Will the spirituality revolution
provide justification for reactionary, anti-progressive and anti-
modern attitudes, or will the new spirituality lead to the creation of
new forms that integrate rather than oppose the progressive
revolutions of society? We may still be a long way from answering
these difficult questions. Before the spiritual impulse can catch up
with society, we have to understand our spirituality in its historical

context, and ask questions about what exactly is 'returning' in us today.

UNHOLY SPIRIT?

The Italian philosopher Gianni Vattimo argues that we long to connect with 'spirit' in our time, but:

> **since the spirit of the times is not the Holy Spirit ... [this longing] is more problematic than ever.**[92]

I take his point, but I am not sure he is right. I agree that 'spirit' in our time is not experienced in terms of the conventional image of the Holy Spirit, as conveyed to us in doctrine or traditional sentiment. Our experience of spirit today appears to break doctrinal rules in its *holistic* rather than perfectionist strivings; in its quest for human authenticity, body–mind integration, psychological health, ecological integrity and sexual wholeness. Might it be that the doctrinal conventions are inadequate, and our traditional images of the Holy Spirit are radically out of touch with the reality of this spirit?

The words 'holistic' and 'holy' come from the same etymological root, and our notion of the holy may be mistakenly skewed towards perfection, away from its true connections with wholeness. Over recent years, there have been numerous psychologists and theologians anxious to prove that the holy and the holistic have more than just linguistic connections, and that the sacred scriptures were actually pointing to a 'holism' that society, culture and church had lost sight of. If this is so, then there has to be a return to the root meanings of scripture, in the expectation that an original wholeness of vision was intended, and posited, in the beginning. The future then becomes a return to the past, to reveal a lost wholeness, in the name of living and embodying that wholeness in the present and future.

If this is true, then God and the Holy Spirit are still valid concepts and realities fashioned by tradition and sentiment so that they are out of touch with their *experiential* reality. If my sense is right, the way forward is not by dropping religion and inventing another one, or adopting a different religion from another culture, but by deconstructing our existing religion, and 'reforming' it in ways that accord with the lived experience of these religious ideas today. This sounds, I know, dreadfully cavalier and bold, but I am wondering if we need a new 'reformation', in which all the traditional ideas are experienced and 'tested' in this new way.

Every cold and non-living element of the former metaphysical universe has to be brought into our experience and refashioned in the fiery furnace of our souls, just as Elizabeth, in the previous chapter, refashioned religious ideas in hers. Not tossing out (atheism), but tossing into the soul (mysticism) could be the next reformation. We 'overcome metaphysics', as modern philosophy has attempted to do (from Nietzsche to Heidegger and beyond), not by abandoning metaphysics but by deepening our experience to discover in our lives the spiritual elements that have hitherto been enshrined in metaphysical theology. Our age, I believe, is destined to discover the divine as a dimension of the human. This was the central project of Mircea Eliade, who called for a New Humanism based on a radically different experience of the sacred.

NEW INTEREST IN ETERNAL QUESTIONS

In 1994, on the Isle of Capri, a group of distinguished European philosophers was called together by the *Italian Philosophical Yearbook* to create a new venture called a *European Yearbook*. The theme of this meeting was to be the condition of 'religion' in society and culture today. Derrida described the candidates at this meeting in this way:

> **We are not priests bound by a ministry, nor theologians, nor qualified, competent representatives of religion, nor enemies of religion as such, in the sense that certain so-called Enlightenment philosophers are thought to have been.**[93]

The first issue to be discussed was what religion could mean today. Is religion a remnant or fossil from an earlier era, which contemporary philosophers should attack in the manner of Enlightenment thinkers? Clearly no, was Derrida's response. Religion should be approached anew, with different assumptions and expectations. This meeting was particularly interested in the fact that, after the fall of the Berlin Wall in 1991 and the collapse of state communism, the people of Eastern Europe seemed to need 'religion'. And in the West, although the churches continued to empty, there was an expressed need recorded in people, the arts, culture and music for 'something more' than material living.

It was difficult for the meeting to define what this 'something' was in Western Europe. But the German philosopher Hans-Georg Gadamer ventured to suggest that the reality of death and the modern person's dim or bright awareness of inescapable and impending mortality had brought about a new interest in the subject of eternity.

Perhaps this was turning towards 'eternity' for enlightened self-interest, but however one wished to name it, it seemed that the eternal questions had returned to contemporary consciousness, and were even 'fashionable' in the arts and music; therefore, philosophy had to engage those questions.

THE RETURN OF THE RELIGIOUS

Religious questions had to be grappled with anew, preferably outside the restrictions of dogma or doctrine, and always with human experience and social reality in mind. Speakers at this symposium kept stating that there was a new feeling of openness and interest about religious questions, although they similarly noted that formal religious practice was continuing to decline. It seemed that the religious and religion had parted company in their understandings, and mostly for the reasons given in Chapter 2 of this book. But unlike my own work, these philosophers refuse to speak of spirituality as such, and instead they keep referring to the idea of the 'religious'.

Derrida's opening paper, 'Faith and Knowledge', deals with the 'return of the religious', as he calls it. His provocative and daring claim is that the religious is returning, and this is uttered with a keen awareness of its monumental significance, not only to philosophy, but also to civilisation and to the very concept of our living in a secular society. It is ironic that Derrida should make this claim, since most universities know him as a key proponent of the idea of deconstruction, namely the art or science of unravelling culture to expose its component parts and inherent assumptions.

This art is mostly practised in a reductive mode, by taking something religious, cultural or spiritual and reducing it to social constructs, power relations or linguistic elements. Derrida has undergone a sea-change, and his deconstruction of culture has led to a deep awareness of and regard for the presence of mystery. Gadamer puts this basic intuition clearly. Philosophy, he writes, has still not been able to 'answer ... the fundamental question as to why there is something rather than nothing'.[94]

Derrida performs linguistic philosophy on the word 'religion', and after claiming that the religious is returning, he shows why this is embedded in the very structure of the word. The letters 're' at the beginning of 're-ligion' ensures that this peculiar phenomenon of human nature and society will re-turn, re-vive, and re-cur. 'Religion', according to Derrida's definition, is 'what succeeds in returning'.[95]

RETURNING TO WHAT?

Derrida's announcement seemed to make the symposium nervous. 'What are we returning to?' cried Gadamer. Derrida indicated that we are not necessarily returning to the churches or to old religious forms, but rather that something primal and basic is returning in us. This return is philosophical and existential, and must not be seen as regressing to past forms.

Some of the philosophers seemed surprised to find themselves announcing to the world that the religious is about to return. This, to me, is what makes the Capri Dialogues all the more moving, compelling and important. We are in the presence of an inspired or even involuntary proclamation. Gadamer, with a slight hint of outrage, reflects on the idea of return (*ruckkehr*), and makes his own position very clear concerning religion. Although describing himself as a Protestant, and indicating that his religious foundation is in the Christian tradition, he announces:

> Clearly 'return' cannot mean a return to metaphysics or to any sort of ecclesiastical doctrine.[96]

Philosophy and religion are still at odds, it seems, and these statements are fired like warning shots to the faith institutions that might want to find comfort or solace in the new turn to the religious in postmodern philosophy.

Just to underscore the fact that postmodern philosophy has not gone soft, lost its radical edge, or somehow becoming nostalgic about religious practice or custom, Gianni Vattimo states:

> Times have doubtless changed since Hegel wrote that the basic sentiment of his time was expressed in the proposition 'God is dead'. But is 'our' time (which, like that of Hegel, begins with the birth of Christ) really so different? And is the phenomenon

known rightly or wrongly as the 'religious revival' (though more in parliaments, terrorism and the media than in the churches, which continue to empty), really anything other than 'the death of God'? That is the question we asked ourselves, as no doubt everyone else is doing today, and it is the question we put to the friends and colleagues we invited to collaborate with us.[97]

Again, I would argue that these philosophers are not making clear enough distinctions between the traditional *images* of God, Holy Spirit or heaven, and the essential realities to which these images point, which may be expressing themselves in new and radical ways. To focus on the breakdown of images only is to end in depression, nihilism and atheism. But to look beyond the breakdown to the new potentials and possibilities is to arrive at a postmodern mysticism, a stage which does not yet seem to be evident, at least not in philosophy where it is only hinted at by Derrida and others.

The philosopher Maurizio Ferraris was even more adamant than Gadamer that a revived Christianity is not about to appear on the cultural horizon. He declared:

Christianity as we have known it in history is disappearing. That is, the Christian religion as a faith whose defences include that of being the most rational, the most true, of a truth that has an essential relation with the truth of history and science, is in the process of dissolving. Nothing will be able to make it rise again.[98]

I am not sure if this philosopher sees the irony of claiming that Christianity, a religion based on the mystery of resurrection, will never 'rise again'. But if it does rise, it will clearly not be in the old form, but in a new form, closer perhaps to historical Buddhism.

COMPELLED TO BE PROPHETIC

What is moving about this collection of essays on religion by postmodern philosophers is their straining towards the prophetic mode. They would like to announce the shape and form of the new, but they are only able to provide a few clues. Gadamer writes, 'Will the world, perhaps, be able to discover an answer which, as yet, can only be guessed at?'[99] Ferraris postulates that what is being prepared could be a 'religion of the other'.[100] Spanish philosopher Eugenio Trias speculates that:

> Perhaps it is a matter of preparing for the emergence of a new religion: the true *religion of the spirit* already prophesied in the 12th century by the Calabrian abbot Joachim of the Flowers and invoked afresh by Novalis and Schelling in the century of Romanticism and Idealism. Perhaps the only way to counteract the wars of religion breaking out everywhere is to lay the basis for a new foundation. But such an event does not come about by force of will alone. For it to occur, a number of different factors must come together. It is a matter, perhaps, of simply preparing the ground in order that the *event* at some point may come about.[101]

At this symposium on religion on the Isle of Capri, most philosophers concurred that a new spirit of the time is expressing itself, and that some ground is being prepared for some event in the future. This is stirring stuff for philosophers generally known for their suspicion of the non-rational and their scepticism towards religion. It is as though, in spite of themselves, they are being urged to be prophetic philosophers, that is bearing witness to the revelation of spirit in contemporary times.

Like so many others in the world today, Gadamer wondered whether the West can be helped out by taking hold of some other religion from a different culture, lest we sink further into the morass of our present materialism:

> We must properly ask ourselves whether other religious and cultural worlds can provide any response to the universality of the scientific enlightenment and its consequences which is different from the 'religion' of the global economy.[102]

Here the attractions of the East, and of Buddhism in particular, come to mind. On my own university campus, the Student Buddhist Society posted flyers that highlighted the attractions of Buddhism for the post-enlightenment West:

> No God. No metaphysics. No overbearing authority.

This sounds like a recipe for sure-fire success in the religious domain; a religion guaranteed to suit postmodern taste and cultural requirements. However, some anonymous undergraduate had scrawled in red ink beneath this list: 'No nothing'. This raised a smile on my face, as I think that, for all the attractions of the East, we do not solve our religious and spiritual problems simply by running away from them and embracing an exotic religion outside our culture.

We can learn an enormous amount from Buddhism, of course, especially how to build a successful religion without the assertive infrastructure of metaphysical machinery. But the Dalai Lama himself is alert to this problem, and during a so-called 'private audience' that I attended in Sydney in 1997, the head of the Tibetan tradition admitted to his audience that too many Westerners are turning to Buddhism for the wrong reasons. Often, he said, Westerners are turning to Buddhism to escape from the dilemmas of the West. He would like to see Westerners solve Western problems in the West, and not use Buddhism merely as a diversion. Gadamer himself recognised that this must be so:

> Whenever it is a question of experience, we should always
> begin from where we are.[103]

The problem is that where we are is a confusing muddle, with no easy solutions or fix-it programs on the horizon. It seems to me that we are waiting, for what I am not sure. But we are clearly suspended between two eras of time, a situation admirably summed up by the Italian Marxist Antonio Gramsci:

> The old is dead and the new has yet to be born; in this
> interregnum there arises a great many morbid symptoms.[104]

We are in-between the times, and many things are uncertain and confusing.

There is often an absurd element in the reflections of the Capri philosophers, reminding us of the enigmatic characters and situations in Samuel Beckett's *Waiting for Godot* (1955) and *Endgame*. 'What's happening, what's happening?' cries Hamm in *Endgame*, and the character Clov replies: 'Something is taking its course'.[105]

'Something is taking its course' is basically what these philosophers were saying on the Isle of Capri and, significantly, many people today say they are not sure about God, but feel that there is 'something there'. The absurd element probably derives from the disjunction between the surety of our feeling and the uncertainty of our thinking. We can 'feel' the new before we can think or see it, a dilemma especially acute in Eastern Europe.

AT THE END OF AN ERA: THE ST PETERSBURG COMPLEX

The continental philosophers keep coming back, time and again, to the example of Russia. It is at the end of a political era, and at the beginning of something as yet unknown. There is a sense that only religion or a new mythology will be big enough to fill the hole left in the psyche of Russia after the collapse of the communist regime. But whose religion, and what religiousness will fill this spiritual void?

It may be salutary in this context to ponder the fate of the city of St Petersburg over the last hundred years, which has seen a series of momentous events and rapid transformations. In its history and suffering, the city reflects the convulsions of Europe as it moved from a traditional religious foundation, to a modern secular-political state, and to the uncertainty and yet spiritual possibility of a postmodern period.

In 1914, the German-sounding name of this city was changed to Petrograd, its Russian equivalent. In 1924, under the control of a communist dictatorship, St Petersburg became known as Leningrad, to honour the memory of the former Bolshevik leader and to showcase state communism. During the early years of Leningrad, religious persecution was rife, as the new totalitarian regime sought to replace the myths and symbols of religion with its own secular myths of utopia and the future. Churches were burnt or destroyed, or converted into storehouses or offices of the Soviet Union.

Then in 1991, after the collapse of the USSR, Leningrad was converted by the will of the people and the energies of a remnant church back into St Petersburg. This symbolises a clash of the titans, Christendom versus Communism, or the Orthodox Church versus Marxism. Religion has been vigorously engaged in what has been called a 'Christian spiritual reconstruction aimed at filling the void of meaning and value left by the dismantled political regimes'.[106]

The transition back to religion has not been smooth. The people have gone through rapid change, suffering and trauma, but religion, although the victim of persecution, appears not to have changed during this long period. We cannot go back and pretend that there has been no rupture, that time has not marched on, or that we can fit neatly into premodern religious categories. As Gadamer puts it, the problems of the present 'cannot be relieved by any homesickness for the simple faith of childhood'.[107]

True to postmodernity, a great many 'new' religions have entered the Russian scene, such as Hare Krishnas, Ananda Marga, Brahma Kumaris, and a host of new evangelical and fundamentalist sects and groups. The Eastern Orthodox church has had to compete with all these new religions for interest and support. But although the collapse of utopian politics has released religious energy and longing, it is by no means clear that 'religion' as such is what the Russian people want, any more than it appears to be what people anywhere want today.

Gadamer continues:

> **Even after the breakdown of the Marxist doctrine of ideological self-deception promulgated from the standpoint of a dogmatic atheism, the various religions still find difficulty in reaching out to people.**[108]

There is religious interest and spiritual need but great uncertainty about what to do with this interest. Gadamer argues that the people of St Petersburg, after a hundred years of dictatorship and oppression, are not attracted to the dogmatic nature of religious faith, and are reluctant to exchange a modern political dogmatism for a premodern religious dogmatism. St Petersburg finds itself in a postmodern rather than a traditional situation. There is an urgent need for 'something' to fill the void, but it must speak to the postmodern condition, and not merely draw people back to a premodern past. Here Gadamer was most uncompromising:

> **No matter to what extent we recognise the urgency of religion, there can be no return to the doctrines of the church.**[109]

The Russian agony over faith, and the desire to believe but inability to do so, is perhaps best summarised by the great novelist Dostoyevsky, who writes in a letter of 1854:

> **I have been tortured with the longing to believe—am so, indeed, even now; and the yearning grows stronger the more cogent the intellectual difficulties that stand in the way.**[110]

What interests us today is what this torturous conflict between faith and doubt will produce in the future. The energy in this conflict is flaming with libidinal intensity, and we can only hope that it expresses itself creatively, and does not explode in socially destructive ways.

THE ESSENCE OF RELIGION

The experiment in pure reason has collapsed, and the time is right for a spiritual revival of humanity. We stand at this juncture needing but not wanting religion. This very word 'religion' seems more problematic than ever. Derrida exclaimed, 'Today the word "religion" is inadequate'.[111] I would suggest that Derrida needs, but does not want, the term 'spirituality'. Philosophers and intellectuals do not like the word 'spirituality', because it seems too subjective, internal and personal or, and this is a more recent problem, too 'fashionable' to be awarded intellectual status. Religion is clearly giving way to individual religious experience, and it seems to me that 'spirituality' is the best term we have to describe such experience.

More than thirty years ago, Mircea Eliade opened his classic book, *The Quest*, with these words:

> **It is unfortunate that we do not have at our disposal a more precise word than 'religion' to denote the experience of the sacred ... But perhaps it is too late to search for another word, and 'religion' may still be a useful term provided we keep in mind that it does not necessarily imply belief ... but refers to the experience of the sacred, and, consequently, is related to *being, meaning,* and *truth.*[112]**

Being 'religious' is for Eliade a natural response to the call of the sacred. In this sense, institutional affiliations and traditional designations fade into the background, and are no longer so very important. What is truly significant is that we *respond* to the sacred, existentially and purposefully. Once one has an experience of the sacred, as Eliade intimates, then questions of 'belief', of subscribing to creeds (Jung), doctrines (Gadamer) or forms (Derrida) become secondary and not primary.

This places us in the territory of William James and his powerful discussions about 'primordial religious experience'. In *The Varieties of Religious Experience*,[113] James argued that what he called 'personal religion', and what we now call 'spirituality', is the primary religious experience, and 'religion' is a secondary phenomenon, or a response to spirituality. It is indeed possible, said James, to have the one without the other, to find religious people who are distantly removed from spirituality, and to have spiritual people who are not connected to formal religion. James argues that spirituality (my term) is a human instinct and a deep-seated personal hunger. It appears in most of us, and is a natural expression of the human longing for God, which is probably our deepest and most profound longing, although some of us manage to hide or disguise it at different times in our lives. Children and young adults have a natural spirituality and a spontaneous interest in the sacredness of life.

James argued that there are two kinds of religion, internal and external, personal and institutional. In *The Varieties*, he chose to 'ignore the institutional branch entirely ... to say nothing of the ecclesiastical organisation',[114] and to focus almost exclusively on 'personal religion in the inward sense'.[115] While admitting that some of his readers will object that 'personal religion' is 'too incomplete a thing to wear the general name [of religion]',[116] he arrived at the astonishing (for its time) conclusion that:

> In one sense at least the personal religion will prove itself more fundamental than either theology or ecclesiasticism. Churches, when once established, live at second-hand upon tradition; but the *founders* of every church owed their power originally to the fact of their direct personal communion with the divine. Not only the superhuman founders, the Christ, the Buddha, Mahomet, but all the originators of Christian sects have been in this case; so personal religion should still seem the primordial thing, even to those who continue to esteem it incomplete.[117]

Needless to say, this statement outraged the religious and theological community of his day, which could not accept the proposition that 'inward' religion was more primary or fundamental than organised religion. James was clearly a hundred years ahead of his time with this formulation. History has vindicated his stance, and we can now go back to read again the Gifford Lectures delivered in Edinburgh in 1902 with an entirely new openness and appreciation of his talented gifts and insights. James' comments were widely regarded as a malicious attack on the institutions of religion, theology and religious education. But I agree with the modern editor of *The Varieties*, who asserts that James was delivering 'neither an attack on nor a defence of institutions'.[118] In hindsight, James' research can be seen not as an 'attack' on the churches, but merely as a statement of fact about the human experience of meaning and its existential priorities. Spirituality or personal religion is 'the primordial thing', and formal organised religion is a secondary phenomenon, a collective and communal response to the truth of spirituality.

PRIMARY AND SECONDARY PROCESSES

James was not always as tactful as he might have been, given the sensitivities of his audience. He possibly ignited potential flames by his use of language and his clear preference for personal religion. One can imagine readers wincing as he wrote that in personal religion 'the individual transacts the business by himself alone' while:

> the ecclesiastical organisation, with its priests and sacraments and other go-betweens, sinks to an altogether secondary place. The relation goes direct from heart to heart, from soul to soul, between man and his maker.[119]

This, we might say, is spoken in the spirit of a radical American Protestantism, with roots in Calvin and Swedenborg. It dismisses tradition with cavalier disregard, and does not manage to understand how 'tradition' itself lives not just 'out there' in externals, but is also alive in the inwardness of the human heart. Perhaps this insight would be too Catholic for the Protestant James to contemplate, and his division into internal/external does seem crudely simplistic and to belong to an outsider's perspective.

But the finer point I would put on James's language is that religion is 'secondary' in logic, not necessarily in value or meaning. Because spirituality comes 'first', it does not necessarily mean that it is 'better' than what is built upon it afterwards. On the contrary, an argument could be developed that says that the primary impulse is raw and unrefined, and often lacking in wisdom. It has the 'immediacy' of experience, but not the subtlety or complexity of the secondary phenomenon. Also, the primary thing is somewhat isolated and removed from community, whereas the secondary development allows us to experience the primordial thing in a much larger, community context. These considerations did not seem to interest James, committed as he was to the American ideals of individualism and pragmatism.

It ought to be possible for us to state that spirituality is primary, without implying that religion is therefore 'merely' secondary. A hundred years ago, religion was still too proud of itself to hear this kind of statement without taking grave offence, or without receiving some kind of insulting blow. Today, with the churches radically humbled by a century of steady decline, faith institutions are perhaps in a better position to listen to what James is saying, and to learn from his discerning eye. But even now it is too easy for the conservative religious to undermine his authority. I have heard James described in conversation as the 'grandfather of the New Age religions'. This is a trivialising of his importance by commentators who are fearful of the appearance of the primordial sacred.

CHAPTER 9

Authenticity and spirituality

What presents itself as spirituality requires discernment.
Sandra Schneiders[120]

When spirituality becomes popular we can almost be certain that some vital elements or ingredients of spirituality have been left out of the popular conception. Things become popular by being distorted, especially by leaving out the hard bits, and emphasising those aspects that seem easy or desirable. The hard bits of spirituality would include sacrifice, discipline, commitment and dedication to the other. A new spirituality arising from society is, at times, going to be 'worldly' and not always 'spiritual'. This should not lead us to reject popular spirituality out of hand, as if it were somehow vulgar or distasteful. We must not become intolerant of the popular just because it is popular.

GIVING BACK TO THE SACRED

Popular spirituality is partly about taking what we can 'get' from the spirit. It is true that the spirit is the fount of our lives, the origin of many gifts, but we must never take the generosity or plenitude of the spirit for granted. The spirit does not exist for our own edification and enjoyment, on the contrary spirituality has traditionally emphasised that we exist to glorify and serve a transcendent reality beyond ourselves. This sense of service, of giving back rather than of taking, of allowing ourselves to be instrumental rather than assuming centrality, can be experienced by the ordinary ego as boring, unattractive or tedious. Our task is to tackle the problem of authenticity in spirituality, and to ask questions about what is true and false in the popular conception of spirituality today.

I am aware that any discourse about true or false spirituality is dangerous and inflammatory. It can be tempting to insert our own preferred kind of spirituality in the 'true' category, while relegating unfamiliar or non-preferred pathways to the 'false' category. I have to admit that what I refer to as true spirituality is a subjective confession about what I see and value within the limitations of my present understanding. The academic in me likes to be definite about these things, but the postmodern thinker in me has to admit that these matters are relative and subject to deconstruction.

THE POPULAR IDEAL OF BLISS

The tendency to idealise and distort the idea of spirituality has been facilitated in our time by New Age industries and enterprises. These industries service the contemporary hunger for spiritual expression, and they often style spirituality as an ego-friendly or utopian experience, presenting the encounter with the spirit as a 'feel-good' encounter. Popular figures such as Joseph Campbell (1988) and Deepak Chopra (1994) have encouraged people to become spiritual adventurers and soulful questers with spiritual reward as the end. Campbell's hugely popular spiritual message in the 1990s, reproduced in the book and television series *The Power of Myth*, was deliberately targeted at our desires for profit and pleasure, as made apparent in its famous slogan 'follow your bliss'.

> Wherever you are, if you are following your bliss, you are enjoying the waters of eternal life, that life within you, all the time.[121]

The waters of eternal life are often presented as idyllic and paradisal, a sort of blue-green sea beside which we relax and become blissfully at peace. But spiritual waters can become grey, dark, stormy and torrential. They can become full of anger and rage at the complacent state of our human existence. These waters may wish to break in upon us, to destroy our peace, to bring suffering and anguish so that something deeper and non-ordinary can be brought to birth in the human heart. The spiritual waters can and do sustain and nourish us, but they can be destructive and wild, especially if our human structures have made no room for the sacred, and have not factored worship into account. In a secular world that has built barriers against the sacred, I do not think Campbell's image of blissful waters is always appropriate, though it is very marketable by spiritual industries seeking to produce designer spiritualities.

SPIRITUALITY AS PAINFUL INTERRUPTION

Bliss is only one aspect of the spiritual, and when it occurs it is often brief and transitory. Truth be known, our entry into spirituality is often unpleasant, difficult and fraught with emotional and social problems. I often speak of 'falling' into spirituality, in the same way as we speak of falling in love. This fall is often involuntary and uncomfortable; it sometimes occurs against our will and in spite of our intentions. To fall into spirituality is to fall into a larger pattern of reality, over which we have no control, and before which we stand astonished, mystified and often disoriented. However, we do not fall into nothingness or emptiness; we fall into relationship with a secret or invisible other. Faith is letting go and knowing that something greater than ourselves is present.

We are overpowered by a force that is greater than we are. This can be miraculous but it can also be dreadful and humiliating to the ego. We are no longer in control of our lives. As such, spirituality is a kind of alien abduction; we are seized, taken over and coordinated by an outside force. This is why it is strange to hear people talk of spirituality as if it were some kind of teddy-bear's picnic, a pleasant event that they look forward to with great interest. Popular language has sentimentalised the spiritual journey, and turned it into something that is ideal, supportive of the ego and full of delight.

Perhaps it is important that we develop these pleasant myths and illusions, because otherwise we might never set foot in the spiritual domain. Spirituality, at least as I experience it, is not something we have or possess for our greater fulfilment, but something that has or possesses us, for the sake of a destiny we cannot know, and another will we cannot fully understand. At times, it is difficult to understand the rush towards spirituality, because if people knew what they were about to experience, they might not be so hasty to leave the cocoon of the protected self and go on the journey. To enter into relationship with the spirit is a fateful and foreboding experience; as scripture informs us:

> **It is a dreadful thing to fall into the hands of the living God.**
>
> **(Hebrews 10:31)**

God has not become destructive in our time, but God often appears to us in negative form, because we are so armoured against the sacred that it has to overtake us before any encounter can take place. The angel has to wrestle us at the ford before we even notice that it exists. When personal breakdown is our only way to break through to the sacred, life arranges obstacles, difficulties, crises or ruptures more often than would otherwise be the case, sometimes repeatedly.

Many of us are dragged down into depth, often with no apparent cause or reason. In Greek mythology, Persephone was picking beautiful flowers in a delightful field, when she was suddenly abducted by Hades, the God of the Underworld. We can feel like Persephone, innocent, naive, contented and going about our pleasant business, when something abnormal and horrible interrupts us. Suddenly, the ground beneath breaks open, exposing a terrible abyss and a dark God. Often, the more we cling to the surface of life, and insist on our innocence, the more violently we are drawn into a strange and difficult terrain, a new dark world that seems so different to normal reality.

The surface of our lives can be punctured by the death of a parent, close relative or friend. Or an intimate relationship crumbles, a marriage falls apart, the children get caught up in drugs, crime or suicidal urges, and chaos breaks loose. Depression, chronic fatigue, ennui, burnout, neurosis, and various kinds of psychosomatic illness are, as it were, the 'left-handed' path into depth and potential spiritual growth.

DENYING THE NEGATIVE SIDE

The difficult, unruly or invasive aspects of spirituality are less frequently engaged or discussed. These darker aspects are conveniently bracketed out of the popular equation, or are projected outside our idealised image of spirituality and placed upon other entities or forces.

It is easy to find scapegoats, or to blame other people or institutions for the mess we are in, rather than see that our mess is part of a greater design, and that such chaos is the crucible in which the philosopher's stone is forged.

Secular or private spirituality can isolate us from others and the wider community. Because so much spirituality operates behind closed doors, in the isolation of our homes or bedrooms, or in the privacy of our own minds, it has just as much capacity to shut us off from community and other people, as it does to open a door to a hidden source or divine power. We often boast about the ability of spirituality to offer us connectedness to nature, others or God, but precisely because this operates in the personal mode it frequently has the reverse effect on our social, familial and communal lives, severing bonds between ourselves and others, and alienating us still further from our social environment.

This bleaker aspect of spirituality is rarely talked about, partly because this would challenge our popular belief in the self-sufficiency of the modern individual, who is supposed to be autonomous and self-contained. If we admitted that spirituality brings as much pain and loneliness as blissful connection with the waters of spirit, we would have to admit that our idealised image of the lone individual before God is inherently flawed and even illusory. But because the secular world is based on a myth of individuality and a cult of individualism, we become like sheep who dare not even raise a bleat against the appalling loneliness that privatised spirituality can bring.

There are numerous difficulties and problems associated with personal spirituality, including the sense of disorientation as one attempts to come to grips with another dimension of the real. This disorientation is all the more acute since more of us in secular society enter into foreign spiritual territory without maps or guides, without direction or counsel from theology, religion, psychology or mysticism. Even Campbell, the advocate of bliss, has to concede, 'If you don't know what the guide-signs are along the way, you have to work it out yourself'.[122] We simply dive in headfirst and wander and roam where we please, often unaware of where we are going, or what we are journeying towards. Do-it-yourself spirituality is potentially very exciting, but when obstacles are encountered or dangers are discovered, we then realise that the path is fraught, and we need lights and illuminations to guide our way.

SPIRITUALITY AS SELF-SACRIFICE

The idea that we enter into relationship with divine forces to gain power over them, or to wrest prestige from them, is a popular marketable fiction. The fact is that true spirituality is not something that makes itself available to our egotistical designs, but rather something that draws us into a larger world and makes us subordinate to a greater will that transcends us on all sides. The credo of true spirituality could be the words of Jesus uttered in despair in the Garden of Gethsemane before the crucifixion, 'Nevertheless, not my will but thy will be done' (Matthew 26:39; Luke 22:42). This is the awesome, foreboding, even terrifying dimension of spirituality, which we might refer to as the not-so-popular aspect of the sacred. Not 'follow your bliss', but 'thy will be done' is the credo for authentic spirituality.

The encounter with the spirit is paradoxical, and our experience of it can split into good and bad aspects when the ordinary ego is governing our standpoint and making our decisions. We designate as bad that which feels uncomfortable, seems overwhelming or compels us to sacrifice, service or subordination. Spirituality is a covenant that offers us the possibility of connection with God, but the price paid for such connection is real and binding. Spirituality satisfies our longing, fulfils our desire, and provides shelter and meaning, but it demands a relative loss of our former freedom and personal autonomy, and entry into the mystery and necessity of sacrifice. We become instruments in the hands of God. Connection to the divine always comes at the cost of losing some element of our former personal freedom.

If we make contact with the sacred, the sacred makes corresponding claims on us. We fall under its direction and become subjects of a divine reality. This involves us in new rules and conditions, including the requirement to follow the dictates of the sacred as they are revealed to us in our experience, prayer, meditation, reflection and spiritual direction. We recognise that we are no longer masters of our fate, as so many modern people like to believe, but become servants of a new reality and participate in a new life that makes considerable demands. Among these demands is not only the need to follow the will of the sacred other, but also to serve the needs of other people and to help others uncover or release the divine potential in themselves. The spiritual life explodes the myths of egotism, narcissism, self-sufficiency, individualism and privatisation. It is completely subversive to modern society and destroys many cherished values of the intellectual enlightenment, especially its idea of freedom.

Our contact with the sacred brings a *metanoia* or conversion within the personal self, which has been popularised in Christian communities as the experience of being 'born again'. Even though we may have embarked on the spiritual journey for purely narcissistic reasons, such as the search for bliss or relaxation, we find that things are not quite as we had planned once the journey gets underway. In spite of ourselves, and regardless of our motives, we find ourselves having to deal with realities that are not pleasant to the ego. This is why Buddhist teachers say that even a spiritual journey begun with 'impure motives' (such as a search for personal power) can actually serve a greater purpose, and can become transformed into an authentic spiritual quest. The ego does not understand what it is letting itself in for. Perhaps these illusions and impure motives are important at the outset, otherwise the ego may not cooperate with what eventually ends up as its own demise, displacement and transcendence. To the ordinary ego, the spiritual experience is a fraud, because it introduces us to the scandal of living otherwards and to being other-directed. The genuine spirit calls us to break our addiction to bliss and to attend to the needs of the other.

SOCIAL RESPONSIBILITY AS A SACRED IMPERATIVE

Although we might initially discover the spirit within ourselves, in quiet introspection, retreat, seclusion or introversion, once spirit is contacted it brings with it an imperative to go outside ourselves and serve others and the world. If we confine the spirit within our own subjectivity, we are liable to explode from the build-up of impossible energy that cannot find fulfilment. Although spirit might be found within us, its 'inwardness' is a temporary dwelling place, because spirit is the fount of human creation and the core of the natural world.

Once released from its hiding place in the self, it rushes out to the wider world, and we need to move beyond ourselves with it, lest we lose the gift of grace that has been bestowed on us. This can cause initial anxiety in many modern people, who may have subscribed to the myth of individualism and are surprised and dismayed by the momentum with which spirit leads them into the world. The narcissistic idea of private spirituality becomes shattered by the spirit as soon as it is awakened. Private spirituality is revealed as an illusion, or as a transitional stage between a former state of sleep and a future mission of social responsibility and commitment. The divine spark inside us longs to become reunited with the universal light, and this is why genuine spiritual awakening is always followed by a centrifugal movement away from the self towards the world and the transcendent.

In our typical human experience, God starts off as 'my' God, my personal redeemer, guiding angel or mentor, and ends up as the supreme and unknowable Godhead, the great mystery who is creator of the world and the reality within every thing. We are drawn out of ourselves and beyond subjectivity, and if we are courageous enough to move with this momentum we find, ironically, true personal fulfilment and individual satisfaction. The secular myth of the individual locks us into a cocoon that is by definition a recipe for despair, depression and frustration. Our real longing can only be fulfilled by contacting the spirit and moving wherever it pleases.

This helps to explain the age-old connection between spirituality and social service, a connection that is being destroyed by the popular myth of spirituality as a private preoccupation and a path of self-development. But this new popular myth is partly right, and provides a necessary compensation to the ideas of formal religion, which have directed our attention to the outer world, forgetting that God resides in the inner man or woman, and can be discovered there through self-reflection. Religion's emphasis on the world and social service needs to be complemented by a new mystical emphasis on the cultivation of the inner life. Once the inner connection is made, the spirit compels us into the world, and we willingly do what religion preaches. But tradition so often misses the inner connection, and engagement with the world soon runs out if we have not nurtured the *religio* or 'binding back' within ourselves. We need both inner life and outer engagement, spiritual contemplation and social action.

MYSTERIUM TREMENDUM

We tend to see spirituality as a preparation for life, a fulfilment of personal hopes and a search for psychological wholeness, but it is also, in its darker aspect, a preparation for death, and a building of a vessel that will carry us into immortal life. For many people, this side of spirituality is too morbid to contemplate, but it is a part of what spirituality is about. The God who gives so much and fills us with life, joy and contentment is the same God who overshadows us with mystery and darkness, and draws us into itself at the time of our death. Rudolf Otto, in his work *The Idea of the Holy*,[123] provides a memorable description of the paradoxical nature of the holy. According to Otto, the experience of the holy is complex and two major aspects may be discerned. The first is the *mysterium fascinans*, and the second the *mysterium tremendum*. The first is the experience of the numinous as fascinating, mysterious, wonderful and elevating. This is the side that is championed today in the popular discussions about spirituality. The second, the holy as *tremendum*, is more foreboding and difficult. It recognises that in our contact with the sacred we encounter something that stands against us, and before which we realise our own frailty, weakness and smallness. In our experience of the *tremendum*, Otto asserts, we are conscious of God as 'a religious object over against the self', and we sense our humanity as sheer 'impotence and general nothingness as against overpowering might, dust and ashes as against majesty'.[124]

The experience of mystery as *tremendum* diminishes our status, displaces human authority, and brings us into relationship with something tremendous and awesome. *Tremendum* relates to the English word 'tremor', as in 'fear and trembling before God'. Otto writes:

> The Hebrew word *hallow* is an example. To keep a thing holy in the heart means to mark it off by a feeling of peculiar dread, not to be mistaken for any ordinary dread, that is to appraise it by the category of the numinous ... The 'fear of God' which Yahweh can pour forth, dispatching almost like a daemon, seizes upon a man with paralysing effect. Here we have a terror fraught with an inward shuddering such as not even the most menacing and overpowering created thing can instil. It has something spectral in it.[125]

The *tremendum* aspect, he continues, is 'the deepest and most fundamental element in all strong and sincerely felt religious emotion'. He argues that throughout history the numinous has been experienced as both wonderful and dreadful, and he arrives at the description of the sacred as a *mysterium tremendum et fascinans*.

In view of this, it would seem that the task of tradition is to remind us of the paradoxical nature of God and spirit. Religion sings praises to God as the creator of life and the universe, but it also recognises in full solemnity that this same God will draw us into itself at our death. The task of religion is to remind us of the complex nature of spirituality, to release the spirit from the merely personal domain, and to broaden its horizon to include the social world, the community and the whole of our experience.

The historical role of religion is to liberate the spirit from personal narcissism, and to introduce a cosmic or universal perspective as well as to keep spirituality firmly related to morality, social responsibility and the remembrance of our own mortality. This role of religion is difficult yet essential; it is compelled to place more emphasis on the *tremendum* than on the *fascinans*, since it is the *tremendum* that we readily lose, repress or ignore in favour of a brighter and more positive or ego-friendly image of the divine. But a creative religion keeps the foreboding and fascinating elements in steady balance, so that religion both inspires our spiritual aspiration and tempers it by reminding us of our boundaries, duties, responsibilities and limits.

AUTHENTICITY AND TRADITION

Tradition enshrines and contains authentic ideas about spirituality, but because tradition has broken down we have to arrive at these ideas in new ways. As we progress along the spiritual path, we often learn to revalue tradition as the historical repository of wisdom, and this can lead to a completely new attitude towards religious tradition. Typically, at the beginning of the spiritual journey, contemporary people often denounce religion as extraneous or external to the self and therefore as irrelevant to spirituality. With greater maturity, a new understanding emerges, but with this maturity comes a new danger: not ditching tradition as irrelevant, but embracing it too fully as the source and goal of one's own spiritual striving.

The contemporary individual may have to distance him or herself from tradition, to emphasise the personal experience of the sacred. This is the archetypal pattern of Buddha, Christ and all religious revolutionaries: to sweep aside tradition so as to get down to a primordial, personal and immediate experience of the sacred. Jung writes: '[our spiritual instinct] leaves the trodden paths to explore the by-ways and lanes ... just as Buddha swept aside his two million gods that he might attain the original experience which alone is convincing'.[126] The historical irony is that the passionate and even fiery individuality of Christ or Buddha gives rise to new religions in which the radical impulses are forgotten, and the revolutionary is then made the head of new social conventions in which the impulse to conform is paramount.

Once personal experience of the sacred has been achieved, in whatever form or expression is appropriate for the individual, there arises a natural desire to link the experience with tradition. It is as if a former rebellious phase has been outgrown, and now there is an opposite desire to embrace tradition and see one's experience in light of the historical process. The spirit, as I have said, hungers for universality, and after an initial period the personal is outgrown and there is a desire to inhabit a much larger world. After pushing tradition aside, we can be assailed by a new problem—a desire to immerse ourselves in a religious tradition, and to abandon individuality in the name of achieving a new authenticity. Formal religion might encourage this as a desirable situation, but it could represent a loss to spirituality.

THE DANGERS OF NOSTALGIC TRADITIONALISM

We must learn to distinguish between traditionalism and authenticity in spirituality. I have observed a number of people, especially around middle-age, who become filled with a desire to lead an authentic spiritual life, and who interpret this as a need to go back to tradition and to bury their individuality in a kind of nostalgic traditionalism. It is as if an Oedipal or rebellious phase has been outgrown, and now there is the opposite desire: not to slay the father of tradition, but to 'marry' the father in an ecstatic merger of self and history. In such a marriage, the pain of isolation is overcome and one attempts to become absorbed in the historical stream. I think this is particularly acute if the postmodern condition has been experienced as flawed, fragmented and disloyal to the past. The maturing person grows out of the rebellious background, and the desire for roots, connections and security makes him or her extraordinarily traditional, as if claiming the authenticity that had been absent in the past.

But authenticity is not to be gained in such a simple way. To be authentic, one must be true to one's own human situation or destiny, and life may be seeking something new or different in and through our individual example. If life wants us to live in the present, and to find a new solution to the religious problem of our time, then a return to the past is not an achievement of authenticity, but an escape from it. We could refer to this as a regressive restoration of the past. People who do this often view themselves as a cut above the general community who are struggling with the fragments and inconsistencies of present social reality. In its extreme form, this longing for certainty and avoidance of the present leads to fundamentalism, extremism and authoritarianism, all in the name of doing what is 'good' for us and others.

One way out of this dilemma is to make distinctions between traditional values and traditional practices. Traditional values include emphasis on the other rather than the self, compassion, respect, charity and sacrifice. While these may need to be embraced in order to discover a new authenticity, traditional practices, creeds and dogmas may simply lead us out of the present altogether in search of an imagined past. It seems to me that the contemporary and the traditional need to stand separate, although linked, with bridges between them. When we abandon the contemporary in a bid to become authentic, we are misunderstanding the meaning of authenticity, that is to be true to what is present in ourselves and in our society at the time. Authenticity means doing what the spirit wants us to do, and to find out what that could be, we need to develop the skills of prophecy and discernment, and not take flight into convention.

Tradition may best be honoured, not by a regressive return to the past, but by a courageous and faithful commitment to the present, and a living of the 'spirit' of tradition in the context of the present. As Picasso once said, tradition is having a baby, not wearing your father's hat. For our purposes, this might mean borrowing from traditional understandings of spirituality, but applying those understandings to the new context of postmodern society, and not betraying the postmodern condition by a flight to the past. As contemporary historians tell us, any reconstruction of the past is a work of fiction anyway, and our image of the past is always an interpretation of history, not a description of it.

How we relate to tradition is a vital element in the spiritual journey. Once some distance and detachment has been gained, we are at liberty to rediscover tradition as a resource. Creative spirituality seems to be a balancing act. The individual must remain true to his or her individuality, and yet also draw from tradition to develop a broader view and to uncover the rich resources needed for the journey. If we are not careful, tradition can exert a mighty gravitational force upon us and draw us into a dull and inert historicism. However, to refuse to dialogue with tradition is a sign of continued youthfulness and adolescence, and a denial of the deep sources that nourish us.

CHAPTER 10

Towards a new image of God

Although I have no problem about the existence of God, I do have a problem with much of the language that is used about God; and I am aware that many people will have a problem with the language I use about God.

Sara Maitland[127]

God is an idea that modernity had rendered obsolete, but which postmodernity is beginning to find attractive again. Until recently, to speak of God was to be classified as a believer of an old religious system that modern knowledge, science and education had surpassed and rejected. The French scientist Laplace was asked by Napoleon about the place of God in the new scientific universe, and he replied, 'I have no need of that hypothesis'.[128] But the kind of modern science that rejected mystery and the idea of God has itself been abandoned and surpassed by the so-called new sciences, which are open to the possibility of mystery and God once more.[129] The return of God in scientific reflection is still highly controversial, and many scientists greet this development with appalled fury, but the old paradigm of science has been challenged and the empire of knowledge is forced to reopen the case about the existence of God.

In a relatively short period of time, the theological universe has been collapsed, declared redundant by those with power and knowledge, and then reopened to new enquiry and sympathetic reflection.[130] Postmodernity has been friendly to the idea of God, partly because it has exposed the constructed nature of the scientific authority or 'objective' knowledge that killed God off in the first place. The idea of God was ruled out mainly because it did not fit the narrow world picture of scientific rationalism, but that picture turns out to have no more or less authority than the cosmology or religious 'myth' it sought to replace. As Sara Maitland the feminist theologian writes, 'Scientism is a myth too, a myth as pernicious an any other sort of fundamentalism'.[131] The demise of arrogant rationality and old-style objective knowledge has opened the door to the possibility of mystery and God. In particular, we have become alert to the tyrannical element in a dominant knowledge system that declares other knowledges to be redundant or invalid.[132] Maitland insightfully remarked:

> Any stance towards the world which holds that it can be read
> off and lived at one level only, and that God must be forced to
> perform according to the requirements of that level, is
> dangerous to our wholeness.[133]

THE CONTEXT FOR A NEW IMAGE OF GOD

The new image of God will not be, and cannot be, the same image that was toppled by scientific knowledge. 'He' won't return in the same form as before, in fact the pronoun 'he' may be dropped altogether, since we no longer believe that God is a man (if we ever did), nor even 'masculine' as a cosmic principle. Yet God will return because God is an archetypal idea, and such ideas are eternal and enormously valuable, although at times they are debunked and declared redundant. In her wonderful survey, *A History of God,* Karen Armstrong wrote: 'Throughout history people have discarded a conception of God when it no longer works for them'.[134] After the collapse of the 'highest value', as Nietzsche called it, it is simply a matter of time before this archetypal idea expresses itself in new ways. God is declared dead, and soon after God is found to be alive again. The new image of God is often not recognised either by the existing religion, which still worships the old image, nor by the debunkers and rationalists, who are still revelling in the glory of their theocidal murder or God-killing.

Apart from anything else, the idea of God has enormous implications for our mental health and well-being, since the idea of the sacred other is integral to the human personality. Even Sigmund Freud, who felt the idea of God was an illusion, could see reason in maintaining this 'illusion' on therapeutic grounds.[135] The self can only come to know itself in relationship with an other, and without a personified absolute other the self lacks identity, definition and form. When God is eclipsed, the self falls victim to insecurity, uncertainty and doubt because there is no spiritual guarantor of its own life. The self eventually becomes narcissistic because it lacks an objective focus for its existence, and psychological interest and energy, in the absence of a higher goal or destination, falls back upon itself. The idea of God stretches the self to its full capacity, draws it out of its cocoon, and links it to the world, to others and the world beyond time. No other idea has such a dynamic consequence, not even the idea of human love or the beloved, who is an earthly version of the mystical idea of God as Divine Lover.

THE ROLE OF ATHEISM IN THE NEW DISCOVERY

Rather than resuscitate the dead God, let us agree that the old image of God is dead and buried. The conventional image of God as a supernatural deity who has an objective existence is a human invention that education and science can no longer sustain. Feuerbach, Marx, Nietzsche and Freud were all correct, in my view, to reject such an image; where they went wrong, however, was in assuming that such an image equated with reality. God was also rejected because the image of God had become equated with an ideal of absolute moral perfection that ordinary mortals could not aspire to or emulate. The figure of God in heaven became synonymous with a persecutory superego (Freud) who looked down upon mortals, judging and often condemning their behaviour. People wanted to be rid of such a life-denying and rigidly moralistic God. Again they were right to do so but wrong to think that such a persecutory figure equated with the reality of God. Today, only sentimentalists, fundamentalists and unthinking people want to return to that antiquated image of the Supreme Being. We need to discover God anew.

The spirit of our time is hugely tied up with atheism, but again the atheist is half-right and half-wrong. The atheist strives to sweep away conventional images and human idols, and emphasise the reality dimension of human and social existence. But the atheist often fails to see that the 'spirit' of God is not demolished by knocking over images and idols; this is where atheism falls short of providing a solution. Nevertheless, an 'atheist' phase is often sobering and salutary for many people, and can be a significant stage in the movement towards a deeper and truer faith. As Paul Tillich says:

> The protest against God, the will that there be no God, and the flight to atheism are all genuine elements of profound religion. And only on the basis of these elements has religion meaning and power.[136]

When I debated with a well-known atheist on national television, a Jewish writer and public leader who wanted to bring down conventional images of God, I agreed with him that we are obliged to deconstruct and disassemble the old God-image. The atheist seemed slightly confused by my position, since I had been invited to the studio to present the case for religious faith.

However, my own faith is certainly not conventional, and I am at one with the intellectual tradition in its desire to critique the ideas and assumptions of faith. I am only interested in a faith that has 'passed through' the fire of atheism, the blaze of modernity, and the critical scrutiny of psychoanalysis and science. What survives after all else has been burnt away, or what rises up phoenix-like after conventional forms have been melted down is the faith that I am interested in. It is the only kind of faith that resonates with the spiritual needs of our extraordinary time.

CULTURAL PERSPECTIVES ON THE RISE AND FALL OF GODS

In every stage of human civilisation, the traditional images of the sacred fade, die or lose their conviction. In ancient times, there were historical crises in which the gods would die, and a cherished icon or deity no longer held meaning. Only the uneducated would keep believing, while the educated would often ridicule and undermine the old cosmology. In the late Greco–Roman world, the mournful cry that 'the great god Pan is dead' was heard throughout the crumbling empire, paving the way for the future ascendancy of Christianity, and the conversion of a declining empire to a new religion from the East. More recently, Christendom, or the 'empire' of Christianity, has met with the same fate that was once reserved for the gods of Olympus and the pantheon of Zeus and Jupiter.

It is a fact that all symbolic representations of the divine die, and society has to set about to renew and remake its sacred images. The new images must carry weight, significance, beauty and conviction, and they cannot simply be invented by human reason, but must well up from the spirit of the people and from the mythopoetic imagination. In such difficult times of transition, we must insist on a difference between the image of God and the essence or absolute reality of God, or between form and spirit. In times such as ours, old images die, but the spirit is released and set free from its old forms. Those who see only the established religious images, and not the spiritual realities behind them, will be sorely alarmed, and will rail against a contemporary world that seems cruel, irreverent, destructive, atheistic and nihilistic. Those who see beyond the old images are already looking forward to the future with anticipation and hope, asking what the new images of the sacred will be.

To focus only on the images brings dread and fear, and to see beyond them brings hope and foresight. At such times, the religious are pessimistic and mournful, anticipating a future of impending darkness and gloom, while the spiritual are optimistic and hopeful. These new sacred images and feelings are apparently invisible to the devoutly religious, who fail to notice them because the new expressions are not conventionally religious. I am sure, for instance, that the new expressions of the sacred will be more holistic and less perfectionist and persecutory; this is what one can discern from the hints and clues in the new sciences, arts and philosophy.

We hear completely opposite statements being made about the state of the world. One person will insist that civilisation is going to the dogs, and we are regressing to paganism, hedonism, and atheism. Another person will argue that the world has never been more spiritual, and that spirituality can be discerned not only in the arts and popular culture, but almost everywhere we care to look. The former will say that people are leaving the churches because they are becoming unholy, the latter that people are leaving churches because they want a more intense kind of spirituality than organised religion can deliver.

Images die, but the sacred never dies; it changes its shape. The spirit needs embodiment and form, and it helps us arrive at such forms through revelation and sacred intercessions. The spirit wants to take form and assume image and symbol, because that is the evolutionary thrust of the spirit, towards embodiment and incarnation. The spirit loves to assume form, but then it apparently loves to unravel it. When the images are taken too literally, are petrified, ossified and turned into idols, they no longer serve the needs of the spirit, and so the spirit turns against religion and attempts to destabilise it. What is sacred and solemn to the churches is no longer sacred and solemn to the spirit. This was the melancholy message of the Danish philosopher Kierkegaard over a hundred and fifty years ago. True faith, he believed, was a leap away from fossilised beliefs into the mystery of the Unknown God.[137]

This is a very explosive situation, where a great deal of hurt and pain can occur. Such pain can be avoided and overcome by increased education and awareness. The person who understands that religious systems are essentially symbolic is in better condition emotionally than the person who is still held in the literalism of religious fundamentalism.

THE RELATIVITY OF SACRED IMAGES

The metaphysical ideas and mythological figures which have come to grief in our time were never synonymous with God, but were only images and conceptions of God, ways of imagining the unimaginable, or knowing the unknown. The sacred is not synonymous with our images of the holy, and to pretend that our images are divine and everlasting is idolatry rather than religion. Religions generally hate to be told by mystics, poets and philosophers that their images are relative, not absolute, because religions always tend towards absolutism in a bid to make their revelations more secure. Perhaps in this regard postmodern philosophers such as Eugenio Trias are right to differentiate between the holy and the sacred:

> The holy refers to what is most profound and sublime; what cannot be touched, even indirectly, by testimony (nor 'looked upon'). The sacred, by contrast, can be touched: it can be used, and in this way may even be destroyed or consumed.[138]

In my own language, the holy would be the absolute other, while the sacred represents our images of the other, which we like to think are absolute but which come and go with the rhythms of culture, history, time and place.

Our relationship with the sacred makes God known and visible, and this is the primary task of religion, to make known to ourselves, each other and the community, the covenant between ourselves and our God. We have a moral and civic responsibility to make the sacred known, and to publicly acknowledge it as the basis of community and the core of our individual lives. But the process of making known can backfire, since religion can lose touch with the spiritual mystery it seeks to serve. When religion serves itself, rather than the abiding mystery, it ceases to be spiritually and socially effective, and disappears into institutional self-concern, where some of our contemporary churches are caught, unable to move forwards into prophecy or vision.

If the Unknown God becomes too known, if the mystery appears wholly familiar and cut-and-dried, if the spirit has stopped leading us into new awareness and we become obsessed with the past, then religion has reached its use-by date and is no longer a vital organ in the social body. We live in a mournful time of the passing of the gods, and mourning is what the churches should be doing, instead of insisting on songs of praise and attitudes of celebration and jubilation that, at the end of the day, are forms of denial and resistance. I find the Western churches sad in their inability to mourn, and their insistence on up-beat and jubilant services which fly in the face of the world's spiritual suffering, gesturing towards a 'salvation' that scripture proclaims, but hardly any of us can feel. If religion knew how to suffer consciously, then we might discover, in and through our suffering, the prophetic spirit that could identify and usher in the new image of God.

THE PRIMARY ROLE OF IMAGINATION AND ART

The avidly religious do not understand that the holy is always above and beyond our formal categories, and no matter how familiar we seek to make God we have never succeeded in capturing God. This is a situation in which further education supports the cause of the spirit, but brings disappointing news to the literal-minded and the fundamentalist. Education can help us appreciate the vital significance of symbolic or analogical representation, and it can help us improve our respect for the imagination and understand its importance in conveying our sense of the sacred. Religion often opposes the development of symbolic awareness, since it sees such education as an evil force bent on undermining its authority. Religion sees such education downgrading religion to cultural symbolism, and with the 'relativisation' of religion it is then a small step to nihilism and despair.

But religion drastically underestimates the symbolic order. It is simply not true that a heightened awareness of the symbolic role of religion is a prelude to loss of faith and nihilism. The symbolic has to be reappraised by a postmodern culture, and given the high status that it fully deserves. The literal-minded tend to confuse symbolic imagination with fantasy, and therefore miss its revelatory significance. They also confuse relativity with relativism, that is a negative ideology that claims that because symbols are relative they are unreliable, untrue or inauthentic. The way to avoid the corrosive effects of nihilism and relativism, and to be open to a potential encounter with the deep mystery of the world, is to increase our understanding and appreciation of the spirituality of symbolic processes.

When a poet, as Matthew Arnold did, announces that the tide is out in the sea of faith, the religious traditions turn their collective back. Come, says religion, come away from the world, with its disbelief, doubt and heresy. We must protect the faith from the world, to protect what we know is good, true and life-giving. But by what authority do the poets and philosophers speak? Surely by no authority greater than ours, for we gain our authority direct from God, and the poets speak for us. This kind of attitude, in which God and the world are brought into dualistic opposition, keeps religion defended and isolated from the world. It also keeps religion alienated from the spirit of poetry, and from the poetic imagination. The divine inspiration of the poets is rejected or ignored, while the poetic and imaginative are banished from religion and dogma. The split between divinity and world diminishes both sides of the divide, and there is no longer any true rapport between God (as conceptualised by religion) and society, or between eternity and time.

Religion needs the poetic imagination and the contemporary arts, because these are the major ways in which 'eternal' truth or the holy become revived and made relevant to the times. It is the poets and philosophers who fashion the new image of God, and so renew the tradition and give it hope and relevance to the present. As the poet A. D. Hope writes:

Yet the myths will not fit us ready made.
It is the meaning of the poet's trade
To re-create the fables and revive
In men the energies by which they live,
To reap the ancient harvest, plant again
And gather in the visionary grain,
And to transform the same unchanging seed
Into the gospel-bread on which they feed.[139]

This is an important statement about the nature of faith, religion and the key role played by the arts. The arts not only serve our aesthetic and expressive needs, but also a spiritual function. In fact they have the capacity to redeem the official image of God of its tiredness and obsolescence. The sacred images of former times never 'fit us ready made', but have to be renewed through contemporary artistic expression. Karen Armstrong again: 'Each generation has to create its own imaginative conception of God, just as each poet has to experience truth upon his own pulse'.[140]

Although traditionalists fear that the arts will create a new religion or an alternative faith system, Hope makes it clear that the true role of the artist is not to invent a new religion, but to award new life to tradition. 'The poet's trade [is]/To re-create the fables and revive/In men the energies by which they live'. Note that the task of the arts is to 'plant again' an 'unchanging' seed, and to reap an 'ancient' harvest. Paradoxically, it is the old that waits to be reborn in the new, and paradox, as we know, is characteristic of the realm of the spirit. Hence in our time, the new image of God is not so new after all, but rather an 'old' or original God is *made new* through the efforts of contemporary culture and understanding. 'There is nothing new under the sun' (Ecclesiastes 1:9), and yet the spirit revels in the feeling and glory of newness.

This view of the role of the arts is close to what the Hebrew tradition refers to as *midrash*, the 'making new' of the ancient tradition, so that it is redeemed of its tiredness, age and weariness by linking it to contemporary awareness and experience. 'Every living culture,' writes sociologist John Carroll in *The Western Dreaming,* 'is inwardly driven to *midrash*'.[141] Jewish culture seems to place much emphasis on this function in theology and religion, but unfortunately Christian culture has no obvious equivalent to the Jewish midrash, and there is no apparent attempt on the part of Christianity to foster and develop the new life of an old and ailing religion.

Morale-boosting efforts to bolster the old are very familiar in Christianity, but this is simply a parody of renewal, and not an equivalent to a truly redemptive *midrash*. Inspired artists and philosophers who seek to bring the new image of God to birth are likely to be condemned as traitors or heretics, rather than revered as prophets or visionaries. Witness, for instance, the treatment of such prophetic figures as Don Cupitt in England[142] or John Shelby Spong in America[143] who have both been rejected and scorned by their own religious institutions. The Christian tradition is wedded to form, and does not look beyond form to the spirit that is moving beneath it. This means that Christian *midrash* is relegated to an underground, or at least is found outside official religious culture, in 'secular' arts, 'heretical' sciences, or 'dangerous' movements such as feminism, psychoanalysis and poetic subcultures.

A WORK IN PROGRESS: RESHAPING THE HIGHEST VALUE

The new image of God is still being developed by the arts, imagination, philosophy and creativity, but we can make some preliminary statements about it. God is no longer seen as a static figure in heaven, a kind of 'person' who 'creates' the world like a master craftsman. In the early depictions of God in the natural sciences, God was the designer of a clockwork universe, who first wound the clock and then withdrew (*deus absconditus*). The emphasis in recent thought is not on God as an object or thing, but on God as a process, force or dynamism. These ideas probably began with the mathematical philosophy of A. N. Whitehead (1926; 1929), and his process thought, which subsequently gave rise to process theology. But from Einstein, Jung and Pauli we developed the concept of reality as a dynamic and purposive process, and the new image of God will be closer to Einsteinian physics, and its concepts of relativity, than it will be to the static physics of Newton or premodern science.

The God of old-style religion is remote, detached, interventionist and supernatural. The God of the new spirituality, however, is intimate, intense and immanent. This is not to say that spirituality's God is not transcendent and sublime, but that this transcendence is imagined differently, not through miracles and magic, but through the radical presence of divine being. God is not conceived as an extrinsic or outside super-reality, but as a mystery at the core of ordinary reality. In other words, transcendence is not imagined literally as an other world, a world 'on top' of or above this world, but as a deeper dimension of the real that transcends our normal perception. For new spirituality, God is not a supernormal being known only to prophets and saints, but is revealed to all and everyone who cares to look, listen and feel deeply enough.

The new God is everywhere and in all things, or to be more precise, all things are in God (*pan-en-theism*). While pantheism reduces God to the shape and size of material things, panentheism allows for the transcendental dimension by recognising that God is greater than things, while also present in them. Spirituality is not tortured by questions about the existence of God, or about proofs for God's existence, as theology and metaphysics so often are. Spirituality does not ask for proofs, because the proof is in the experience itself. Old-style religion is plagued by doubts about God's existence, because it realises that its own conceptions are difficult to believe. It tries to bury its doubts in repeated assurances, dogmas, creeds and articles of faith. When religion is based on distant belief, rather than intimate experience, it has to summon all manner of props and bulwarks to keep the sense of the holy alive.

Spirituality does not require bolstering and support, team assurance or incantatory magic. It is enough for spirituality to realise that there is mystery and presence in the ordinary world. The world itself is revelatory of God's presence, so the intense rituals, liturgies and chants become less important in developing and maintaining a compelling sense of the sacred. Reality does not have to be broken by ritual to reveal the sacred, and time does not have to be suspended to admit the eternal. Rather, time contains the eternal as a dimension of itself, and reality is felt to be part of the sacred reality, which gives a pregnant, meaningful or ritual dimension to all our human experience. God reveals itself to us not only in scripture, creation and tradition (the three official sources of revelation), but also in the minor revelations of everyday life, in our encounter with the known, which is made mysterious and wonderful when we see the known as an analogy for the unknown, that is as symbolic and sacramental.

GOD AS RADICAL ORDINARY PRESENCE

We see one thing and comprehend another, or we see a sacred reality as we are perceiving an earthly or ordinary thing. Spirituality gives us double vision, and at first we think we are 'seeing things', imagining things, or making things up. But the echo or shadow of the real is the sacred drama itself, which stands behind the real and acts as its guarantor, benefactor, source and support. In the future, theology will need to develop into *theopoesis*, that is a recognition of the living God and the mystery of spirit at the very core of our universe. God speaks to us analogically, saying one thing through the agency of another, and often through something simple and quite ordinary.

We cannot know the Unknown God directly, through metaphysical encounter, for God is not a thing, an idol or figure in space, but something greater than our rational thought can comprehend. I like the mystical description of God as a circle whose centre is everywhere and whose circumference is nowhere. God is radically present with us and closer even than our own breath, a presence that is nearer to us than is comfortable to admit. It is easier to imagine God as an old man in the sky, for that puts God outside us. Eventually, we have had to realise that this conventional image of God has to be destroyed so that the deeper reality of God can be experienced.

It is the fullness and abundance of God that becomes known to spirituality, and eventually this fullness, which is hidden or obscured to normal perception, is revealed and made known to a mature spiritual awareness. Spirituality notices God, whereas other kinds of perception see only surfaces, literal forms or the absence of forms. William Blake famously declared that the poetic task is to 'melt apparent surfaces away, displaying the infinite which was hid'. He writes:

> If the doors of perception were cleansed every thing would
> appear to man as it is, infinite. For man has closed himself up, till
> he sees all things thro' narrow chinks of his cavern.[144]

When the opacity is cleansed from our perception, when the scales are taken from our eyes, when the familiar is broken and defamiliarised, when clichés, platitudes and hackneyed conventions are removed, then spirituality's God is experienced. It is by taking away the familiar that the hidden mystery is revealed, it is by puncturing the surface that the sacred depth is made manifest. God is present all the time, whether we realise it or not. The task of poetry and metaphor is to shatter the surface appearance, so that we can see things in a new light.

This is where religion becomes defensive again. Religion replies: do you mean to say that God is merely a figment of our imagination, that we invent God simply by an act of poetic imagination? Religion suffers from a very low opinion of the imagination, which it confuses with fantasy, day-dream or invention. Spirituality has to patiently and tolerantly reply that imagination in this deeper sense is not invention but an act of revelation in the Blakean sense of 'melting away' the surface appearances. The poetic imagination is a central organ of theology and the perceptual mechanism of the spirit. Sara Maitland again: 'Imagination, creativity, narrative seems to be the way God is revealed in the world of matter'.[145]

REDISCOVERING GOD IN THE CATHOLIC TRADITION

I would like to consider the problems faced by the theologically literate Catholic in the contemporary world. I take the Catholic example, because Catholic faith has been traditionally based on a sacramental, ritualistic and communal faith, precisely the kind of faith that has been destroyed by modern perception. Catholic theology is far beyond a 'magical' interpretation of sacramental process, but at the parish level, of which I have some experience, the magical view of God and sacrament seems to have remained dominant, due to a lack of adult faith development. My key text in this discussion is Hans Kung's inspired essay, 'Rediscovering God'.[146] A further discussion of these problems can be found in Kung's work, *Does God Exist? An Answer for Today*.[147]

The educated Catholic is in a crisis, because he or she has to catch up with his or her Protestant cousins, who have been grappling with the problems of modernity for a longer period of time. The Catholic has to reach a postmodern image of God, before having achieved a specifically modern perception in the Reformed sense. There is, however, not much solace for the Catholic in a Protestant-style faith. It is too rational, cerebral, wordy and not sacramental enough. To enter the current era of faith, with its emphasis on justice, ethics, worldly concern, and a social gospel based on the historical life and moral example of Jesus, is to enter barren territory. It is to relegate to the category of medieval superstition much of what the Catholic worshipper has held dear.

The Catholic mass has always promised, and often delivered, an experience of the nearness of the sacred. Catholic liturgy and ritual has been based on the assumption that the presence of God is near, and that such presence can be heightened and intensified in high liturgical moments. To enter a 'modern' faith, where God is distant and remote, and where Jesus is a moral example rather than a spiritual presence, is a colossal leap into disenchantment for the Catholic. It is little wonder that 'lapsed' Catholics are attracted not to Protestant-style churches, but to the New Age movement, and to Eastern religions such as Tibetan Buddhism, Zen and gnostic philosophies, because such pathways offer the possibility of a recovered sense of spiritual presence and contact with spiritual reality. This modern stage of faith is not attractive because it is unspiritual, disenchanted and a reflection of the worldliness that mystical faith seeks to overcome.

The problem facing the educated Catholic is how to conceive of God's presence in creation and sacrament. In the past it was conventional to adopt a basically supernatural understanding of God's presence. In this model, the priest is a sort of latter-day shaman or magician who performs magic in the sacraments, waving his hands over the eucharistic elements and turning them into the body and blood of the Redeemer. In this model, God is a supernatural being living in heaven, a bit like Zeus or Jupiter, who intervened in the course of history at his desire, creating miracles and wonders to make things better on earth, or to cause the faithful to strengthen their belief.

It is this supernatural model of religion that is dissolving rapidly, causing many Catholics to abandon their faith because it is no longer tenable. 'I cannot accept it,' I sometimes hear them say, 'I cannot accept all this fairytale stuff, and need a different approach to God'. Thinking people require new models and understandings of the presence of God in the world. Hence, the relative urgency of reaching, describing and communicating a new model of religious life that is neither a return to magical thinking (that is reactionary conservatism), nor a capitulation to the hopeful yet bland liberalism of the modern era (characteristic of 'progressive' attitudes).

Hans Kung understood this task:

What is called for [in theology today] is not first and foremost originality, but personal involvement from one's own experience, an account with something to say to other people. The question is whether the theology we live with doesn't simply sustain its own system, confirm its own plausibility and coherence, reach only theological insiders, for the most part priests and catechists, only talk about itself and to itself. The question is whether it really talks to the people of today about God, and whether it talks about the real God, whether it lives on experiences of God and discoveries of God and is capable of leading people to find them anew.[148]

Kung realised that many are rejecting faith because it seems implausible. This does not mean that such people are rejecting the idea of God or the possibility of God, but the picture of God as it is presented in traditional teaching. It is lack of belief in this old model and its archaic language, rather than lack of faith in God as such, that is causing decline everywhere. Kung went on:

I start from the premise that for many people this subject is one of acute urgency, particularly for all those who, with almost no religious upbringing, are engaged in a permanent quest for themselves, for identity, security, community and meaning, and at the same time, openly or in secret, are looking for religious experiences. If they often fail to find them, this is largely the fault of a theology and preaching which is still too much in the head, choked with dogmas and pastorally inefficient: theology for theologians, dogmas for dogmaticians.

There are countless unbelieving people in whose experience God simply does not appear, but who would be prepared to accept God anew, to rediscover God. In this human sense the question 'Is God coming?' may have meaning: God can come again in a new way as an experience for countless people.[149]

Kung was suggesting that the secular or non-religious person, as well as the lapsed Catholic, may be invited into a new understanding of the Western religious tradition, if only a new language can be found that is meaningful and effective. God can 'come again' for those who have rejected God, and for those who have never accepted God into their lives. Kung argued that theology must focus on the real God, and that, of course, leads us back to the question with which we started. Who or what is the real God for us today? How to conceive of God in the postmodern world?

NEITHER LIBERAL NOR CONSERVATIVE: THE MYSTICAL APPROACH

Kung's responses suggest that, like Karl Rahner before him, he saw personal and mystical encounter with the fact of God as the only way forward for a dying tradition. God is an immediate experience, discovered through prayer, meditation and sacraments. God somehow 'inheres' in all things, but we do not know how this works, only that it happens to be so, and can be verified through prayer and experience. 'God is not 'available' to the 'neutral observer', Kung conceded, in a tone much more humble than traditional Catholic claims.[150] God is a hidden yet sometimes discernible presence in the world, whose divine presence is rendered transparent and more present by sacrament and liturgy.

The priest is not a magician who goes zap or says 'abracadabra' and causes God to be present but a poet or bard who reveals to people the God who is already present. The function of the clergy is not down-graded to good fellow or everybody's mate who provides racing tips and football jokes, as in the liberal model, but nor is the priest a stern supernaturalist who has a hotline to the 'man upstairs', a phrase still dominant in parishes and in the magical model. Rather, in the mystical model I am outlining, the priest is the figure who transforms our lives and sufferings by reconnecting—'binding back' (*religio*)—our lives and sufferings to a deeper, more profound presence. In the mystical vision, God is close at hand but hard to discern, and the priestly function is to bring God closer, or to bring us closer to God. The New Age says that God's proximity to us renders irrelevant the role of the priest or minister as 'middleman', but this is not so. The presence has to be seen clearly, discerned and acted upon.

Kung suggested that the Catholic Christian, and indeed any Christian, has to divest traditional elements and expectations to experience this new dimension of God:

God is not in a simple way 'out there', where a priest, bishop or pope 'celebrates', 'pontificates', and sometimes puts on a performance at the altar; and God is also not in a simple way 'up there', where the heavenly world where God dwells has evaporated since Copernicus and Galileo, when not even a baroque art heaven can conjure him back again, just as no arbitrarily ruling Church hierarchy, attempting to push itself in as a 'mediator' between God and human beings, can obscure him.[151]

He also acknowledged that the experience of God as object or person has to be radically challenged now and in any future religion:

If the word 'God' is to mean anything at all, then it cannot mean an object like other objects, a being among other beings, a person like other persons. If the word is to retain a meaning today, it must denote the invisible and inaccessible, first and last reality which determines and permeates everything. And this reality would then be, not just another level, but a completely other dimension, which cannot be discovered by the use of some sort of super x-rays. No, God would not be God if he could be empirically detected, worked out or deduced by mathematics or logic.[152]

The fact that God exists, said Kung, 'is not a matter of rational demonstration, as many Catholic theologians believed in the Middle Ages'. Nor is the idea of God 'a matter of irrational experience or feeling, as many Protestant theologians assumed in the face of post-Enlightenment difficulties'. Kung concluded that, in the postmodern context, the existence of God is 'a matter of reasoned trust'—in other words, an act of mystical faith. Any confidence in the existence of God today must have passed through our individual human experience of the ground of reality itself. We can no longer have faith merely because tradition tells us about it, or because an authoritarian church commands us to do so.

Kung supplied a fascinating existential twist to the justification for faith for the contemporary person:

And why is this confidence in a totally different, 'invisible' reality reasonable and intelligible? Because it is supported, justified, tested, verified, in the context of our lived experience ... God has been obscured in our churches, and often by their actions, so that the only remaining possibility is to close one's eyes in order to turn inwards and find the all-encompassing, all-directing God in the secrecy of my inner self, to sense, feel, and experience him at the core of my being.[153]

This is Kung sounding very much like Jung, who made virtually identical statements over sixty years earlier, and from a Protestant, not a Catholic, point of view. But at this existential level, questions about Protestant or Catholic identity are virtually irrelevant. Everyone is in the same boat, on the same stormy seas, tossed in every which way, and hoping the boat does not capsize and throw them out. We are all wrestling with the same issues, although arriving at these issues from different contexts and directions.

The writings of Kung and Jung, and of most contemporary thinkers on these matters, would lead us to conclude that religious tradition, if it is to survive, must add a fourth source of revelation to the 'big three' of scripture, tradition and creation. This fourth source has to be individual experience, or perhaps 'conscience', though this latter term sounds too clinical. This direction was strongly advocated in the 18th century by the philosopher Friedrich Schliermacher, for whom 'religious faith could not be confined to the propositions of creed: it involved an emotional apprehension and an interior surrender'.[154]

Tradition will dig in its heels and resist this 'romantic' or 'mystical' movement, because it does not want the grandeur of God and the greatness of the holy to be dependent on such an apparently whimsical and fickle basis as individual human experience. But in real terms, such greatness and grandeur are indeed dependent on the frail human being for recognition, acceptance and creative relationship. This is the great risk that God took in the beginning and throughout the course of history—the risk that the creation would not recognise the creator, and would ignore the imperatives inherent in the experiment of life. If God is prepared to take this risk, then the institutions of faith acting in God's name should be prepared to take them as well.

PART 4

Concluding reflections

CHAPTER 11

Youth, cultural crisis and ecospirituality

Will the intimations of catastrophe inspire a psychospiritual renewal, a global blitz spirit?

Richard Neville[155]

I continue to be impressed by the vitality and strength of youth spirituality, and its astonishing appearance in the midst of a secular education system that does not encourage it, a religious system that does not understand it, and a materialist society that gives no official sanction to it. It is in youth culture that we see the revolution most powerfully and persuasively at work; here we recognise that Western civilisation is in transition, and that our institutional structures are out of date and unable to cope with the spirit of the new.

It is of the nature of the 'new' to be carried and expressed by the young, since they are the ones who are least defended against the spirit of the time, and the ones most deeply, if not always consciously, embedded in it. This is why we should pay close attention to developments in youth and popular spirituality, because in and through our youth we see most clearly the stirrings of the *zeitgeist*. Youth provide not only a divergent or alternative expression of religious life, but they also provide glimpses into the future shape of religious culture, a kind of window into the future of our world. The expressions of spiritual life in our youth are prophetic, and show us in what direction the spirit is moving or 'blowing' in the public domain. In particular, youth spirituality points to the future integration of spiritual and ecological revolutions.

THE SOCIAL CRISIS OF MEANING

People are aware of the midlife crisis, and how it forces those who encounter such an experience to reconsider one's direction in life and to come to terms with deeper, spiritual issues that may have been neglected in earlier years. Young people are obviously not subject to a personal midlife crisis, but it seems they are the victims of a social situation that is similar to a 'midlife' crisis on a massive, collective scale. Society as a whole has been plunged into doubt, despair and disorientation, and regardless of our individual age we are all drawn into this turbulent crisis, and forced to deal with deep philosophical issues that would not normally be presented to us in a time of social stability. Because they are so sensitive to the underlying issues of the time, youth are living and grappling with the problems and crises of meaning that many older people are used to fobbing away or ignoring. In this respect, youth can often appear older than their years, because they frequently adopt a philosophical attitude to life that makes them wiser than they are supposed to be.

Mature-aged people often hide behind various defensive postures and survival mechanisms, and chief among these is the mechanism that allows us to live in the face of evident meaninglessness and lack of purpose. The young are much less defended against these harsh realities, and are less expert in the art of 'getting on' with the business of living in the absence of soul or meaning. Young people who become depressed, suicidal or fatigued in response to the hopelessness that confronts the world are living symbolic lives. Their struggles with meaning are not just personal struggles. They are trying to sort out the problems of society, and their sufferings, deaths and ruptures are not just personal tragedies but contributions to the spiritual dilemmas of the world.

Youth are moving in a post-secular culture that has experienced the death of God and is now, as it were, moving beyond the spiritual wasteland to a recovery of God and a rebirth of meaning. Formal religion does not fully comprehend the enormous rupture in the mind and soul of the secular world. It represents an established and continuous faith tradition that has not died, and therefore it does not see the need to be reborn. There is a certain complacency in a religious tradition that does not attempt to reach across the gap that separates it from the anxieties and confusions of society.

The secular world is filled with a spiritual longing that it is trying hard to fathom and interpret. The secular is being besieged by repressed sacred impulses, but religion as it stands cannot relate to these impulses because they speak a different language. They speak the language of raw emotion, of barely understood inward impulses, as something new demands to be born. These impulses can, however, be accessed and understood by the new sciences, including depth psychology, quantum physics, ecology and postmodern philosophy. Hence youth feel that although these new sciences and knowledges are speaking to them, formal religion exists in a time-warp, is out of touch, and not speaking a language to which the age can respond.

Students adopt the view that churches have ignored the challenges of humanism, secularism, existentialism, atheism, nihilism and postmodern philosophy. They appear ignorant of the great modern and postmodern thinkers, philosophers, poets and movements. Western religion has not integrated the lessons of these contemporary movements, and so has marginalised itself from society and life, a tragic situation that has prevented it from showing leadership in the rediscovery of God. Religion has stopped having a conversation with culture, and young people live under a cloud of darkness that the churches do not understand.

WALKING AMID THE RUINS

A culture that has lost its shared cosmology no longer provides any emotional or psychological shelter beneath which youth can enjoy their youthfulness, but urges on them an existential attitude that causes them to lose some of their innocence at an early age. This, I take it, is one of the dire consequences of our living in a spiritual wasteland where, as T. S. Eliot said, religious symbols have collapsed into 'a heap of broken images', and where the tree of life 'gives no shelter'. One of my students wrote the following in a class paper on spirituality:

> Like so many of my generation, I have had to walk among the
> ruins of what was once a stable, mighty spiritual empire; an

empire that took millennia to build and only a few hundred years to collapse.

It seems as if the collapse has been accelerating in recent times. I don't know anyone today who attends religious services, but only two generations ago people seemed to belong to one or another religious tradition, or so I am told. It is hard, actually, to imagine that our society was governed by religion so recently, because from today's perspective, we seem to be incredibly secular.

(Peter, 23, 2000)

This student sees himself as walking amid the ruins of Christendom, and later in this essay he expresses a difficult dilemma. He says he cannot embrace a tradition that is dying and collapsing, and yet he has spiritual urges and impulses that seek outward and social expression. If he turns to Christianity, he says he will be labelled a 'born-again Christian'; if he turns to Buddhism he will be labelled a 'New Ager', and if he turns to nature and the earth for spiritual solace he will be labelled a 'Greenie' or a 'Gaia worshipper'. No matter where he turns, or what he does with his spiritual longing, mainstream society will have some hurtful tag or reductive label to attach to his interest. This is one of the ways in which secular society expresses its revenge against the return of the spiritual dimension, by representing it as aberrant, silly or escapist. Still, he perseveres and tries to move ahead, like so many others like him.

This 'making do' with the little we have after the collapse of religion is not only a theme of Eliot's 'The Waste Land' (1922), but also a major theme of W. B. Yeats, who writes in his last major poem, 'The Circus Animals' Desertion':

> Now that my ladder's gone
> I must lie down where all the ladders start
> In the foul rag and bone shop of the heart.[156]

Spiritual cosmology and shared mythology were conceived by Yeats as ladders to the higher world of meaning, myth and spirit. Our secular culture has taken away our ladders, or rather the ladders have been allowed to fall into ruin and disrepair, so that we can no longer climb upon them to reach a higher spiritual state. We can no longer rely on inherited wisdom or traditional faith to give us a glimpse of transcendence, but instead we are forced into an existential mode, where we must start with the 'foul rag and bone shop of the heart'.

This is what many young people are forced to do today. They have an innate distrust of religious tradition or authority, and always attempt to consult their heart, conscience and personal feelings, almost as if these were their only guides to truth. To more conservative people, they appear to be somewhat self-oriented, and a few in the churches argue that they are narcissistic and morbidly inward. But they are true to their time and, as the poets foretold, they are thrown back on themselves, without spiritual ladders, without a sheltering tree of life, and without much to rely on except their heart and conscience.

D. H. Lawrence wrote this about the modern condition:

> Ours is essentially a tragic age, so we refuse to take it tragically.
> The cataclysm has happened, we are among the ruins, we start
> to build up new little habitats, to have new little hopes. It is
> rather hard work: there is now no smooth road into the future:
> but we go round, or scramble over the obstacles. We've got to
> live, no matter how many skies have fallen.[157]

Youth today are living in the existential landscape mapped out and described more than seventy years ago by Eliot, Yeats and Lawrence. Our youth are the inheritors of a 'modernist' condition that has experienced the death of God, the collapse of Christendom, and the loss of certainty and truth. Earlier generations had managed to stave off the sense of cataclysm by ignoring it, by getting on with the business of living, or by telling ourselves that things were getting better all the time. But the present generation sees through any denials or pretence, and understands the deep spiritual plight in which we live. For them, spiritual meaning is not just a game we play with life, but a serious business that can cost us our life if we get it wrong or go off the rails. The problem of youth suicide is intimately connected with the spiritual side of youth experience, and when meaning or truth cannot be found, lives can be broken or lost by the terrible discovery that the spiritual vacuum in society has not been filled by a personal encounter with meaning.

The down-beat, dismal or negative tone of much youth culture derives from the sense that the skies have fallen (Lawrence), spiritual ladders have collapsed (Yeats), and religious symbols are a heap of broken images (Eliot). Western culture and religion can appear to youth as a rubbish dump or junkyard, where everything is meaningless, broken or profoundly out of joint. They whistle and kick cans through this junkyard, often paying little regard to the things they see, including an old religious system, a collapsed theology, and a church that barely manages to keep the rumour of God alive.

STIRRINGS BENEATH THE RUBBLE

In a collapsed or post-holocaustal culture, the things that appear to thrive are the weeds and hybrid growths, that is virulent and uncontrollable forms of capitalism, materialism, consumerism, nihilism and escapism. Many youth fail to see the signs of hope, or the signs that God is still alive, and the 'death of God' is manifest for them in the culture of greed, heartless economic rationalism, accelerated community breakdown, and in various kinds of social evil, especially depression and despair. Many feel themselves to be nothing more than the rugged and street-wise survivors of the wasteland. If they prefer grunge to high culture, punk to high art, heavy metal and techno to the classics, and New Age parodies to religious tradition, this is because, from where they are situated, their discordant and irregular culture speaks to them of the rubble and dissonance, the horror and the terrible beauty of what lies about them.

Nevertheless, for many youth new life stirs in our Western soul. Some youth appear to be turning to the East, especially to Buddhism, Zen and Hinduism, because there is a feeling that the West is a spent force in religious and metaphysical matters. But even the journey to the East is often a metaphorical journey into a different aspect of the Western psyche, a dimension so 'foreign' to society that it is symbolised by a journey to a foreign culture. Although some appear fascinated by the continued dissolution of the West, there are increasing numbers who speak about re-enchantment. It is too early to say whether this movement of the spirit will lead to a revival of Christianity, but it does suggest that we are witnessing a revival of the spirit, which may impact upon our faith institutions further down the line once they have understood what is happening.

A new enchantment seems to be emerging from deep sources in the Western psyche, from beneath Eliot's 'heap of broken images'. It is as if Eliot's heap has decomposed into a pile of organic compost, giving off new life and new forms, some of which, admittedly, are eccentric, strange and difficult to comprehend. Nature goes to work in the junkyard of modernity, disassembling and dissolving the old, and manufacturing the new. 'Nature abhors a vacuum', not only in the physical sense, but in spirituality as well. And to counter-balance all the internal, cerebral and philosophical exploration taking place at the moment, nature itself is emerging as a major site for re-enchantment and an important *locus* for the recovery of the sacred.

NATURE AND SPIRITUAL RENEWAL

Peace comes within the soul of people when they realise their relationship, their oneness, with the universe and all its power.
Black Elk[158]

Many young people are finding themselves drawn to 'ecospirituality' and to what could broadly be called the spirituality of nature. At least, this is true in my own country, and many of the writings I receive on spiritual experience are concerned with 'ecospiritual' encounters. Such encounters change lives and expose young people to the mystery and presence of the sacred within themselves, even as they are moved by the sacred in nature.

This is a cutting-edge interest and there has not been a great deal written about it, which is hardly surprising given the materialistic bias of modern knowledge. But we are witnessing an emergence of ecospiritual concern at the grassroots level, and researchers have not begun to discern what this could mean in terms of a cultural shift away from materialism to a new awareness of living in an enchanted spiritual universe. Nor have we begun to absorb what ecospirituality could mean for changes in youth culture, in identity formation, and in rites of passage into adulthood. It seems that a universe of possibility lies ahead, and I hope some of this possibility is realised in the near future, since youth urgently require a foundation for their experience of the sacred. Nature is certainly a greater and more rewarding foundation than, for instance, experimentation with drugs or mind-altering substances.

I have noticed that ecospirituality looms large for young people in primary and secondary schools, and in universities and colleges. Nature is being experienced in intensely passionate ways and, in literary terms, it seems that a movement close to Wordsworthian romanticism is upon us. But 'romanticism' may be the wrong term, or introduce inappropriate associations. This new interest is not a romantic escape into the ferny woods or sylvan forests, but a very real interest in the politics of nature, in the extent of the ecological emergency, and in activist programs and undertakings to set right what humanity has put wrong in its exploitative attitudes to the natural world.

In other words, this is a political as well as a spiritual movement, with very real social and economic consequences. This movement has much to tell us about our place in the larger scheme of things, and about meaning and purpose discovered through the re-placement of human identity in the context of the natural environment. In psychological terms, the modernist ego has been dis-placed and de-centred by postmodern experience, and our identity appears to be in search of a re-placement that brings us into a new relationship with nature. We are revisioning ourselves and our world, and this revisioning is not just a poetic or mystical flight of fantasy, but a holistic process involving political awareness, economic understanding and a philosophical spirituality.

FALLING IN LOVE WITH THE WORLD

The revelation of the sacred as immanent and worldly comes to us with a specific sense of ecological and environmental urgency. This urgency has to do with the imperilled nature of the material world and its threatened biological existence. The abuse of human power, especially in areas of technological advancement and economic progress, has put in jeopardy the integrity and the future of life on earth. If there are intelligent forces in the universe, these forces have to mobilise themselves to ensure that the experiment of life is not wiped out by human greed, egotism and destructiveness. By a meaningful conjunction or synchronicity, we are becoming more receptive to the immanent aspect of the sacred when the world needs it most. The creational face of the sacred reveals itself to us just in the nick of time.

Perhaps Gaia, the Earth Mother, or the feminine face of the divine, has placed a spell on us, forcing some men, women and youth to fall in love with her. The Earth knows that she can only be saved by care and attention, and if humans proceed on their present course she will be destroyed by a human-generated series of catastrophes. Perhaps she looks up to the planet Mars, fearing that some day her cosmic green and blue will be replaced by the scorched and arid reds of our desolate warlike neighbour. How, then, can she make us shift from ego-centrism to eco-centrism? Thomas Berry arrived at the formula some years ago. The 'dream' of nature is to compel us to apprehend the world as a communion of subjects, rather than as a collection of objects.[159] Nature wants to be apprehended as a living subject and not as a dead object and, to achieve this end, we have to expand our subjectivity to include the realm of nature.

We human beings are vain, proud and self-centred, and we only care about what we are in love with, or what we feel is intimately 'ours'. If we can be made to fall in love with the world, it may be revealed to us that the world is 'ours', the world is us, and that the world intimately matters. The sure way to get humans to care about the environment is to expand our narcissistic boundaries so that these boundaries include what we used to call the 'external world'. By making the world part of our subjectivity, and by connecting us to the world by an act of spiritual identification, the physical world protects itself from a destructive consciousness that has conceived itself as being 'outside' the physical world. Causing us to fall in love with the world may be the world's best insurance policy against ecological devastation and a scorched earth scenario.

WHAT DRAWS YOUTH TO NATURE

Youth are receptive to the love of nature for a variety of reasons. First, nature looms large for young people precisely because it represents an absence, a lack, an emptiness that creates psychological longing and desire. Arguably, most young people today experience less outdoor activity than ever before in human history, especially those who live in big cities, but even those in country areas and smaller towns seem to be drawn indoors by the new technologies. We find ourselves enclosed in houses, offices, bedrooms, classrooms and public buildings, and when we venture outdoors much of our time is spent in cars and vehicles. We find ourselves staring often into computer screens and visual display units, and in this context nature beckons with enormous nostalgic longing for what we have lost.

Youth are beginning to champion and idealise nature because they normally see so little of it, appear shut out from it, and feel removed from it. There is an awareness in many young people that this disconnection is abnormal, dangerous and out of balance. The desire to bridge the gap between society and nature is therefore a way of reconnecting society with a natural sanity or a restorative wisdom. Society is a source of fascinating technology and endless inventiveness, but the wisdom, health and groundedness that makes life meaningful and endurable come from nature, not from society.

Second, the imperilled nature of the environment brings out the heroic dimension of youth, and gives them a rallying-point around which they can make informed accusations at adult society. Youth culture sees that adults, and previous generations of adults, have 'stuffed up' the environment, as they often say. Anyone with eyes to see can recognise this, but youth culture is especially alert to the environmental crisis because its sympathies are more with the wounded and debilitated earth than with the commercial companies and economic interests that persist in abusing the environment and its resources. As Gary Hamel, the influential writer in business leadership, says:

> **Unless you are an industry leader in an unassailable position, you probably have a greater stake in revolution than preserving the status quo.**[160]

Youth culture has become the conscience of the modern world. It studies environmental degradation, deforestation, salination, worldwide pollution, global warming, extinction of animal and plant species, loss of biodiversity, and asks, why is this happening?

This questioning makes adult society feel uneasy, anxious and threatened. The answer to this question is that a fundamental lack of balance has brought about all these crises, difficulties and disasters. This lack of balance has been created by our tilting of the scales of life in the direction of human greed, and by an insatiable appetite for progress at all costs. Our society is heavily invested, financially and psychologically, in the over-development of nature and the exploitation of the environment, so the voices of protest at our environmental degradation arouse an enormous amount of guilt and shame from adult society.

But when young people grow older and become adults will they maintain their youthful idealism? What guarantees have we that they will 'maintain the rage', and continue with their opposition to exploitation? Will they switch sides, from embattled nature to aggressive society, when they decide, as adults in search of careers and financial stability, that benefits and profits are to be had through investment in social development, rather than through the protection of nature? It is easy to be angry and revolutionary when young, but does their 'spirit' shift its allegiance from nature to society when they become socially adapted and society-identified? Or will they work to break down the dualism between society and nature by focusing upon sustainable development and environmentally conscious planning?

Perhaps youth will learn to redefine progress; certainly it is the hope of the Earth that this is achieved. We must learn to see that progress as generally conceived is a euphemism for destruction and devastation. Enormous effort must be put into redefining social and economic progress, and society has to reconstruct itself so that it does not oppose nature, but learns to live in a new relationship with nature. When a positive, relational ethic is established that bonds society to nature, young people will not feel impelled to 'betray' nature when they join society as successful and participating adults.

A third factor that draws youth to nature is their search for moral and spiritual values. It is this factor that shifts environmental interest beyond the level of heroic or activist concern. The search for ethical values and spiritual affinity with nature transforms environmental concern into ecospirituality.

Youth need to believe in truths, values and visions greater than themselves. Beyond the flux of change and the ebb and flow of human opinion, there is a need for a firm spiritual foundation, an experience of something extra mundane that can ground life in deeper meaning and give our fluid existence solidity and security. This need for a firm spiritual foundation is especially marked in adolescence, when the individual is traversing the difficult terrain that separates childhood from adulthood. During the adolescent 'rite of passage', life is full of uncertainty and it is of great personal, moral and spiritual value to have a strong and sturdy foothold upon existence.

In the past, spiritual meaning was provided by society and generated by its various institutions such as the family, religion, law, government, education and health. But now this empire of symbolic meaning has crumbled. It is in these social conditions that ecospirituality gains enormous popular support. If we cannot have faith in our institutions or traditions, where else can we turn but to nature, which does not lie or cheat, which makes no pretence, and which is not manufactured by human hands. We are looking to nature for truth, guiding principles, moral categories and personal meaning. There is a desire today to enter desert places, to have wilderness experiences, to get in touch with primal nature, not to convert nature into any usable resource, but to find new spiritual bearings in the scheme of things.[161]

THE HEALING WHOLENESS OF THE EARTH

The testimonies of young people who have been involved in nature experiences or bush camps often contain references to spirituality and meaning. I take here a sample of comments from essays I have read:

> After an argument with my family, I went on a nature camp at a seaside park. One night, I walked along the beach, listening to the sound of the waves. The moon arose above the horizon, and I felt bathed in its healing light. A deep peace came over me, and I forgot about the strife at home. I felt connected with sea, sky and moon, and this filled with me joy. I have often tried to recapture this feeling, especially in times of difficulty or when problems arise.
>
> (Mandy, 19, 2000)

> Once, in the outback with a group of friends, I had a powerful sensation of the earth as a living, breathing being, with myself connected to it as a smaller being. This feeling of aliveness extended to the galaxies above, and to the night sky teeming with points of starry light. This changed my perspective on everything. It is hard to describe how this changed me, but I am grateful for the experience.
>
> (Melissa, 18, 2001)

> Looking out across the land from the hilltop, I felt a sense of holiness in the scene around me. I will always be thankful for this experience, and to nature for showing me my path and making me focus on the important things in life.
>
> (Lisa, 19, 1999)

> The age, wisdom, and endurance of the land had a big impact on me. I felt so peaceful, words cannot describe the feeling. It was spiritual for me.
>
> (Bronwyn, 18, 2000)

The pattern here, as elsewhere in my reading of such experiences, is simple and yet profound. Nature provides a sense of peace and harmony, and this has the effect of reducing anxiety in the human observer, who not only observes the peacefulness around him or her but somehow participates in it. This, at least, is the obvious interpretation of such events.

The psychological or archetypal understanding of such experiences might be more complex. With Eliade and Jung as our guides, we might say that nature carries for some of us the image of a primordial, intricate and undivided whole. Nature in this sense is more than 'nature', it is a cosmos, or a carrier of a Platonic wholeness. When conditions are appropriate and the person is receptive and relaxed, this cosmic image shines through nature, or we might say that nature gives birth to a cosmic image. In participating in this event, the individual has a 'cosmic' experience, and is transformed by it.

It seems that the human 'part' is changed and healed by its contact with the cosmic whole. The part 'remembers' who and what it is, recognises its relationship with the whole, and its sense of purpose is restored or discovered for the first time. Human beings need experiences such as this, to secure our sense of identity, to relate us to a larger design, and to reduce alienation and separateness by confirming our embeddedness in a mystical whole. The impact of such experiences can hardly be underestimated, since they virtually function as conversion experiences, in which the part recognises the sacred whole, and is made more complete in this realisation. This awards not only peace and healing, but also a sense of destiny and purpose, expressed colloquially by thanking nature for 'showing me my path and making me focus on the important things in life'. Obviously nature does not literally 'show us' the path we have to take, but somehow the path is revealed or recognised in this heightened experience.

The joy of the part is not only in seeing the whole but in serving and devoting oneself to it. Thus, after such experiences, young people can often demonstrate radically different behaviour, such as helpfulness towards others, volunteer work for society, and a conciliatory and cheerful disposition. Such changes seem miraculous at first, especially if the young people were previously selfish, egocentric or antisocial. In denying us spiritual experiences of this kind, society does itself and its citizens a grave disservice, because the positive results of such experiences are clearly evident, and apparent to all who care to notice. We are more than human beings, we are cosmic beings, 'formed from stardust', and when we catch a glimpse of this deeper belonging, we suddenly feel 'at home' in the universe, and we desire to work for the good of the whole, rather than strive only to satisfy the part. The paradox of spirituality is that in serving the whole the part is truly satisfied. This is the testimony of saints and martyrs throughout history, and we can experience this for ourselves today.

The opportunities for 'nature therapy' strike me as enormous for society, schools and colleges, and especially for wayward or criminal youth in correction centres and prisons. The criminal or antisocial impulse arises when we do not know who we are, when we fail to understand our relation to society and others, and when we are unaware of our place in the universe. If nature can help provide us with a sense of moral proportion and spiritual connectedness, then the social and personal advantages of nature experience, which acts as a contemporary form of conversion, speak for themselves. Those who have lost their way, and that includes all of us at some moments in our lives, are in need of renewal and redirection, and nature can provide this if we are receptive to it.

We have to admit that our new interest in nature is not innocent, not completely altruistic. We are asking nature to tell us who we are, and where we belong. We go on wilderness journeys and outback adventures to discover an inner peace or silence that eludes us in the cities. Nature has become a hugely important spiritual resource, and this attachment appears to be spiritual, not consumerist. These people are not insisting on 'owning' land to find security; they are advocating a more subtle and elusive contact with the natural world. The experience of peace and harmony in nature brings self-definition and a deep sense of purpose, even if we cannot always put these experiences into words.

Students often write that words fail them at this juncture. In a sense, ecospirituality is not about words, it is about experiences. It is about moments of passion, peace and belonging, and because these rewards are so profound, they are also priceless and beyond reckoning. But we cannot expect to achieve a constant 'high' in nature, only moments of recognition, where we remember who we are. This is remembrance in the Platonic or spiritual sense, before our ego-centredness broke up this original unity and made us feel separate, alien, apart. It is from these fleeting experiences that we find strength to face the ordinary disappointments, and develop a sense of security that can sustain us through the various trials of life.

CHAPTER 12

What can religion do?

*The Christian of the future will be a mystic or he or she will not
exist at all.*

Karl Rahner[162]

I have spoken at length about the problems facing religion, the 'split'
between religion and spirituality, and the fact that young people in
Western societies are not responding to formal religion. What can
religion do? How are those of us who are concerned about religion to
deal with this crisis? Some rush in to prop up the ailing structures, in
the hope that what is good and true in religion can be protected from
further collapse, if only we can shore up the orthodox core of the
tradition. In religious institutions, there is a pervasive sense of gloom
and despondency, as if the sacred heart of civilisation is about to
expire or be extinguished. Internally, religious institutions oscillate
between a defensive bolstering of the central core, and a blatant
denial of the dire reality facing religion in postmodern society.

PROPHETIC DISCERNMENT

It is important to look beyond the organisational response to this
crisis, which looks mainly at performance-based factors, and becomes
depressed at declining numbers. A prophetic or spiritual response
might find in this crisis an opportunity for new thinking, new ways of

'doing' religion and being religious. The demise of the old forces us to contemplate new directions, but there is in religious structures enormous resistance to discovering the new. This is understandable, because if religion already contains sacred revelation and the holy then why must it change? Why should mere mortals and contemporary thinkers such as myself meddle with something as important and vital as our traditional vessels of the sacred? There is a tendency in religion to treat reformers and thinkers as trouble-makers and rebels, because it is felt that religion is already perfect, fully revealed and complete.

But religion is not complete unless it is communicating effectively with the world. Religion may enshrine what is eternally true, but if religion does not successfully communicate this truth to the world we have to think again about the religious enterprise. Religious authorities must not suppose that refined dogma, wonderful liturgy, or even committed social service, are the bases of a 'successful' religion. A religion that fails to communicate its message, and so fails to transform the world by its message, is a religion that has to examine itself and adopt a self-critical attitude.

There are too many people in authority who treat religion like a great masterpiece or classic work that can only be admired and never altered or improved. I would contend that such an attitude, although adopted with reverence, can actually be seen as destructive, since there is often little effort to build bridges of communication between religion and the world.

MYSTERY ABOVE ORGANISATION

If we only admire religion, and do nothing to halt its radical demise, such admiration is counter-productive and a kind of false conservatism that preserves the religious form but kills off its essence. If we care enough about religion, we have to be prepared to take risks and support the spiritual essence of religion in a new way. Clearly, religion must engage in what Walter Brueggemann, the American theologian,[163] calls prophetic criticising, so that the spiritual life is allowed to be drawn out and shown to the world. If religion wants to have a future, it must allow itself to be seen not only as an institution, but also as a mystery that can feed and nourish the spiritually starving world. Many people I meet see religion merely as an empty structure, or as a human institution. If religion wants to survive, it will have to reach into itself, and reveal the mystery that forms the basis of its light and wisdom.

Only the rediscovery of this mystery, and the sharing of this mystery with the world, can ensure any real future. The community will always be receptive to mystery if it can be expressed in valid and contemporary ways, because the community never loses its spiritual thirst, even though it loses its taste for formally-expressed religion. Therefore, less 'self-preservation' (or organisational concern) and more 'expressive spirituality' (or revelation of mystery) is the way forward for religion. By clinging to the past, we not only lose sight of the present and but we fail to allow the future to be born. If we risk cultural form in the name of the spirit, renewal can take place. We might almost say, in a new adaptation of scripture: He who has his faith shall lose it, and he who loses his faith for the sake of the spirit shall find it.

THE BROKEN VESSEL OF FAITH

In the past, many of us understood religion in terms of a 'passing on' of the faith from one generation to another. One was simply born into a religious tradition at birth, and that was that, so long as we obeyed certain practices, conventions and observances. Faith was conceived as a fragile family monument, like a precious vase or chalice that was handed down through the generations. But at some point in our recent history, this fragile vase was dropped, and the precious object of inherited faith shattered into pieces.

In recent times, we see the breakdown of inherited faith in countless ways. Children can no longer accept the faith of their parents, grandparents or natal tradition, and instead they go on individual searches for meaning and value. Many parents have begun to doubt and question the faith that they once held dear, and wonder whether their children are right to reject the inheritance. Beyond the family, more people are doing without traditional faith, and going in search of individual meaning.

What must we do? Must we get down on the ground and collect the broken shards and fragments, so that the holy vessel of inherited faith can be restored to its former shape and beauty? This might seem like a natural human response, to pick up the pieces, recover the fragments, and find the glue and adhesive to restore the holy chalice.

IS SPIRIT BREAKING THE OLD WAY?

But there is another way of doing things, and this is what I have spent recent years exploring in my writings. We have to acknowledge the brokenness of the old vessel and search within ourselves and the community for the new vessel. We must acknowledge that the old way of conceiving faith as some external cultural object has broken down, and rediscover faith in an entirely new way, not through received belief, but through the lived experience of the spirit. The old vessel has broken for good reason, perhaps because the time-honoured path of inherited or extrinsic faith no longer serves the purposes of God.

I sometimes imagine that the so-called 'demise of religion' has been orchestrated by the spirit itself, which may have grown tired of our external or extrinsic faith, and may be urging us to a deeper experience of the spirit. The present challenge, it seems to me, is to shift from extrinsic to intrinsic faith. This deeper experience of faith is not based on unconscious family inheritance, religious routine, external performance of rituals or automatic church attendance. Rather, this new experience of faith is based on an existential grappling with the reality of the living God. God is not some static figure or some vague theistic background to our lives. God seeks continual and dynamic incarnation in creation, society and human consciousness.

God is serious about incarnation, and is never content with 'eternity', but wants to risk an adventure in time and space. There is urgency and force in God's direction towards the world, and if religion is no longer successful in carrying forwards this divine power into the world, then God may be behind the so-called demise of religion. God may be saying to us, 'I will take away the traditional vessels from you, and see what creativity might arise. I will break the religious clichés and images, and see whether something new can be fashioned from the direct experience of spiritual life'. God is serious about spiritual mission, and serious enough to take action if religion appears to be falling short of the mark. God might be saying, 'I don't want blind belief, or worshippers who are content with a mere rumour of my existence. I want people to experience me in their hearts and lives; I want transformation, conversion and encounter'. The spirit of God wants to lead us on, and yet our attachment to old forms may be preventing this spirit from being realised.

MOURNING FOR CHRISTENDOM

It is important that religious traditions take this challenge seriously, and do not attempt to hide from it. I often find these traditions in various states or stages of denial. They see the collapse of religion in society, but continue to operate in a mood of celebration, and to insist on the health and well-being of their church. I think, on the contrary, it might be more instructive to face the crisis and mourn the collapse of the old.

Religion is good at ritual, and it should develop rituals to help us come to terms with our repressed or denied grief. But religion is largely in denial, and perhaps is even choking on its own unwept tears.

FROM DEVOTIONALISM TO SPIRITUALITY

Religion has to make itself more spiritual, and change its churches from places of devotional worship to centres of existential spirituality. When society was more stable, when we felt we knew what God was and signified, then devotional worship was appropriate, and the correct form of sacramental life. But today, we must first find God before we can worship him (or her, or it). Our time is forced to be 'spiritual' before it can be 'religious'. Once we have had an experience of spirit, then religion makes more sense, so long as we have tools to decipher its symbolism and understand its language. Today, we cannot sit in pews and pretend we understand who God is and what religion is about. The sacred chalice has broken, and this means our understanding, assumptions and values have broken too.

We have to go in search of God again, and discover the primordial religious experience in which God can be located and found. Another way to put this is to say that religion has to shift from moralism to mysticism, with less emphasis on the God 'out there' and more emphasis on the God within. Perhaps in the past we did not need to relate personally and intensely to the God within, because the God without was already convincing, powerful, mighty and self-evident—this God focused our attention. But with the collapse of belief in the traditional image of God, we have to find God in a new place, and the most convincing place of all will be our own human hearts. This does not mean that God will be a merely personal experience, locked away in the closet of introspection, but rather the discovery of God in our interiority will be the basis for a new appreciation of God in the world. As Meister Eckhart wrote in the 14th century, when God disappears from culture, we have to learn to give birth to God in the soul.

Religion needs to understand this shift from outside to inside, and to avoid the typical conservative reaction that such interiority is somehow narcissistic. True, interiority can become narcissistic if it is conducted in the wrong way, but when the spirit is encountered we are immediately led out beyond our subjectivity to a new ethical involvement with others and the world. There is no danger of narcissism, so long as this interior journey is performed with discernment and prophetic criticism.

FROM BURDEN TO GIFT

In his *Theological Investigations*,[164] Karl Rahner said that we have to stop trying to pump religion into people's lives, and start drawing it out of people's lives. This gets the new approach to religion precisely. It must be 'led out' or 'educated' from within, and this has to begin in spirituality and not in propositional statements of an outside system. If religion could shift from imposing itself on people to drawing out the spirit, we would have an immediate revolution of religious life. Today, countless people in the community say that religion is external and irrelevant, an outside burden of dogma. This is a two-way breakdown. People cannot see what religion has to offer, and religion has failed to speak to the personal experience of the spirit.

If religion could learn to lead the spirit out, it would no longer be conceived as a burden, but as a boon or gift. Religion would then speak *to* us instead of *at* us, and its message would help to liberate us from our personal isolation. Today countless 'secular' people are engaged in personal spiritual journeys, and many claim that such journeys are fulfilling and rewarding, but I think we are masking internal pain and suffering. The personal spiritual journeys that are so popular are very often journeys into isolation, despair and fragmentation. Many people will not admit this pain, because they might have to revise their views about individuality.

Much of the hype about popular spirituality is deliberately masking the yearning of the human heart for fellowship and community. The fact is that the spirit within us longs, even craves, for community and fellowship. The spirit is not our personal possession; we might experience it as a reality 'within' us, but it is not private. Rather, it is our intimate experience of the universal love and power of God. It is this innate human need for community that will build religion again, but meanwhile, with this lack of fit between spirit and religion, our world falls into fragmentation, and religion and spirituality do not converse with each other.

When religion gets into a new relationship with spirit, it will cease to be experienced as a burden, and begin to be experienced as a personal liberation. We will be liberated from personalism and isolating secularism, and enter again into the joy of shared spirituality. The churches of the future that can manage these transformations will be able to say, 'Take my yoke upon you, and learn from me; for I am gentle and lowly in heart, and you will find rest for your souls. For my yoke is easy, and my burden is light' (Matthew 11:29–30).

EXPANDING RELIGION, INCLUDING THE WORLD

If religion wants to play a role in the future, it will have to start listening to the world and discerning the presence of God in it. What may be breaking down in our time is the old dualism between church and world, a dualism that may have been useful once but is no longer beneficial. The churches should regard dialogue with popular spirituality as part of their ministry and mission. They should not view popular spirituality as a competitor in the field of transcendence, nor should they imagine that God is only inside the institution, or that popular spirituality is somehow godless or without the divine. The spirituality outside the institutions of faith is certainly outside tradition, but it is not outside God or the spirit. Therefore, nor is it outside 'religion' in the broad sense, if by religion we mean that which is concerned with the holy.

God cannot be neatly separated from the world, or marshalled into a corner of reality marked 'formal religion'. Nor is God's work kept alive by organisations acting in God's name. God is much larger than our organisations, and the divine work and mission far exceeds the boundaries of any institutional aspiration or religious assumption. This message needs to be sent to the institutions loudly and clearly, and it is heartening to see Bishop John Shelby Spong,[165] among others, engaged in precisely this kind of work. Spong challenges the churches with this important corrective, 'Your God is too small'.

Apparently, Spong pinned this notice to the doors of churches in his area in New Jersey. If the traditional churches are dying, it is partly because their image of God is too narrow, too small and too human. Some think that because traditional practices are diminishing God is being diminished by this process. This represents a narrowly human and anthropocentric perspective on the experience of God. What may be falling into decline is an out-of-date image of God that has held God away from life, and thus withheld life and vitality from God. Religion has a responsibility to expand its sense of mission and relate more fully to the world.

CATCHING UP WITH THE BIGGER PICTURE

Harvey Cox, the 1960s champion of the so-called social gospel, sounded this message from Harvard University some decades ago:

> The secular world is the principal arena of God's work today. Those who are religious will have to enter more vitally into the secular world if they are to be agents of God's reconciliation.[166]

Cox reversed the traditional prejudice that placed the churches above the world, and argued that they were lagging behind the work of redemption already taking place in the world:

> The church . . . must run to catch up with what God is already doing in the world.[167]

Sara Maitland expressed the gap between God and the human understanding of God in this way:

> God is up to something larger, more complex and more refined than we seem able to imagine.[168]

If religion is to survive in the future, it will have to think outside conventions, and here David Hay's research on the spirituality of adults suggests ways in which this might be possible. In *The Tablet*, David Hay and his associate Kate Hunt write:

> The Holy Spirit speaks to everybody, whether or not they are the kind of people who believe in God, or who turn up in church on Sunday. In Christian terms, this new spirituality may strike us as very thin. In many cases (but by no means all) it is cramped and impoverished because of the secular nature of our culture.
>
> In these circumstances the church's major concern should not, in the first place, be about filling empty pews. The first thing is to observe how God is already communicating with

these many millions of people. They need to feel that even in a highly secularised culture, there is still *permission* to develop the natural spirituality that is within them. The people we have been talking to in recent months tell us again and again that the church is out of touch. This may be a wearisome platitude, but perhaps we should face up to the reality behind it. Perhaps the cliché is telling us that we are not in touch with the ways in which God the Holy Spirit is already communicating with his secularised children.[169]

The research of David Hay and Kate Hunt in Britain is moving towards a new definition of mission and evangelisation, the kind that is needed in the postmodern society. Their work suggests that the churches should place less emphasis on the old model of parish life, with its stable and tight sense of community, and become public voices for good and God in the wider community, giving people 'permission' to develop the natural spirituality that is within them. I would add not just permission, but discernment to tell true from false spirituality. If the churches could focus on this task, they might worry less about dwindling numbers, and focus on a new future in which religion can regain its authority and presence in the world.

People need to be told that although they are outside institutional structures, they are not outside religion in the broadest and best sense of the word. The 'secular' must not be confused with the 'profane', since the secular is a condition in which God and spirit resides, though often in a veiled, hidden or obscured way. The idea of leading a religious life can no longer be confined to conventional patterns of behaviour, but must be broadened to include all those who feel that there is 'something there' and who wish to enter into personal and direct relationship with this presence.

MINISTERING TO THE SCATTERED COMMUNITY

Religion in the past has been based on the idea of ministering to a gathered community. Today it has to work towards a new model, offering guidance, support and spiritual discernment to the scattered community. The postmodern society is a plural, fragmented society, and it is doubtful that our society will quickly recover the cohesion and uniformity that it had even a few decades ago. The churches will need to think in more fluid, open and expanded ways about the future; not in terms of closely-knit, stable and parochial communities, but in terms of loose networks, drop-in centres, and small groups or 'cells of evangelisation'.

This is not to abandon the traditional notion of church, but to return to its beginnings. Christ did not direct everyone into sacred buildings or structures, but rather he moved into the world, going to the people, healing their ailments, and binding their secular lives to the sacred. Those lives were then transformed by virtue of their new relationship with the sacred. The way of the future will be the way of the founder: not to expect the world to submit to clerical authority, but to transform the world by revealing the presence of God where it least expects to find it, in the everyday and the ordinary.

The challenge is to allow all people to see that they are 'chosen' people, and to show that the sky under which they live, labour and love is a sacred canopy, ennobling their actions by a divine presence. For those who so choose, the holy sanctuaries will be ready and available, not only for devotional worship, but for quiet reflection, conversation and spiritual direction. In many ways, the task ahead for religion is to get connected with the spirit of the time and the spirit in the individual, showing people how and why religion is relevant to their lives.

CHAPTER 13

The spirituality gap: credibility and supernaturalism

The spirituality revolution is of the time, and yet also ahead of the time. There is a gap between this new social awareness or movement and our established practices, values and attitudes. Many people are interested in exploring spirituality, but the social, cultural, educational and religious institutions that purport to represent the community are still grounded in a former era, prior to this uprising of spiritual interest. A serious gap has arisen in society, between those people who are inspired by the prospect of spiritual discovery, and the traditional institutions and establishments, which remain sceptical about spirituality as a viable or credible personal and cultural endeavour.

PROBLEMS OF CREDIBILITY

Most of our social institutions are grounded in an intellectual point of view that is inherently critical of the idea of spirit. To these institutions, spirit is a sort of chimera or illusion, or a mystifying idea that religion has used merely to enforce order and authority upon the community. Secular or non-religious institutions have thus viewed spirit through jaundiced eyes, as a sort of mystification which in the past allowed formal religion to impose conformity, authority and fear upon the people. It is therefore problematical to expect these institutions, formed in historical opposition to religion, to suddenly turn around and validate the idea of spirit in a new, post-secular context.

Spirit has the inherent problem of being invisible, or at least, it is invisible to those who do not have the inner vision or insight to see it. But while spirit is invisible, its effects and influences are not. It is possible to see the spirit moving in culture and life, illuminating our experience, changing our lives, providing direction and improving health and well-being. The lived experience of spirituality must become better known and more readily recognised than it is. Those who fail to see the spirit as a transcendent reality might still be persuaded to see its effects in this world.

The secular often insist that only faith can give us the eyes to see the spirit, but I do not agree with this. I think faith intensifies our awareness of the presence of spirit, but that anyone, with or without faith, can notice the effects of the spirit in culture and life. The wind is invisible to our eyes, but its effects certainly are not, and one does not have to 'believe' in the wind in order to see its effects in trees, skies, clouds and landscapes. As with the wind, so with the spirit, which similarly blows where it wills and causes great change and sometimes upheaval. I do not think we can expect the secular society and its institutions to turn overtly 'religious', but we might anticipate that society can begin to embrace the concept of spirit in a universalist or non-sectarian context.

RELEASING SPIRIT INTO LIFE

To cross the spirituality gap, it is important to uncover spirit from within its traditional encasements. The secular insist on neat separations between the secular and the religious, but these separations have to be subverted. If only the faithful can see the spirit, then only self-declared 'religious' people can see it, and this is a myth that is convenient for the secular society to adopt, since spirit becomes a rarefied object observed only by those who are predisposed to see it. In other words, spirit, like God, is 'there' only for people who believe in it. For others, it is not 'there' at all. We have to subvert these comfortable categories of secular society, designed to imprison spirit in a religious worldview that the secular society seeks to discredit.

To liberate spirit at this stage in our human history, we therefore have to step aside from the exclusively religious aspect and affirm the human or existential factor. We cannot afford to have the recognition of spirit to be dictated by dogma, because it is actually prior to doctrine, an essential part of human experience. Today, some authorities in our institutions find talk about the 'spirit' to be incredible in any context, because we are referring to something that cannot be verified by science or experimentation, nor confirmed by the senses. When claims are made about the power and effectiveness of spirituality, its ability to change lives, deepen our experience, open our eyes, and give renewal and inner reward, some authorities stop listening to this discourse and refuse to take it seriously. It seems to be mumbo-jumbo and nonsensical, or a kind of fantasy wish fulfilment, about as credible as magic and superstition.

This block against spirit has to be overcome. It is important that spirit is not typecast as irrational or superstitious, but released from these mental prisons and freed into our lives. If, as I contend, the recognition of spirit has huge impact on our mental and physical health, on our relationships, personal identity, work relations and adaptation to the psyche or soul, it becomes vitally important that spirit is not held hostage by belief, prejudice or ideology. Spirit has to be 'naturalised' and brought into human reality, making it an essential aspect of human experience. Whether or not we are religious, superstitious or mystical, spirit is already present and has to be taken into account as an existential reality.

SPIRITUAL PATIENTS AND MEDICAL DOCTORS

I first heard the term 'spirituality gap' from a psychiatrist friend of mine, who mentioned that some colleagues of his in the Royal College of Psychiatry had begun to use this term. It is apparently used to refer to the ever-present and persistent gap between patients who report that 'spirituality' is an important element in their personal identity and mental health, and doctors who have no way of entering, at least professionally or 'legitimately', into this spiritual language and terminology. He said large numbers of patients speak in the clinic and in therapy about their spiritual lives and problems, but the medical doctor or professional health worker often has no way to reach into this kind of discourse.

Spirituality is not on the training agenda in medical school, and health professionals frequently feel unprepared to engage the spiritual longings or aspirations of their patients. Even if the health professional has a private faith or a religious practice of his or her own, he or she has been instructed by a code of ethics not to impose this religious belief upon others, but to keep matters of faith private and confidential in the pursuit of a medically or scientifically based process of healing. However, if patients are pleading for discussion about spiritual issues, what do doctors and health workers do?

Those who are sceptical about these matters might be tempted to suggest to their clients that spirituality is part of their problem, and they would be best advised to drop the idea because of spirituality's capacity to distort the mind and create further mental illness through dangerous illusions about self and world. Perhaps, in some cases, these doctors are right to think in these terms, given the fact that the term 'spirituality' includes a multitude of perceptions and practices, some of which may indeed be classified as sick, wacky or pathological. How can these doctors decide what kind of spirituality is authentic and what kind is pathological, if they have no training in these areas, and therefore no way to discern between good or bad spirituality? Such decisions can hardly be informed or reliable if there has been such a gap in professional training.

SPIRIT BEHIND CLOSED DOORS

Doctors and therapists who possess a personal faith of their own are obviously able to use this faith to speak to patients in spiritual need, even contrary to the code of ethics. But once again, how do we know that doctors are able to deal sensitively and appropriately with these issues? A doctor may possess impressive medical knowledge, but be poorly developed in the area of the human spirit. A doctor might be a fundamentalist who believes that his or her chosen religious belief is of absolute, binding and universal significance. I have met such a doctor myself, and I was alarmed to think of what might take place in the consulting room, before vulnerable and suggestive clients. Such doctors may seek to impose their viewpoint upon the patient, in the belief that spiritual cure is synonymous with adopting the religious attitude of the doctor.

Everywhere we turn in this field, there are gaps, holes and inconsistencies. We will not be able to cross the spirituality gap until society as a whole, including its traditional institutions, has taken up the challenge of a postmodern and perhaps even post-religious, or certainly anti-fundamentalist, spirituality, and has understood the urgent need for a universal language of the spirit that does not collapse the spirit into one or another of the competing religious traditions. Clearly, the crossing of the spirituality gap involves us in at least two huge steps. One is to get over the secular prejudice that spirituality is falsity, superstition or escapism, and the other is to develop a universal language of the spirit that is not always dependent on religious affiliations. We can no longer afford to have religions declaring a monopoly on the sacred, but nor can we afford to dismiss religions from the postmodern scene, since they are the historical containers of spiritual wisdom. This conundrum is central to our present cultural dilemma.

SPIRITUAL RESEARCH AND EMPIRICAL COURSES

As in health, so in education. But in education the 'threat' of spirituality comes from two sides, and so is perhaps more complex and difficult to avoid. The discourse about spirituality arises not only from below, that is from clients 'up' to the professionals, who must respond to the grassroots challenge, but also from the top or uppermost levels of professional enquiry and research. In education, spirit comes from below (the students) and from above (some leading international researchers), and those in the middle often feel besieged and uncomfortable.

Most of us are aware that spirituality and mysticism have become important areas of speculation and theorising in such areas as the new physics, new biology, organisation and systems theory, economics, ecology, ecopsychology, management and human relations. But the universities and institutions of knowledge do not generally incorporate these new developments into the core curriculum. There is a considerable time-lag between cutting-edge research and the educational establishment and its course offerings. But when the cutting-edge research actually abandons the intellectual paradigm or model in which the discipline is conventionally situated, no amount of time will actually overcome the gap separating such research from the mainstream discipline.

Hence the time-lag is not the real issue here. We need to speak of a paradigm clash, at the core of which is the problem of spirituality. The disciplines of knowledge, institutionalised in organisations with roots going back to the Intellectual Enlightenment, remain grounded in rational, empirical and historical approaches to the various subjects, and in this way the incursion of spirit into knowledge is severely curtailed and reduced. We might speak of the repression of spirit in each individual case, except that what is taking place is not some nasty master-plan designed to subvert and destroy the spiritual life, but simply a paradigm clash in which the knowledge of the spirit is excluded from the knowledge of the world and its history.

I realise that many undergraduate students can become quite agitated and even paranoid about such systematic exclusions, and begin to imagine world-wide conspiracies against spiritual truth, but we need to go back to Thomas Kuhn and understand this situation in terms of the grinding conflict of one paradigm against another. The ideas that are put forward in *The Structure of Scientific Revolutions*[170] can be readily appropriated and applied to the spirituality revolution. Revolutions share common structures and patterns, even though their contents might be radically different, and these common structures, involving an epic conflict between old and new knowledge, are relatively similar throughout history. The old paradigm might look like the evil empire in its merciless exclusions and vigorous policing of its boundaries, but such activities are to be seen as routine and unsurprising, given the social production of knowledge and the conflict-torn history of ideas.

UNHOLY SPIRITUAL DESIRE AND RELIGIOUS TEMPERANCE

The spirituality gap is also felt and experienced in religion. Increasingly, parishioners and church-goers of many traditions and denominations are developing interest in spirituality. Many are saying that traditional forms of worship, based on devotional practices, extrinsic faith and creeds, are no longer adequate to their spiritual needs. They do not want to be told to believe in a religious mystery by authorities outside or above them. They want a deeper and more abiding relationship with their faith. They want a personal and intimate connection with the mystery to which their religion points. Ironically some, in their frustration, have left the churches and the institutions of faith to pursue a deeper connection to faith outside the institution.

The parish priest or local minister can be taken by surprise by this behaviour. He or she sometimes wonders why people have become so impatient with the old forms of worship, and why they want so much more. Some priests and ministers report that the word 'spirituality' hardly entered their training at theological institutes and seminaries, and like the medical doctor or health worker, they feel unprepared and unable to take up the new challenge before them.

This is doubly ironic, because often medical practitioners advise patients to consult a priest or minister for advice and counselling in spiritual matters. But the kind of spirituality that the patients have in mind is a far cry from the religion that most ministers and priests are able to supply. Basically, the difference is this: interiority and the cultivation of the inner life. The spiritual urge seeks an inner journey and understanding, but conventional religion remains external to the self and far too historical.

We witness the same paradigm clash in religion as we do in health and education. The new paradigm is based on the idea of the interior journey, and the story at the heart of the new paradigm is that God or spirit is an inward experience, not just something in scripture, liturgy or historical time. Our age has grown weary and longs for renewal and rejuvenation. It has grown tired of the world, and seeks to return to the source of its being for life-giving water and energy. It is no longer impressed by traditional methods in health, education, religion, law or ethics, but seeks a new answer based on direct and personal experience of the ground of our being.

Even if the priest or minister has developed a personal spirituality of his or her own, this does not mean that he or she is in a position to develop this inward, living connection to faith in other people. The traditional forms of worship are collective, communal and devotional, and mostly do not follow the detailed contours and shifts of the personal spiritual journey. The priest or minister can be speaking at cross-purposes to the modern person in search of spirit, unless the modern person can be satisfied with traditional and objective answers to personal problems in which case he or she can be returned to the sanctified fold of group experience of the sacred. But where such group experience does not satisfy, the person is left to fend for him or herself, and to find an individual solution to personal spiritual hungers and desires.

Formal religions hope and pray that people will have deeply meaningful and transformative experiences of the faith, but the process by which this happens, namely spirituality, is often beyond their grasp or understanding. Spirituality is often viewed as a matter of divine grace, or a gift from the spirit, that is as something given by God and not by men or women. But our age is not content to wait gracefully for spirituality to descend from above; instead, it is anxious, irritable, impatient and hungry, and is committed to going in search of spirit right away. There is an unholy desire in contemporary spirituality, which the faith institutions find hard to comprehend.

THE WIDENING GAP: OTHERWORLDLY SPIRIT

What exacerbates the spirituality gap is the fact that spirit can present itself to our experience initially as disembodied spiritualism rather than as integrated spirituality. When it appears in the guise of spiritualism, spirit is even less likely to be embraced by society or its rational institutions, since this kind of spirit is otherworldly, arcane and esoteric, and often strongly opposed to rationality or common sense. In this mode, spirit is viewed as a power that can reverse the natural order, move mountains, bend spoons, break glass, and reveal itself in marvellous ways that the credible find compelling and the sophisticated find utterly appalling, distasteful and repellent.

Spiritualism is often championed by people who are poorly educated, socially maladapted, sensationalist, literal in their thinking, and wedded to a tabloid-style understanding of the spirit. When spirit is caught in these subcultures, it has no chance to come out of the 'weird' closet, or to present itself as a serious force in society. Society, understandably, rejects it as a form of irrationality.

In providing a critique of spiritualism, I am critiquing aspects of my own background and personal experience. As a young child, my own grandfather frequently dabbled in the occult, and the rest of the family was at a loss to know how to relate to this activity. Some of us gave his activity grave respect, while others expressed dismay and protest at his concerns. There was a sense in the family that occultism was wrong. We did not like the fact that glasses would explode while grandfather was meditating, but this was generally dealt with by referring to our 'Irish roots'.

In the 1970s, in search of an understanding of spirit, I found my way into various occult and spiritualist networks. Even as I engaged these networks and groups, however, I felt there was something essentially ill-conceived about their concerns, but could not quite articulate the problem. One difficulty I had was the relatively trivial and often ridiculous nature of the spiritual revelations. For instance, a 'message from the beyond' is communicated as 'your dead Aunt Agnes says hello from the other side and hopes all is well', or the 'power' of spirit is revealed as the ability to move an upside-down glass on a table. Nevertheless, I think spiritualism can be a prelude to spirituality if we are prepared to educate and develop our interests.

SPIRITUALISM AS AN ARCHAIC LANGUAGE OF SPIRIT

In spiritualism, spirit remains marginal, eccentric, exotic, and outside society as it is normally conceived. Of course, that is part of its attractiveness, that it remains beyond the norms of ordinary life and represents a kind of exotic place to which we can flee as an escape from the real. So long as it is outside society, removed from science, beyond the rational, it inhabits a fairytale space that has more in common with fable, legend or entertainment, than with spirituality or religion. Locked in this distant, fabulous, fairytale space, spiritualism places no real demands on the personal self, and does not compel us towards spiritual change or moral transformation in the ways demanded by true spirituality.

Spiritualism is concerned with the occult pursuit and discovery of hidden spiritual forces in what appears to be a very busy parallel universe. By all accounts, there is constant traffic in this otherworld, and such movements can be plotted and chartered by such occult practices as mediumistic trances, witchcraft, seances, channelling, astral travelling, occult divination, fortune telling, lucid dreaming, auras, ghosts and luminism. These and other conceptions of the spirit world represent literal patterns of thinking about the realm of spirit, patterns that may have been useful in the past but have no real place today. They belong to an outmoded mythology and depend almost entirely upon a mechanical notion of metaphysics. Spiritualistic conceptions can be seen as interesting metaphors about the soul and spirit, but generally those who uphold these conceptions are not interested in viewing them through a metaphorical lens.

I often attract students who imagine that spirituality consists of these occult phenomena. They see my own project of re-enchantment as a concern for spells, visions and occult channelling. In the popular mind there is basic confusion, I believe, between the pursuit of spirituality and the practices of spiritualism. This is not surprising given that the advocates of spiritualism like to represent their interests as spirituality, since this validates and ennobles their concerns, while the agenda of debunkers of the spirit is to pretend that all spiritualities are essentially the same, and all share the same implausibility and irrationality. The cause of ignorance and prejudice is always furthered by lack of differentiation and discernment.

THE COMMERCIAL VALUE OF SPIRITUALISM

Spiritualism has enormous commercial appeal and marketing potential, because the businesses and industries of consumer capitalism are always striving to produce, package and sell things that will give life that extra boost or that missing dimension. In an exhausted, flat and spiritually empty society, spiritualism appears as one of our favourite addictions, since it presents spirit as a fabulous product to be consumed, or a toy to be played with in our boredom and depression. It is eminently marketable, and supplies us with parodies of spirit in a society that can no longer tell the difference between genuine spirituality and spiritualistic diversions or entertainment. By fixing spirit in a fabulous space readily manipulated by commercial industries, we are prevented from discovering richness, depth and transformation in the spaces that we normally inhabit.

Popular culture, including fiction, cinema, videos, music, games, books and cartoons, finds the construction of a supernatural parallel universe to be irresistible. It appeals to our desperate need to imagine other worlds, and represents an escape from the mundane and the ordinary. It also appeals to our power urge, our desire to be more than we already are. In the anonymous wasteland of secular society, our desire to make contact with a greater world, to be part of a larger universe, a new world of depth, colour, excitement and power is considerably intense. Rather than discover the otherworld in this one, it is far simpler and easier for commercial businesses and industries to supply us with alternative worlds that exist alongside or in addition to this world.

These industries know that our desire to break out of the mundane is great, and that we all want to be liberated from banality and flatness. They actually prey upon our own unexpressed spiritual urges. Our undeveloped spirituality is exploited by popular culture, and used as a recipe for enormous commercial success. If we fail to break through the hidden layer that withholds the mystery of life from our eyes, that is to cultivate creative spirituality, popular culture is only too happy to step into this void, and to offer us *ersatz* versions or parodies of the spirit.

MISUNDERSTANDING THE OTHERWORLD

It often seems to me that spirit presents itself as spiritualism in people who do not have a naturally intuitive sensibility. Those who are gifted with intuition and insight are generally not seduced by the false pretensions and glittering yet hackneyed illusions of spiritualism, which represents a low-level in spiritual understanding. Those who lack intuition and hence fail to comprehend the subtle, immanent reality of spirit and its symbolic language, seem to want to conceptualise spirit as a separate super-reality, a second world of forces, demons and spirits outside or parallel to this world. In occultism, this second world of forms, energies and ghostly essences can be entered and contacted by people with occult powers. At times, this otherworld intersects with this reality, creating anomalies, miracles and wonders, demonic possessions, visitations or other strange events.

Some people can be offended by sweeping denunciations of the spirit worlds in which they strongly believe. To attack such worlds, they say, is to have a closed mind, to be narrow and bigoted. They vehemently believe in another universe containing spirits of the dead and the unborn, as well as archetypal powers and grand forces, which can be contacted and conversed with by various esoteric techniques and magical acts. It is true that none of us, ultimately, can know the nature of reality, and there may be a spirit world in which the dead, the unborn, angels and demons reside. But I doubt this very much, at least as it is popularly described. The otherworld of occultism seems utterly banal and all too human to me, an obvious product of human fantasy, escapism and literal thinking about the realm of spirit.

There is indeed an other world, but it is not the Disneyland of the spirit that occultism imagines, which is a pale and shallow parody of the spirit and its transformative powers. Like many educated people, I find myself unable to subscribe to a spiritualistic view of the world, and in some ways I find the spiritualistic conceptions to be abhorrent. It seems to be based on a metaphysical worldview that cannot be supported by science, art, poetry or religion.

SORCERY IN THE SUBURBS

Bored people in the city or suburbs take to sorcery and occultism with unusual delight. At first, it seems that occultism will open them to the secret forces of the universe, and their boredom will be dissolved by a dizzying array of supernatural forces. The flat universe will suddenly become high, deep and wide, by virtue of their exposure to the secret energies in a parallel universe. Moreover, their social alienation and personal disempowerment will be eclipsed in an instant by their immersion into omnipotent forces. Although anonymous and impotent in life, in the spirit world they can become powerful, charismatic and all-conquering. If others around them can be convinced of their special charisma, they acquire a completely new status in the community, or at least in the subcultural community that upholds these beliefs.

If criticised, such groups usually protest that they are involved in 'white' magic, and only seek to do good works in this world and the next, by liberating trapped spirits, facilitating communication across the worlds, and so on. The typical Christian response is that such activity is dangerous and should be stopped. The fundamentalist Christian position is more strident, claiming that such activity involves Satanism and Devil worship. It is easy for the fundamentalist position to be laughed at and derided by secular people and New Age enthusiasts, but as with many religious claims, there is an element of truth in the fundamentalist attack.

Fundamentalists are often involved in sensationalist, high-pitched and far-fetched moral accusations, but there is often a kernel of meaning in what they say. This is especially the case if we take their comments out of the mythological framework in which they are embedded, for example references to Satan, Devil and Hell, and translate these comments into a psychological frame of reference. If Satan is viewed symbolically as the impulse towards power and control in the human character, with special emphasis on power and control in the spiritual world, then spiritualism may be seen in this light, as a human attempt to usurp power from the sacred. Spiritualism is often an attempt to establish power, even if this is done under the pretext of 'helping' the spirits of the dead, which may not require help at all. In this activity, there is an inflated concentration on the self, and a desire to make the self grandiose in the eyes of the occult arts.

True spirituality is about the cultivation of a right relationship with the sacred, and this relationship usually involves a displacement of the ego and a willing acceptance of the secondary or instrumental role of the human being. But when the focus is overtly or covertly upon the personal ego, then we can suspect that the forces of darkness, as it were, have been unleashed. The forces of darkness are simply another way of talking about the lust for power and prestige, the 'principalities and worldly powers' that turn attention away from the divine light of the sacred, towards fixation upon the self and its inflated importance. Whenever we lose sight of 'thy will' and become focused on 'my will' then, in mythological terms, Satan has triumphed, and God has been defeated. From personal and anecdotal experience, there is a great deal of neurotic power-play and narcissism in the cultural trend towards supernaturalism and sorcery, and we would do well to regard such activity with scepticism and doubt, rather than see it as a legitimate expression of the spirituality revolution.

SPIRITUALITY AS AN ART OF IMAGINATION

In one sense, spiritualism involves a failure of imagination, as well as a hijacking of the spirit by the ego and its power principle. Poets and visionaries like Blake and Yeats have always emphasised that the seeing of spirit is an art of imagination, and that to see spirit correctly involves an education or development of the imaginative faculty. In order to see spirit at work, we have to see through the literal and the concrete to the unseen forces that rest at the heart of creation. These forces express themselves through symbol, image and myth, but of course these symbolic constructions are not to be taken literally, that is as metaphysical entities in another time-space universe. These forces are at the heart of this reality, and they can only express themselves indirectly through symbolic forms, because they have no form as such.

This does not mean that imagination is a form of delusion, or an act of obscuring the real. On the contrary, imagination liberates the real by giving form to things unknown. Imagination is an act of revelation, and the true nature of the real is discovered in imaginative forms. But if we take these forms literally, and confuse the signifier with the signified, then the process is no longer revelatory but delusional. The realm of the spirit is 'real', but not in the sense in which the ego or the conscious self understands reality. When the limited ego constructs the spirit in its own image, we lose the essence of spirit and surround ourselves in the dance of *maya* or illusion.

The mystery of spirit cannot be reduced to the ego's understanding of the real, because the ego's world is finite and mechanical, whereas the spirit is infinite and mysterious. The task of the spirit is to constantly defeat and annul our images of the spirit, because when we become too wedded to our own images we are no longer relating to spirit, but only to the projections of the ego. My own views on the nature of reality are closely related to those of Buddhism, Christian mysticism and mystical poetry such as that of Blake and Yeats. Every expression of spirituality in art, scripture or poetry is an interpretation of the spirit, not a description.

FUNDAMENTALISM OF THE SPIRIT

For me, spiritualism stands in relation to spirituality as fundamentalism to religion. It is a crude and idolatrous interpretation of its subject, full of philosophical problems, epistemological flaws, ontological illusions and category errors. Spiritualism is too simplistic and too human; a reductive interpretation of spirit that believes too strongly in itself, and is fostered and encouraged by uninformed thinking. Spiritualism occurs most often when the nature of reality has been defined in cramped, narrrow or limiting ways. If reality is mundane, predictable and boring, then the reality of spirit is felt to be something eccentric and otherworldly, something out there, beyond and remote.

This same kind of thinking, given a technological twist, ends up arguing that spirit is embodied in alien beings from other planets, and hence *Ufology* becomes a modern myth of our time, linked with cosmological fantasies about supernatural realities. Such thinking is often found mixed with traditional religious thinking, so that on one occasion a man at a faith development group at a Catholic church told me without any humour or irony that God is an astronaut at the edges of the galaxy. People who have not reflected deeply on the spiritual side of life often grasp onto these hackneyed formulae, and believe in them with extraordinary conviction. Spirituality seeks to deepen the nature of reality to expose the indwelling presence of the numinosum, while spiritualism seeks to impose a super-reality onto a mundane reality that remains essentially unchanged and untransformed by the presence of the spirit. The one deepens what we have, the other abandons what we have in favour of flights of fantasy and supernaturalism.

Spiritualism can be an important precursor to a mature spirituality, the vulgar or crude form in which something 'other' first insinuates itself into any life, making that life aware of something alien, outside and beyond itself. The spirit will latch onto these suggestive images, and may become entombed by them, unless we engage in an educational process that allows us to grow beyond these crude or early forms. This is especially so for young people, who may have an early intuition of an other or grander life, and yet lack the understanding to grasp this as mystery and imminent presence. In this case, spirit may be visualised as alien outer space life—forces from another galaxy or visitors from other planets.

Television programs such as *Star Trek* and other late-night offerings do much to provide story, narrative and character to these nascent or barely developed intuitions of an other world. Spiritualism, science fiction and fantasy narratives may therefore be useful preludes to spiritual awareness, insofar as these forms break open the mundane world and admit an alien 'otherness' that was not there before. The hope of culture and religion is that these infantile versions of otherness can be transcended and replaced by deeper and more profound understandings of the spiritual life. Religious adults have to be careful not to squash or destroy a young person's belief in the supernormal or the parapsychological, lest we destroy the very germ from which a more developed sensibility might grow. This possibility has a lot to do with readiness, maturity and the ability to replace a nascent form with a more mature and ripened understanding of the spirit.

COLLAPSING THE DUALISM OF SPIRIT AND WORLD

The urgent task of a true or sensible spirituality is to show that spirit is indeed a separate reality to ours, but it is in our reality and not apart from it. Although spiritualism sees itself as daring and challenging, the truly radical position is not supernaturalism but a spirituality that urges us to transform the world we have, rather than invent another one. The supernatural world is a poor substitute for the spiritual worldview, and it also creates a dependency on external things such as gurus, occult masters, hierarchies of supernatural powers, magicians, conjurers, outerspace aliens, spells, potions and cinema technologies. As soon as we grow up and realise that the mystery of spirit is before our eyes and already present with us, we can bid farewell to the powermongers and predatory entertainment industries that seek to produce this otherworld for the secular society.

In effect, we need to take the supernatural, dualistic conception of the world and collapse it, so that the mystery of spirit is revealed at the heart of the one world. There is no need for a fantasy second world, a supernatural elaboration, if spirit can be reconceived as the unknown depth dimension of the world we already have. When that transformation occurs, which is achieved through the education of our souls and the development of our imagination, we no longer need be bothered by supernatural worlds and psychedelic preoccupations. When reality is revealed as fundamentally numinous, we no longer require supernatural tricks or special effects to give us an elevated experience of life.

CHAPTER 14

Winning back our connections

Spiritual adjustment is the problem.
C. G. Jung[171]

The new attention being given to spirituality is not just some
fashionable interest in esoteric matters, nor is it an escape from the
real or an intellectual enquiry into human nature. It is an emotional
and urgent reaction to widespread alienation, disempowerment and
disillusionment. It is an almost panic response to the apparent lack
of relationality and connectedness in contemporary life. To call for
spirituality is to call for healing and reconnection. It is to admit that
we are divided and long to become whole. It is to acknowledge that
our lives are fragmented, and that we hope for some mystery that will
fit the broken parts together.

A sceptical part of the mind sees that hope as vanity and
delusion, while a deeper part of us sees it as the wellspring of
personal sanity and public health. We only call for spirituality when
our brokenness has reached a high point, when we can no longer
bear our alienation and call out for some greater authority to heal
our emotional suffering. We only cry for the spirit when alienation
is advanced, when we feel debilitated and numbed by our
dividedness.

NAMING THE SPIRIT

In stable social times, such as the 1950s, I believe that spirituality is present but not always named. It is a felt but not articulated experience found in the fabric of society and its rituals, forming the sacramental basis for human community and sociality. But in critical periods, where spirituality is no longer felt or readily discerned in official society, it must be named, described, articulated and conjured up, usually by creative artists, writers and individuals working away from or even against the 'progressive' social current. We are forced to name and describe the invisible thing that brings sustenance and comfort, in the hope that, by naming and calling out for healing, this invisible reality might spring forth in response to our cry.

In critical times, there can be a lot of endless talk about spirituality because it is sorely absent and needs to be drawn up from the depths. In critical times, we feel the loss of our soul acutely, and there are many attempts, some manipulative and exploitative, others creative and profound, to win back the soul to society and life. Language is usually the key to our success—to find, and use, the right words to say the things that need to be said. There are so many words today, some of them evasive, useless and unable to release our anguish or name our pain. The writer Richard Hames said, 'What is reported by the media is ultimately of little consequence now. What remains unsaid and unsayable is more significant'.[172] But what remains unsaid and unsayable in the media is nevertheless sayable in the arts, music, literature and the realm of imagination, which is our true hope for spiritual renewal.[173]

NEW RESPECT FOR THE SACRED

The realm of spirit is powerful and constitutes perhaps the largest portion of human reality. This realm is not a fantasy invention of the mind, but a living reality that we have to regard with great respect. It is for this reason that all indigenous and traditional cultures have been based on respect for the sacred. Respect for the sacred is the basis of cultural sanity, since such respect enables us to honour and acknowledge the eternal mystery from which life springs. If we deny the sacred, we not only harm the spirit but we also harm ourselves, as we are more dependent on this reality than we can ever realise with our ordinary commonsense.

The modern is one of the few civilisations that has not been based on respect for the sacred, and it remains to be seen whether our civilisation can endure since it has placed itself in a precarious and dangerous situation. If we can imagine humanity as a living tree, we could say that the sacred constitutes our largely invisible root system, and to cut ourselves off from this system of deep and dark relations is a catastrophe of enormous magnitude. The effects on us are manifold. Severed from our invisible roots, we feel a loss of orientation and purpose, and an existential shudder goes down the nervous system of humanity. We feel strangely different, disconnected from mystery, spiritual guidance and the past.

After this initial existential shock, we suffer a moral and ethical decline, because we have privileged the human fragment or part above the divine whole, and it is only connection to the larger sacred whole (however we like to envisage it) that brings natural morality, responsibility and justice. Emphasis on the part, the fragment, can only bring selfishness, greed, immorality and exploitation, the very things that destroy civilisations and bring about their downfall.

In the midst of moral decline and ethical anguish, the people begin to speak about spirituality, and the need for something to guide them that is greater than the human, because the human has become monstrous and mad. We look around for religious direction, and see that the God of religion is too familiar and 'known' to provide an elemental counterweight to our human madness. The churches themselves, to some eyes, look too identified with the social establishment, and seem distant from the radicality of spirit or 'otherness' of the sacred. This was one of Nietzsche's most powerful and trenchant criticisms against Christianity:

> What do we do with a human God, when we turn to God
> precisely because we are disgusted by mankind? What do we do,
> not just with a God that is human and our brother, but with a
> religion in which there is no mystery?[174]

THE BREAKDOWN OF SOCIAL RELATIONS

What modernity failed to realise was that community is based on the same invisible ties and sacramental bonds that it sought to destroy. The art of community is the art of the soul, and community is what happens when deep, invisible bonds are shared, and when deep meanings are communicated between people, especially in the act of public ritual and in the presence of the sacred. 'When two or three are gathered together in my name'. Community is not a rational activity, but is nourished and nurtured by forces much deeper than the rational.

We could say that all connectedness, invisible and visible, human and divine, is based on the spirit and becomes realised in the presence of spirit. Thus, it is hardly surprising that as we lost or destroyed our invisible connections to the sacred, we found that our wider circles of identity began to be eroded and undermined. Our human ties and communal bonds began to weaken, because as the spirit withers, the human, social and ecological communities disintegrate. Family communities have been disintegrating rapidly in recent times. Initially pressures were exerted on the extended family, now the nuclear family is exploding as well, with divorce and separation rates soaring in the Western world.

All sorts of human situations are suddenly revealed as explosive and uncontainable, including financial, economic, sexual and physical situations, as we learn to battle with strange and difficult problems in our human and social interactions. It is as if some demon had been let loose in the human domain, and we are at a loss to know what to do. We invent all manner of rational solutions to our problems, but our problems are essentially spiritual and irrational. We are going crazy because our super-rationality is a form of contagious madness. The spirit at the heart of life and of all human endeavour is not being acknowledged or respected, and it is thrashing around in disturbed, manic and uncontrollable ways, driving us to frenzy and neurosis.

'The Gods have become diseases', wrote Jung in 1929 in his commentary on a 'The Secret of the Golden Flower'.[175] More recently, the novelist Christopher Koch wrote in *The Year of Living Dangerously*, 'The spirit doesn't die, of course; it turns into a monster'.[176] Interestingly, both these comments by Western writers, Jung and Koch, derive from their responses to Eastern texts or social philosophies. Jung is commenting on an ancient Chinese alchemical text, and Koch is articulating the wisdom of an Indonesian character in revolutionary Jakarta. The idea that the immortal, spiritual element in the human soul can become diseased or monstrous is often found in Eastern literature and tradition, although it is rarely evident in Western religion, except in the Old Testament where old Yahweh pours forth his wrath and rage upon his people if they deny, betray or forget him. 'The fear of Yahweh is the beginning of knowledge' (Proverbs 1:7).

But Western understandings of the God realm are generally far too caught up in idealised and sentimental images of the deity to understand much about the disastrous human and social effects of the repression of sacramentality. Our religion seems too abstract and remote from human experience, and does not have enough psychological knowledge of the catastrophic effects of repressing the realm of sacred relations over large periods of time, and increasingly over larger tracts of land now that secularism is spreading its market economy and ego-mania into all parts of the world. The spirit is our vital and deepest human and social function, and when it is repressed the consequences are even more serious than the effects of sexual repression, which as Freud documented are serious enough.

THE DAMAGE TO SPIRITUAL AND NATURAL ECOLOGIES

D. H. Lawrence was a literary genius who contained both the wisdom of Freud and Jung. He understood sexual repression, and wrote extensively about it, but he also wrote about the consequences of our spiritual dissociation, often in the same texts that are better known for their sexual themes. In *Lady Chatterley's Lover*, originally banned for its sexual explicitness, Lawrence writes:

> Oh what a catastrophe for man when he cut himself off ... from his union with the sun and the earth. This is what is the matter with us. We are bleeding at the roots, because we are cut off from the earth and sun and stars, and love is a grinning mockery, because, poor blossom, we plucked it from its stem on the tree of Life, and expected it to keep on blooming in our civilised vase on the table.[177]

The tree of man cannot live for long without its secret root system. Lawrence argues that we have done this to ourselves; we have blindly and stupidly plucked the top, showy part of the human system from its dark, invisible roots, upon which the whole structure is based. Here he echoes Nietzsche, who cried that God is dead because we have murdered God. We have committed these crimes knowingly, and we have called them works of liberation and freedom. Perched in our civilised vase on the table, we wonder why we feel so bad, so ill at ease, so unsupported and cut off.

Eventually, the effects of our uprooting ourselves from the invisible roots become biological, physical and environmental. Our lack of organic connection to the whole of life begins to take its toll on the physical world, as we have not understood the delicate balance of our ecological relationship with nature. We exploit the whole of nature to serve the human part, and we ignore sustainable development to meet short-term and egotistical goals. In the same way that severance from our invisible roots destroys the ecology of the soul, so this same severance destroys the ecology of the environment.

This withering decline affects our bodies, health and vitality. The pollution of the atmosphere and the poisoning of the earth for industrial goals begins to invade our bodily systems. There are pesticides, chemical residues and toxic elements in our organs and bones, in our blood-stream and immuno-vascular system. Our vitality begins to wear down, even our sexual potency and sperm-count becomes depleted. The erosion of the ozone layer mirrors the erosion of protecting layers and nurturing canopies in the human soul. The combination of factors, environmental and spiritual, biological and moral, wears heavy on the body-psyche. Some suffer from chronic fatigue, burnout, exhaustion and allergies, and wonder why. Depression, predicted by experts to be the major health problem of the new century, threatens to engulf society like a wave of melancholy sadness, and society wonders why. The limbs and branches of the tree of man grow heavy, lifeless, weary.

The artist Michael Leunig explores the crisis and disequilibrium of the soul in these terms:

> **We are in the midst of the pillaging and rape of the psychological ecosystem, the ecology of the soul. There's a great, delicate, interconnected ecology that goes on in people's lives. We're defiling it, plundering it, exploiting it, and this will have tremendous consequences for the emotional health of society.**[178]

The phrase 'the ecology of the soul' is brilliantly descriptive and sums up the situation well. Formerly, we were not aware of this ecology, as spiritual things were taken for granted when they were in good order. When life is not broken, we do not need to understand how it works. But when life is radically fragmented, we have to learn how to repair it, and suddenly this strange new ecology emerges before us as something we have to attend to.

The ecology of the soul and the ecology of the natural world are intimately related, and both have been disturbed by a consciousness that has privileged the human part above the spiritual or cosmic whole. The human part has abused the ecology of the soul and the unity of nature, and we are now realising the tremendous consequences of our actions. The crises within and about us are forcing on us a new kind of reflection, and many are being forced into a philosophical mode even against our natural inclinations.

We desperately look around for our lost roots, hoping we can graft our dying tree onto some mysterious and subterranean root system. Some fear that the roots themselves have died from the violent and brutalising separation of visible and invisible worlds. Even theologians and religious begin to doubt the endurance of God through all of this upheaval, and so we find a 'death of God' theology, which is like a ritual mourning for the lost invisible roots. But the roots themselves have their foundation in eternity, and they never wither, even though the branches, fruit and leaves wither on the tree. This is the great wonder of faith and the mystery of life, that our deep roots remain eternally present and alive with new potential, even if we spite them or cut them away from us. Jung became so convinced of this process that he had engraved above the front entrance to his house in Switzerland this affirmation, 'Called or not called, God is always present'. In a secularised society, God is mostly not called, but nonetheless is present.

THE SPIRIT IN SEARCH OF ITS CREATION

In our new call for spirituality, something mysterious is present in our call. It is not just the ego that calls for spirit, not just our helplessness that cries out to be healed. Above and beyond our anguish, the spirit can be heard calling out to us, inviting us to change, hoping that we do not destroy the whole experiment in life and creation from our narrow-mindedness and egotism. We experience not just a human craving for the sacred, but also a sacred craving for the human. To return to the tree metaphor, it is as if the mysterious roots are now searching for us. Spirit is seeking us, because there is some intelligent force in creation that wants to live and desires to be realised on earth, in space and time. Christians speak of the 'coming of the kingdom', and never have we needed metaphysical support more than in the present era. Jung, the great prophetic voice in modern science, wrote that a mysterious wholeness is seeking us, even as we, in our brokenness, seek wholeness.

There is something else going on in spirituality, something that impinges on the nature of the divine, and its need to ensure that life remains on earth, that its reality can be incarnated and developed in time and space. The sacred sees that the very existence of life is now threatened, and if life is destroyed, God is diminished and has to return to the uncreated cosmos. The intelligent force in creation, call it God, Gaia, Sophia, Spirit or Wholeness (depending on our viewpoint), is tenacious, committed and does not seek annihilation. The return of spirituality in a desperate time is further evidence (if we ever needed it) of the continued presence of the sacred in creation, and the unwillingness of this sacredness to let us go and see us destroy ourselves and the entire planetary system. It will not let go, even though we have officially let go of it, and have repeatedly abused, betrayed and persecuted it. The Spanish writer Maurizio Ferraris put this in an ironical formulation, 'God has need of man, who for just this reason no longer has, in principle, any need for God'.[179]

DAWNING RECOGNITIONS

As Yeats predicted, when the creature no longer respects the creator, when the falcon no longer hears the falconer, things fall apart, the centre cannot hold, and anarchy is loosed upon the earth. Today, in the face of so much shocking alienation and destruction, our hunger for connectedness has broken through, and in this sense the hunger for spirituality is not so much a voluntary choice in favour of the metaphysical, as it is an involuntary and instinctive reaction against social conditions that are inimical to life and to our planetary survival. How rational, we might ask, is economic rationalism in view of these imminent disasters? How sensible is the kind of 'commonsense' that destroys mystery and life? How enlightened is the kind of knowledge that attacks the very links that hold things together? It is worth remembering the scriptural warning, 'Where there is no vision, the people perish' (Proverbs 11:14). We know that civilisation is going downhill, and we do not want it to happen. Instinctively, we listen to the heart, and to its silent cry for spirituality and connectedness.

The ecological revolution, which is welling up from below and from the grassroots level of community, is a spontaneous and vitally important counter-reaction to the unchecked madness and so-called progress of the world. We call for sustainable development, not for the delusory limitless development that harms so much of life and the environment. In the same vein, we call for 'sustainable' levels of alienation and disconnection, by seeking to compensate the harsh realities of fragmentation by inventing new stories and sciences about interconnectedness and interrelationship. Significantly, science is inventing new myths of connectedness, even though 'science', or rather scientism (an ideology, rather than a method of investigation), was the culprit which effectively destroyed the invisible connectivity that tied and bound creation together. It was science and industry that declared myths and religions to be nonsensical, and that replaced religious myths with new 'physical' understandings about how the world works.

Today, the new sciences, particularly theoretical physics, biology and maths, keep telling us that there are no separate parts in the universe, that everything is in dynamic relationship with everything else. These insights are also emerging from environmental philosophy and deep ecology, just as they are from systems theory, management theory and the new economics. It is cold comfort to our displaced and debunked mystical systems, such as cosmology, alchemy, religion and Platonic philosophy, that these insights into mystical unity are now returning to a respectful place in the social and cultural order. The ancient mystical systems have always taught that the world is a dynamic whole, that energies, vibrations, currents, and forces bind everything together in an indivisible cosmos. The debunked and refuted cosmological systems can now be recovered and appreciated in a completely new way, and ironically it is the sciences that are today making this recovery of the past and retrieval of ancient wisdom possible.

The compensatory and salvational desire for reconnection will involve us in enormous changes of philosophy, psychology, theology, social policy, ecology, land-use and religion. The development of a new worldview in which relationship, not isolation, is of central importance, in which responsibility, not freedom, is the object of desire, in which cooperation, not competition, is the key dynamic of social enterprise, will take a long time to come to fruition. No doubt, such development will meet with resistances, objections, rivalry and jealousy, with disbelief and rejection, and we will have to stand firm in the conviction that a new paradigm needs to be born, so that the things that have fallen apart can be put together again.

CONNECTIVITY AS A PARODY OF SPIRITUAL CONNECTEDNESS

The difficult thing today is how to make this dream of reconnection happen. We know what we want, but how do we get it? Spirituality, happiness and reconnection is at once more simple and more difficult than we realise. The simplicity is that it is available to us always, at all times, and if we make an attempt, we may find healing and renewal. The difficulty is that our normal, everyday mind gets in the way of this reconnection, does not know how to go about it, and can often be a real obstacle to its achievement.

But when we want something desperately enough, technology tries to supply it. This has been the habit of the modern West for a long time—to satisfy deep longings with material goods, advances in science and new technology. A new secular myth has grown up in our midst, to replace the myth of utopian politics, and this is the myth of technological *connectivity*. It is a direct copy of our deep spiritual yearning, our desire to overcome our alienation, and it is doing very well at copying this yearning, and that is why connectivity is the number one international industry in the world today. It is where most of the big money and corporate action and postindustrial excitement is to be found.

Our secular, technological inventiveness has invented a brave new world that we all believe we have to have and are told we must be part of. This brave new world is based on computers, Internet, World Wide Web, email, link-ups and mobile phones, a proliferation of new and marvellous inventions that seek to put us in touch with each other. Once we enter this new world our isolation will be overcome, and we will feel marvellously interconnected, hooked-up, linked-in. These are the same sorts of statements that were basic to the seductions of state communism and ideological capitalism; as soon as we accept the new ideology, our lives will be changed and our human lot improved. The old propaganda and rhetoric is now employed in the service of high technology. We do not see this high-tech world as mythology because we are far too identified with it, but it is a new myth based on a profane interpretation of sacred desires.

The new connective technologies do what they claim to do, at least at one level. They link us through information, and they make global and local communications possible in an instant. But they are largely symptomatic attempts to address the larger and deeper problems of alienation that beset us. They give us a substitute connectedness through the sharing of information, but they do not, and cannot, give us the authentic experience of connectedness. The new technology is a parody, an imitation which copies a spiritual connectedness that many of us have never experienced, but can only guess at.

The secular version of connectedness promises this: every man, woman or teenager with a mobile phone, Internet and email need never feel alone again. This is the new panacea, the social utopia, the dream of interconnectedness. A new cult has arisen that believes 'www' will bring about a new world order. The web is certainly unlimited, respecting no boundaries, subject to limited censorship, and heeding no national or state borders. The potential is present for the good, but in our technological excitement and fervour we can blind ourselves to the evils of these new systems.

The problem with our technological visions is that they must always, by definition, fall short of the mark and meet with human disappointment and failure. It is not that the material world is incapable of sustaining us. Earthly contentment is possible if we know how to live within its bounds. Rather, we overburden the earthly and the technological with impossible longings, and these cannot sustain the weight of this burden, and collapse in the confusion and chaos of emotional overload. It is not the material level that collapses, but our expectation that it can deliver us the happiness and fulfilment for which we crave. Our deepest hopes and dreams are not rational at all, they are irrational, intangible and well up from invisible regions of the soul. It is our habit, however, to project them upon people, objects, things, policies, gadgets and programs.

A person who is asked to name his or her dream might reply 'to own my own home', 'become wealthy', 'drive the best car', 'own the newest information technology'. But these are not their dreams at all, they are the manufactured dreams of our consumer industries. We should be able to see through this charade, but we do not. Theologians might suggest that our problem is one of original sin or exile from the divine. Sin means falling short, and we are always falling short of our goals and making 'category errors' about our deepest desires. The anthem of the postmodern world is described in a popular song, 'I still haven't found what I'm looking for'.

We never find what we are looking for, until we have a *metanoia*, a conversion, and realise that we have been looking in the wrong places for our fulfilment. Many of our human activities are copies or reproductions of impulses that are invisible, hard to discern, and poorly described in the over-used word 'spirituality', but it will have to do. The real thing is so beyond us, while the copy, the reproduction, can be worked up in a jiffy. Give me two seconds, here it is, there you are, not a problem. But it is a problem, because the deeper impulse has not been satiated, just temporarily relieved by vicarious displacement, by a stop-gap or addictive behaviour.

The dominant cultural style or literary mode of the postmodern period is parody and imitation. The addictive society cannot access the spiritual life or undercurrent that would bring creativity and originality, so we become obsessed with reproducing the known, 'playing it again', doing what we already know and what brings sentimental comfort or nostalgia. In her book *For Common Things*, Jedediah Purdy writes:

> There is a perception that the world has grown old, flat and sterile, and that we are rightly weary of it. There is nothing to delight, to move, inspire, or horrify us. Nothing will surprise us. Everything we encounter is a remake, a re-release, a rip-off, or a re-run. We know it all before we see it, because we have seen it already. What has so exhausted the world for us?[180]

What exhausts us is the lack of connection to our invisible, life-sustaining roots. Why do we delight so much in imitation and parody? Partly because it is easier to reproduce something than to make something new.

'Making new' calls for connection with the deep roots of creativity. But we do not have control over the deep roots or over what they produce for us, whereas we have a sense that a reproduced version is something we can control or manipulate. Perhaps this is what Eliot meant when he said that we cannot stand much reality. The living reality baffles and eludes us, but it is worth trying to reach out for it, to catch hold of the real thing. The hope for the future is that we can overcome our obsession with imitation, stand-ins, substitutes and copies, and face the nature of the real. Not just the surface real, but the deep real, from which surprising, alarming and transforming things emerge.

ACKNOWLEDGEMENTS

The Spirituality Revolution is part of my ongoing project of reading human experience through psycho-spiritual perspectives. My previous works have considered the American New Age movement (Tacey 2001), Australian spirituality (2000), the American men's movement and feminism (1997), landscape awareness and Aboriginal spirituality (1995), and a writer's struggle with spirit (1988).

While avoiding academic jargon wherever possible, this book is based on readings that are often felt in the background and not overtly discussed. I have been inspired by the philosophical ideas of Hegel, Nietzsche, William James, and A. N. Whitehead. The writings of the historian of religions Mircea Eliade are constantly in my mind. In recent philosophy, I have been influenced by Gadamer, Levinas, Gianni Vattimo, and Eugenio Trias. The ideas of C. G. Jung are foundational to my thinking, and I could not have conceptualised spiritual experience without the support of Jung's writings.

My reflections have been helped by the political writings of Joel Kovel and Andrew Samuels, the mythopoetics of John O'Donohue and Thomas Moore, the ecological reflections of Thomas Berry and Paul Collins, and the spiritual studies of Sandra Schneiders. In theology, I am inspired by Paul Tillich, Hans Kung, Tony Kelly, Sara Maitland, Karen Armstrong, and Sally McFague. Conversations with Don Cupitt, Ian Player, John O'Donohue and Clare Wilde have been significant. On the subject of the re-enchantment of science, I am grateful for discussions with Daryl Reanney, Rupert Sheldrake and David Suzuki.

I acknowledge the creativity of those who are working in the field of spiritual education in the UK, especially Ron Best, Mark Chater, Clive Erricker, Jane Erricker, David Hay, Cathy Ota, and Jack Priestley. In Australia, I thank Greg and Pip Burgess, Janine Burke, John

Carroll, Maryanne Confoy, John Fisher, William Johnston, Rachael Kohn, Michael Leunig, David Ranson, Peter Ross, Maria Vella, Pamela Webb, Michael Whelan, and others for illuminating discussions.

I thank my research associate Patricia Dutton for her insight and careful attention to draft versions of this book, and I am grateful to my publishers, Cathy Jenkins and Helen Littleton, and editors Bridget James and Sandra Rigby for their advice and support. Finally, I am grateful to my students, who have given generously of themselves in writings and discussions on spirituality. Where relevant, I have referenced student writing by indicating the first name only, the age of the student, and the year of the course.

David Tacey, Ph.D.
Associate Professor and Reader,
School of Arts and Critical Enquiry,
La Trobe University, Melbourne, Australia.

References

All references to the works of Jung in the *Collected Works* are to paragraph numbers, not to page numbers. References to the *Collected Works* will be indicated by the essay or chapter, followed by *CW*, and the volume number. Such references are to *The Collected Works of C.G. Jung*, translated by R.F.C. Hull, edited by H. Read, M. Fordham, G. Adler and William McGuire, and published by Routledge in London and in America by Princeton University Press, 1953–92.

With regard to the Bible, several editions and translations have been consulted and compared, including *The English Revised Version* (1885), *The Revised Standard Version* (1952), *The Jerusalem Bible* (1966), and *The New International Version Study Bible* (1995).

1. Hooks, Bell 2000, *All About Love: New Visions*. New York: William Morrow, p.82.
2. Armstrong, Karen 1993, *A History of God*. London: Heinemann, p.398.
3. Tacey, David 2000, *Re-Enchantment: The New Australian Spirituality*. Sydney: HarperCollins, p.190.
4. Zinnbauer, Brian 'Religion and Spirituality: Unfuzzying the Fuzzy', *Journal for the Scientific Study of Religion* (Utah), Vol. 36, No. 4, 1997, p.561.
5. Schneiders, Sandra 2000, 'Religion and spirituality: strangers, rivals, or partners?'. In *The Santa Clara Lectures* (California), 6 (2), p.1.
6. Hay, David & Hunt, Kate 2000, 'Is Britain's soul waking up?' In *The Tablet*. London, 24 June, p.846.
7. Ibid.
8. Bloom, Harold 1996, *Omens of Millennium*. London: Fourth Estate.
9. Lyotard, J. F. 1984, *The Postmodern Condition*. Manchester University Press.
10. Spretnak, Charlene 1991, *States of Grace: The Recovery of Meaning in the Postmodern World*. San Francisco: Harper.
11. Griffin, David Ray (ed) 1988, *Spirituality and Society: Postmodern Visions*. Albany: State University of New York Press.
12. Hay and Hunt, op. cit., p.846.
13. Eliade, Mircea 1976, *Occultism, Witchcraft, and Cultural Fashions*. University of Chicago Press, p.iii.

14. Eliade, Mircea 1975, *The Quest: History and Meaning in Religion* (1969). University of Chicago Press.

15. Tillich, Paul 1963, *The Shaking of the Foundations* (1949). Harmondsworth: Penguin, 1963, p.56.

16. Arnold, Matthew 1983, 'Dover Beach' (1867). In Allison, A.W. (ed) *The Norton Anthology of Poetry*. New York: W.W. Norton.

17. Hegel, Georg, 1974, 'The phenomenology of spirit' (1807). In F.G. Weiss (ed.) *Hegel: The Essential Writings*. New York: Harper Torchbooks, p.v.

18. Derrida, Jacques & Vattimo, Gianni (eds.) 1998, *Religion*. Stanford University Press, p.41.

19. Moore, Thomas 1983, *Rituals of the Imagination*. Dallas: Pegasus, p.2.

20. Freud, Sigmund 2001: 'The Future of an Illusion' (1927). In vol. 21, *The Standard Edition of the Complete Psychological Works of Sigmund Freud*. London: Vintage.

21. Kovel, Joel 1991, *History and Spirit: An Inquiry into the Philosophy of Liberation*. Boston: Beacon Press, p.225.

22. Faber, Mel D. 1996, *New Age Thinking: A Psychoanalytic Critique*. University of Ottawa Press.

23. Jung, C.G. 1964, 'The Spiritual Problems of Modern Man' (1928/1931). *CW* 10, 162.

24. Jung, C.G. 1959, 'Aion' (1951). *CW* 9, part 2, 67.

25. Johnson, Robert 1993, *Owning Your Own Shadow*. San Francisco: HarperCollins.

26. Jung, C.G. 1980, 'Does the world stand on the verge of spiritual rebirth?' (1934). In William McGuire & R.F.C. Hull (eds) *C.G. Jung Speaking*. London: Picador, p.224.

27. Ibid, p.81.

28. Jung 1980, 'On the frontiers of knowledge' (1959), op.cit., pp370–72.

29. Eliot, T.S. 1978, 'The Waste Land' (1922). In *Collected Poems*. London: Faber, p.75.

30. Jung 1980, 'Does the world stand on the verge of spiritual rebirth?', op. cit., p.81.

31. Das, Surya 1999, *Awakening to the Sacred*. New York: Bantam, p.19.

32. Schneiders 2000, op. cit., p.2.

33. Eliot 1978, op. cit., p.63.

34. Weber, Max 1922, *The Sociology of Religion*. Boston: Beacon, 1964.

35. Jung, C.G. 1958, 'Psychology and Religion' (1938/1940), *CW* 11 and Claxton, Guy 1996, *Beyond Therapy*. Newton, Dorset: Prism Press.

36. Schneiders, Sandra 1989, 'Spirituality in the Academy'. In *Theological Studies*, 50 (2), p.681.

37. Ibid.

38. Jung, C.G. 1946, 'The Psychology of the Transference'. *CW* 16, 396.

39. Jung, C.G. 1955, '*Mysterium Coniunctionis*'. *CW* 14, 503.

40. Tillich, op. cit., p.98.

41. Yeats, W.B. 1991, 'The Second Coming' (1920). In Timothy Webb (ed) *W.B. Yeats: Selected Poetry*. Harmondsworth: Penguin, p.124.

42. Schneiders 1989, op. cit., p.679.

43. Heagle, John 1985, 'A new public piety: reflections on spirituality'. In *Church*, 1 (2), p.53.

44. Schneiders 2000, op. cit., p.2.

45. O'Donohue, John 1997, *Anam Cara: Spiritual Wisdom from the Celtic World*. London: Bantam.
46. Mowaljarlai, David 1993: *Yorro, Yorro: Everything Standing Up Alive*. Broome: Magabala Books.
47. Atwood, Margaret 1972, *Surfacing*. London: Virago.
48. Anderson, Jessica 1984, *Tirra Lirra By the River* (1978). Melbourne: Penguin.
49. Eliade, Mircea 1965, *Rites and Symbols of Initiation*. New York: Harper & Row.
50. Op. cit., p.119.
51. Anderson, Sarah 1997, *The Virago Book of Spirituality: Of Women and Angels*. London: Virago Press, p.vii.
52. Ibid, p.vii.
53. White, Patrick 1966, *The Solid Mandala*. Harmondsworth: Penguin, 1986, p.1.
54. James, William 1982, *The Varieties of Religious Experience* (1902). New York: Penguin, p.53.
55. Freud, op. cit.
56. Kelly, Tony 1990, *A New Imagining*. Melbourne: HarperCollins.
57. Griffin, David Ray (ed) 1989, *God and Religion in the Postmodern World*. Albany: State University of New York Press.
58. Derrida, op. cit., pp96–9.
59. Ibid, p.41.
60. Ibid, p.34.
61. Ibid, p.36.
62. Ibid, p.79.
63. Barthes, Roland 1980, *Mythologie* (1957). London: Granada, p.37.
64. James, op. cit., p.12.
65. Ibid, pp 11–13.
66. Berry, Thomas 1988, *The Dream of the Earth*. San Francisco: Sierra Club Books.
67. Jung, C.G. 1971, 'Psychological Types' (1921). *CW* 6, 630.
68. James, op. cit., p.11.
69. Tacey, David 2001, *Jung and the New Age*. London and Philadelphia: Routledge.
70. Jung 1964, op. cit., 193.
71. Ibid, p.187.
72. Heelas, Paul 1996, *The New Age Movement: The Celebration of the Self and the Sacralization of Modernity*. Oxford: Blackwell.
73. Hegel, op. cit., p.6.
74. Ibid, p.2.
75. Ibid, p.190.
76. Ibid, p.v.
77. Ibid, p.329.
78. Eliot, T.S. 1968, *Murder in the Cathedral* (1935), London: Faber, p.76.
79. Weber, op. cit.
80. Nietzsche, Friedrich 1967, 'The Birth of Tragedy from the Spirit of Music' (1872). In Walter Kaufmann (ed) *The Birth of Tragedy and The Case of Wagner*. New York: Random House.
81. Schneiders 2000, op. cit., p.2.
82. Ricoeur, Paul 1974, *The Conflict of Interpretations*. Evanston: Northwestern University Press.

83. Best, Ron 1996, *Education, Spirituality and the Whole Child*. London: Cassells.
84. Hegel, op. cit., p.208.
85. Eliade, Mircea, 1987, *The Sacred and the Profane* (1959). New York: Harcourt, Brace & World, p.204.
86. Schneiders 2000, op. cit., p.1.
87. Eliot, T.S. 1978, 'Four Quartets' (1942). In *Collected Poems*. London: Faber, p.218.
88. Ibid, p.222.
89. Schneiders 2000, op. cit., p.2.
90. Otto, Rudolf 1980, *The Idea of the Holy* (1923). Oxford University Press.
91. Derrida, op. cit., p.33.
92. Ibid, p.x.
93. Ibid, p.7.
94. Ibid, p.211.
95. Ibid, p.39.
96. Ibid, p.207.
97. Ibid, p.ix.
98. Ibid, p.172.
99. Ibid, p.204.
100. Ibid, p.175.
101. Ibid, pp99–100
102. Ibid, p.204.
103. Ibid, p.205.
104. Gordimer, Nadine 1979, *July's People*. Harmondsworth: Penguin, p.1.
105. Beckett, Samuel 1982, *Endgame* (1958). London: Faber, p.17 and 1990, *Waiting for Godot* (1955). London: Faber.
106. Derrida, op. cit., p.95.
107. Ibid, p.208.
108. Ibid, p.202.
109. Ibid, p.207.
110. Armstrong, op. cit., p.412.
111. Derrida, op. cit., p.36.
112. Eliade 1975, op. cit., p.i.
113. James, op. cit.
114. Ibid, p.29.
115. Ibid, p.30.
116. Ibid, p.29.
117. Ibid, p.30.
118. Ibid, p.xx.
119. Ibid, p.29.
120. Schneiders 2000, op. cit., p.5.
121. Campbell, Joseph & Moyers, Bill 1988, *The Power of Myth*. New York: Doubleday, p.150.
122. Ibid, p.2.
123. Otto, op. cit.
124. Ibid, p.21.
125. Ibid, pp13–14.
126. Jung 1964, op. cit., p.192.
127. Maitland, Sara 1995, *A Big-Enough God*. London: Mowbray, p.15.
128. Davies, Paul & Gribben, John 1991, *The Matter Myth*. London: Viking, p.27.

129. Davies, Paul 1992, *The Mind of God*. London: Simon & Schuster.
130. Griffin, op. cit.
131. Op. cit., p.186.
132. Foucault, Michel 1980, *Power/Knowledge*. Brighton: Harvester Press.
133. Op. cit., p.186.
134. Op. cit., p.408.
135. Freud, op. cit.
136. Op. cit., p.52.
137. Kierkegaard, Soren 1946, *Kierkeguard's Attack Upon Christendom* (1854). London: Oxford University Press.
138. Derrida, op. cit., p.110.
139. Hope, A.D. 1992, 'An Epistle from Holofernes' (1960). In *Selected Poems*. Sydney: Angus & Robertson, p.56.
140. Op. cit., p.403.
141. Carroll, John 2001, *The Western Dreaming*. Sydney: HarperCollins.
142. Cupitt, Don 1980, *Taking Leave of God*. London: SCM Press and 1984, *The Sea of Faith*. London: British Broadcasting Corporation.
143. Spong, John Shelby 1991, *Rescuing the Bible from Fundamentalism*. New York: Harper and 1998, *Why Christianity Must Change or Die*. New York: Harper.
144. Blake, William 1976, 'The marriage of heaven and hell' (1793). In Geoffrey Keynes (ed) *Blake: Complete Writings*. Oxford University Press, p.154.
145. Op. cit., p.189.
146. Kung, Hans 1991, 'Rediscovering God.' In Philip Hillyer (ed) *On the Threshold of the Third Millennium*. Special Issue of *Concilium*. Londond: SCM Press.
147. Kung, Hans 1980, *Does God Exist? An Answer for Today*. New York: Doubleday.
148. Kung 1991, op. cit., p.86.
149. Ibid, p.86–7.
150. Ibid, p.102.
151. Ibid, p.90.
152. Ibid, p.87.
153. Ibid, p.90.
154. Armstrong, op. cit., p.402.
155. Hames, Richard 1997, *Burying the 20th Century*. Sydney: Business & Professional, p.iii.
156. Yeats, W.B. 1991, 'The Circus Animals' Desertion' (1939). In Timothy Webb (ed) *W.B. Yeats: Selected Poetry*. Harmondsworth: Penguin.
157. Lawrence, D.H. 1994, *Lady Chatterley's Lover* (1928). Harmondsworth: Penguin, p.5.
158. Van Ness, Peter (ed) 1996, *Spirituality and the Secular Quest*. New York: Crossroad, p.421.
159. Op. cit.
160. Hames, op. cit., p.iv.
161. Zelinski, Mark 1991, *Outward Bound, the Inward Odyssey*. Hillsboro, Oregon: Beyond Words.
162. Rahner, Karl 1981, *Theological Investigations. Volume XX: Concern for the Church*. London: Darton Longman & Todd, p.149.
163. Brueggemann, Walter 1978, *The Prophetic Imagination*. New York: Doubleday, p.150.

164. Op. cit.
165. Op. cit.
166. Cox, Harvey 1965, *God's Revolution and Man's Responsibility*. Valley Forge: Judson Press, p.1.
167. Ibid, p.24.
168. Op. cit., p.7.
169. Hay and Hunt, op. cit., p.846.
170. Kuhn, Thomas 1970, *The Structure of Scientific Revolutions*. University of Chicago Press.
171. Jung, C.G. 1973, 'Letter' (1949). In G. Adler & A. Jafrfe (eds) *Letters of C.G. Jung*. Vol. 1. Princeton University Press, p.537.
172. Hames, op. cit., p.ix.
173. Tacey 2000, op. cit.
174. Derrida, op. cit., p.174.
175. Jung, C.G. 1968, 'Commentary on *The Secret of the Golden Flower*' (1929). *CW* 13.
176. Koch, Christopher 1978, *The Year of living Dangerously*. London: Michael Joseph, p.236.
177. Lawrence, op. cit., p.323.
178. Leunig, Michael 1995, 'Drawing the line on creativity and other curly issues'. *The Age* (Melbourne), 5 August, p.20.
179. Derrida, op. cit., p.171.
180. Purdy, Jedediah 1999, *For Common Things*. New York: Alfred A. Knoff.

A SELECT LIST OF FURTHER READINGS

I am frequently asked by individuals, organisations and conferences for a list of recommended readings in spirituality and, in particular, for reliable works that relate spirituality to various fields of knowledge and enquiry. The works on spirituality and its application are now so vast it is virtually impossible to keep watch over these numerous domains. The study of spirituality has exploded traditional boundaries of knowledge, and has spilled over most academic disciplines, as Diarmuid O'Murchu said:

> No one discipline, no matter how sanctioned by time, will enable us to comprehend this new upsurge; it requires a multi-disciplinary analysis.

Of course, when such a vast and all-inclusive concept as 'spirit' arises in our time, we should not expect it to conform to existing categories of knowledge or specialisation, especially since many of these categories are defined by secular authorities. There is hardly any field of knowledge that has not been affected by the new interest in spirituality. Often, the introduction of spirit simply means viewing a traditional field in a slightly different light; sometimes, however, the eruption of spirituality means that an entire area of knowledge has to be revisioned from first principles, as for instance, in recovery from addictions.

I struggle to keep abreast of the application of spirituality in the domains, because this means reading across dozens of different areas and disciplines. My areas of formal education are in literature, philosophy, art history, education theory and analytical psychology. But my interest in applied spirituality has led me into such diverse fields as nursing and health care, physics and the new sciences, physical and outdoor education, Western religion and theology,

Eastern religions and philosophies, anthropology, sociology, ecology, and business management and leadership.

Because these fields are numerous and innately different, it is often the case that people in one field know little or nothing about similar kinds of development, that is the introduction of spiritual perspectives in other fields. This means that the spirituality 'wheel', as it were, is often being reinvented, as knowledge is not communicated across conventional borders, even if people are distantly aware of similar developments elsewhere. My advice to readers and students in these areas is always to look sideways at what others are doing in different fields, and not just ahead at the goal of our striving. It may be that by glancing sideways we find more efficient ways of moving forward.

It must be admitted that not all writing in the field of spirituality is good. Some of it is fuzzy and unclear, some is indulgent and sentimental, and some stretches the boundaries of reason too far. Spirituality is a field that attracts the best and worst of culture, the most sublime thoughts and the most baleful nonsense are often found together. Some writers take their own concepts and frameworks too literally, failing to realise that spirit is not a static thing or an object in metaphysical space, but a fluid reality that is best grasped by metaphor and symbol. If there is no awareness of the play of symbolic imagination, and an absence of humour or self-criticism, then we should become suspicious. Most of what appears in this list I have consulted, and can endorse so long as it is read with a critical attitude.

I emphasise that this list is provisional, sketchy and selective. A separate book could be devoted to a bibliography of writings in spirituality and its fields of application published since 1970. This list serves as an introduction to the nominated areas, and I hope it will be useful to readers, students and teachers.

SPIRITUALITY AS AN EMERGING FIELD OF KNOWLEDGE

DEFINING AND DESCRIBING THE FIELD

Cousins, Ewert 1994, *World Spirituality: An Encyclopedic History of the Religious Quest*. A 25-volume series on spirituality. New York: Crossroad.
Harvey, Andrew 1991, *Hidden Journey: A Spiritual Awakening*. London: Rider.
Hinnells, John R. 1997, *A New Handbook of Living Religions*. Cambridge, Mass: Blackwell.
O'Murchu, Diarmuid 1997, *Reclaiming Spirituality*. Dublin: Gill & Macmillan.

Schneiders, Sandra 2000, 'Religion and spirituality: strangers, rivals, or partners?' *The Santa Clara Lectures* (California), 6 (2).

Van Ness, Peter (ed) 1996, *Spirituality and the Secular Quest.* New York: Crossroad.

Zinnbauer, Brian 1997, 'Religion and spirituality: unfuzzying the fuzzy'. *Journal for the Scientific Study of Religion,* 36 (4).

JOURNALS

The International Journal of Children's Spirituality. Brighton, England, 1998+.
Studies in Spirituality. Kampen, Holland, 1991+.
Spirituality Today. Chicago, 1978+.

A HOLISTIC APPREHENSION OF HISTORY, SCIENCE, NATURE AND PHILOSOPHY

Capra, Fritjof 1983, *The Turning Point: Science, Society and the Rising Culture.* London: Fontana.
——1989, *Uncommon Wisdom.* London: Flamingo.
Dillard, Annie 1982, *Teaching a Stone to Talk.* New York: HarperCollins.
Wilber, Ken 1995, *Sex, Ecology, and Spirituality.* Boston: Shambhala.
——1997, *The Eye of Spirit.* Boston: Shambhala.
——1998, *The Marriage of Sense and Soul.* New York: Random House.

MODERN MASTERS IN THE INTELLECTUAL TRADITION

Eliade, Mircea 1959, *The Sacred and the Profane.* New York: Harcourt, Brace & World, 1987.
——1969, *The Quest: History and Meaning in Religion.* University of Chicago Press, 1975.
Huxley, Aldous 1946, *The Perennial Philosophy.* London: Chatto & Windus.
James, William 1990, *The Varieties of Religious Experience* (1902). Penguin Books.
Jung, C.G. 1964, 'The Spiritual Problem of Modern Man' (1928/1931). *CW* 10.
——1964, 'Modern Man in Search of a Soul' (1933b). *CW* 10.
——1958, 'Psychology and Religion' (1938/1940). *CW* 11.
——1964, 'The Undiscovered Self, Present and Future' (1957). *CW,* 10.
——1973, *Memories, Dreams, Reflections* (1961). New York: Random House.
Nietzsche, Friedrich 1967, *The Birth of Tragedy and The Case of Wagner* (1872). New York: Random House.
——1978, *Thus Spoke Zarathustra* (1885). Harmondsworth: Penguin.
——1973, *Beyond Good and Evil* (1886). Harmondsworth: Penguin.
Otto, Rudolf 1980, *The Idea of the Holy* (1923). Oxford University Press.
Teilhard de Chardin, Pierre 1959, *The Phenomenon of Man.* London: Fontana.
Tillich, Paul 1949, *The Shaking of the Foundations.* Harmondsworth: Penguin.

THE PRESENT MOMENT IN TIME

Bellah, Robert 1970, *Beyond Belief.* New York: Harper & Row.
Bloom, Harold 1996, *Omens of Millennium.* London: Fourth Estate.
Campbell, Joseph & Moyers, Bill 1988, *The Power of Myth.* New York: Doubleday.

Das, Surya 1999, *Awakening to the Sacred*. New York: Bantam.

Drury, Nevill 1999, *Exploring the Labyrinth: Making Sense of the New Spirituality*. Sydney: Allen & Unwin.

Eliade, Mircea 1976, *Occultism, Witchcraft, and Cultural Fashions*. University of Chicago Press.

Fox, Matthew 1983, *Original Blessing: A Primer in Creation Spirituality*. Sante Fe: Vear.

——1991, *Creation Spirituality: Liberating Gifts for the Peoples of the Earth*. San Francisco: Harper & Row.

Haule, John Ryan 1999, *Perils of the Soul: Ancient Wisdom and the New Age*. York Beach, Maine: Samuel Weiser.

Hay, David & Hunt, Kate 2000, 'Is Britain's soul waking up?' *The Tablet*. London, 24 June.

Raschke, Carl 1980, *The Interruption of Eternity: Modern Gnosticism and the Origins of the New Religious Consciousness*. Chicago: Nelson-Hall.

Van Ness, Peter 1992, *Spirituality, Diversion, and Decadence: The Contemporary Predicament*. Albany: State University of New York Press.

Whitmont, Edward C. 1982, *Return of the Goddess*. New York: Crossroad.

ACADEMIC CRITIQUES OF SPIRITUALITY IN POPULAR CONTEXTS

Faber, Mel D. 1996, *New Age Thinking: A Psychoanalytic Critique*. University of Ottawa Press.

Heelas, Paul 1996, *The New Age Movement: The Celebration of the Self and the Sacralization of Modernity*. Oxford: Blackwell.

Heelas, Paul; Martin, David & Morris, Paul (eds) 1996, *Religion, Modernity and Postmodernity*. Oxford: Blackwell.

Lau, Kimberly 2000, *New Age Capitalism: Making Money East of Eden*. University of Pennsylvania Press.

Rhodes, Ron 1990, *The Counterfeit Christ of the New Age Movement*. Michigan: Baker.

Tacey, David 2001, *Jung and the New Age*. London: Routledge.

Yoffe, Emily 1995, 'How the soul is sold: James Hillman and Thomas Moore.' In *The New York Times Magazine*, 23 April, 44–49.

SPIRITUALITY AND ITS APPLICATION IN THE FIELDS

Note: The point of this listing is to show spirituality in new and 'secular' fields of knowledge; I have not included the world religions in this list. The following categories are arranged in alphabetical order:

ABORIGINAL CULTURE

Hammond, Catherine (ed) 1991, *Creation Spirituality and the Dreamtime*. Sydney: Millennium.

Pattel-Gray, Anne 1996, *Aboriginal Spirituality: Past, Present, Future*. Melbourne: HarperCollins.

Tacey, David 1995, *Edge of the Sacred*. Melbourne: HarperCollins.

AMERICAN SOCIETY

Albanese, Catherine 1977, *Corresponding Motion: Transcendental Religion and the New America*. Philadelphia: Temple University Press.

Bednarowski, Mary 1995, *New Religions and the Theological Imagination in America*. Indiana University Press.

Bloom, Harold 1992, *The American Religion: The Emergence of the Post-Christian Nation*. New York: Simon & Schuster.

Ellwood, Robert S. 1979, *Alternative Altars: Unconventional and Eastern Spirituality in America*. University of Chicago Press.

Wuthnow, Robert 1998, *After Heaven: Spirituality in America since the 1950s*. Berkeley: University of California Press.

ART AND LITERATURE

Abrams, M. H. 1971, *Natural Supernaturalism*. New York: Norton.

Apostolos-Cappadona, Diane (ed) 1984, *Art, Creativity, and the Sacred*. New York: Crossroad.

Baggley, John 1987, *Doors of Perception*. London: Mowbray.

Eliade, Mircea 1992, *Symbolism, the Sacred, and the Arts*. New York: Continuum.

Lipsey, Roger 1988, *The Spiritual in Twentieth-Century Art*. Boston: Shambhala.

Mercier, Jacques 1997, *Art that Heals*. New York: Museum for African Art.

Tacey, David 1988, *Patrick White: Fiction and the Unconscious*. Melbourne: Oxford University Press.

BUSINESS MANAGEMENT AND ORGANISATIONAL LEADERSHIP

Cairnes, Margot 1998, *Approaching the Corporate Heart*. Sydney: Simon & Schuster.

Chappell, Tom 1993, *The Soul of a Business*. New York: Bantam.

Chopra, Deepak 1994, *The Seven Spiritual Laws of Success*. San Rafael: Amber-Allen.

Greenleaf, Robert K. 1991, *Servant Leadership* (1977). New York: Paulist Press.

Owen, Harrison 1999, *The Spirit of Leadership*. San Francisco: Berrett-Koehler.

——2000, *The Power of Spirit: How Organizations Transform*. San Francisco: Berrett-Koehler.

Ray, Michael & Alan Rinzler (eds) 1993, *The New Paradigm in Business*. New York: Jeremy Tarcher.

Wheatley, Margaret 1992, *Leadership and the New Science*. San Francisco: Berrett-Koehler.

CHILDREN AND EDUCATION

Best, Ron 1996, *Education, Spirituality and the Whole Child*. London: Cassells.

Erricker, Jane, Ota, Cathy, & Erricker, Clive (eds) 2001, *Spiritual Education: Cultural, Religious and Social Differences*. Brighton and Portland: Sussex Academic Press.

Hay, David & Nye, Rebecca 1998, *The Spirit of the Child*. London: HarperCollins.

Myers, B.K. 1997, *Young Children and Spirituality*, London: Routledge.

Neville, Bernie 1989, *Educating Psyche*. Melbourne: HarperCollins.

Plunkett, D. 1990, *Secular and Spiritual Values: Grounds for Hope in Education*, London: Routledge.

Thatcher, Adrian (ed) 1999, *Spirituality and the Curriculum*. London: Cassell.

DREAMS

Johnson, Robert 1989, *Inner Work*. San Francisco: Harper & Row.

O'Connor, Peter 1986, *Dreams and the Search for Meaning*. Sydney: Methuen Haynes.

ECOLOGY

Berry, Thomas 1988, *The Dream of the Earth*. San Francisco: Sierra Club Books.

Boff, Leonardo 1995, *Ecology and Liberation*. New York: Orbis Books.

Collins, Paul 1995, *God's Earth: Religion as if Matter Really Mattered*. Melbourne: HarperCollins.

Kinsley, David R. 1995, *Ecology and Religion*. Englewood Cliffs, New Jersey: Prentice Hall.

Lovelock, James 1979, *Gaia: A New Look at Life on Earth*. Oxford University Press.

——1988, *The Ages of Gaia: A Biography of Our Living Earth*. London: Norton.

Rockefeller, Steven & Elder, John (eds) 1992, *Spirit and Nature: Why the Environment is a Religious Issue*. Boston: Beacon.

Suzuki, David 1997, *The Sacred Balance*. Vancouver: Greystone Books.

FEMINISM AND FEMINIST THEOLOGY

Adams, Carol (ed.) 1995, *Ecofeminism and the Sacred*. New York: Continuum.

Christ, Carol & Plaskow, Judith (eds) 1992, *Womanspirit Rising: A Feminist Reader in Religion*. New York: HarperCollins.

Hooks, Bell 2000, *All About Love: New Visions*. New York: William Morrow.

Plaskow, Judith & Christ, Carol (eds) 1989, *Weaving the Visions: New Patterns of Feminist Spirituality*. New York: Harper Row.

HEALTH AND RECOVERY FROM ADDICTIONS AND ILLNESS

Baumeister, Roy F. 1991, *Escaping the Self: Alcoholism and Spirituality*. New York: Basic Books.

Garrett, Catherine 1998, *Beyond Anorexia: Narrative, Spirituality, and Recovery*. Cambridge University Press.

Kurtz, Ernest & Ketcham, Katherine 1992, *The Spirituality of Imperfection*. New York: Bantam.

Morgan, Oliver & Jordan, Merle 1999, *Addiction and Spirituality*. St Louis: Chalice Press.

Riekman, G. F. 1978, *The Holistic Health Handbook*. Berkeley: And/Or Press.

Wilson, Bill 1952, *Twelve Steps and Twelve Traditions*. New York: Alcoholics Anonymous.

——1988, *The Language of the Heart*. New York: A.A. Grapevine.

HISTORY AND POLITICS

Kovel, Joel 1991, *History and Spirit: An Inquiry into the Philosophy of Liberation*. Boston: Beacon Press.

Neubauer, John 1999, *Cultural History After Foucault*. New York: Aldine de Gruyter.

Page, Benjamin (ed) 1993, *Marxism and Spirituality*. Westport, Conn: Bergin & Garvey.

Paris, Peter 1995, *The Spirituality of African Peoples: The Search for a Common Moral Discourse*. Philadelphia: Fortress.

Jung and Analytical Psychology

Bolen, Jean Shinoda 1985, *Goddesses in Everywoman*. New York: Harper Colophon.
——1989, *Gods in Everyman*. New York: Harper Colophon.
Johnson, Robert 1984, *The Psychology of Romantic Love*. London: Routledge & Kegan Paul.
——1989, *Ecstasy: Understanding the Psychology of Joy*. San Francisco: Harper & Row.
Jung, C. G. 1963, *Memories, Dreams, Reflections*. New York: Random House.
Singer, June 1973, *Boundaries of the Soul*. New York: Anchor.
Ulanov, Ann 1999, *Religion and the Spiritual in Carl Jung*. New York: Paulist Press.
Young-Eisendrath, Polly & Miller, Melvin 2000, *The Psychology of Mature Spirituality*. London and Philadelphia: Routledge.

Medicine

Cassileth, Barrie R. 1998, *The Alternative Medicine Handbook*. New York: W. W. Norton.
Fuller, Robert C. 1989, *Alternative Medicine and American Religious Life*. New York: Oxford University Press.
Gevitz, Norman (ed) 1988, *Other Healers*. Baltimore: Johns Hopkins University Press.
Hammerschlag, Carl A. 1993, *The Theft of the Spirit: A Journey to Spiritual Healing with Native Americans*. New York: Simon & Schuster.
Peck, M. Scott 1978, *The Road Less Travelled*. London: Arrow Books.
——1993, *Further Along the Road Less Travelled: The Unending Journey towards Spiritual Growth*. London: Arrow Books.

Men and Masculinity

Bly, Robert 1990, *Iron John: A Book About Men*. Reading, Mass: Addison-Wesley.
Corneau, Guy 1991, *Absent Fathers, Lost Sons*. Boston: Shambhala.
Hillman, James, Bly, Robert, & Meade, Michael 1994, *The Rag and Bone Shop of the Heart: An Anthology of Poems for Men*. New York: HarperCollins.
Johnson, Robert 1974, *He: Understanding Masculine Psychology*. New York: Harper & Row.
Tacey, David 1997, *Remaking Men: Jung, Spirituality, and Social Change*. London: Routledge.

New Age

Bloom, William (ed) 1991, *The New Age: An Anthology of Essential Writing*. London: Rider.
Button, John & Bloom, William 1992, *The Seeker's Guide: A New Age Resource Book*. London: The Aquarian Press.
Campbell, Eileen & Brennan, J.H. 1990, *The Aquarian Guide to the New Age*. Wellingborough: The Aquarian Press.
Campbell, Bruce 1980, *Ancient Wisdom Revived*. Berkeley: University of California Press.

Ferguson, Marilyn 1981, *The Aquarian Conspiracy: Personal and Social Transformation in the 1980s*. Los Angeles: Jeremy P. Tarcher.

Redfield, James 1994, *The Celestine Prophecy*. London: Bantam.

NURSING AND HEALTH CARE

Barnum, Barbara Stevens 1996, *Spirituality in Nursing: From Traditional to New Age*. New York: Springer.

Catalano, Joseph T. 2000, *Nursing Now*. Philadelphia: Davis.

Cassidy, Shiela 1991, *Sharing the Darkness: The Spirituality of Caring*. New York: Orbis.

Cooper, Carolyn 2001, *The Art of Nursing*. London: W. B. Saunders.

PAGANISM AND WICCA

Adler, Margot 1986, *Drawing Down the Moon: Witches, Druids, Goddess-Worshippers, and Other Pagans in America Today*. Boston: Beacon Press.

Albanese, Catherine 1990, *Nature Religion in America*. Chicago University Press.

Crowley, Vivianne 1989, *Wicca: The Old Religion in the New Age*. Wellingborough: The Aquarian Press.

Drury, Nevill 1987, *The Shaman and the Magician*. Harmondsworth: Arkana.

PHILOSOPHY

Derrida, Jacques 1989, *Of Spirit: Heidegger and the Question*. University of Chicago Press.

Derrida, Jacques & Vattimo, Gianni 1998, *Religion*. Stanford University Press.

Hadot, Pierre 1995, *Philosophy as a Way of Life: Spiritual Exercises from Socrates to Foucault*. Oxford: Blackwell.

Hart, Kevin 1989, *The Trespass of the Sign*. Cambridge University Press.

PHYSICAL AND OUTDOOR EDUCATION

Raines, Howard 1993, *Fly Fishing through the Midlife Crisis*. New York: Doubleday.

Rogers, Susan (ed) 1994, *Another Wilderness: New Outdoor Writing by Women*. Seattle: Seal.

White, Jonathan 1994, *Talking on the Water*. San Francisco: Sierra Club.

Zelinski, Mark 1991, *Outward Bound, the Inward Odyssey*. Hillsboro, Oregon: Beyond Words.

PHYSICS AND THE NEW SCIENCES

Bohm, David 1980, *Wholeness and the Implicate Order*. London: Routledge.

Capra, Fritjof 1976, *The Tao of Physics*. London: Fontana.

Capra, Fritjof & Steindl-Rast, David (eds) 1991, *Belonging to the Universe*. New York: HarperCollins.

Davies, Paul 1983, *God and the New Physics*. London: Dent.

Reanney, Daryl 1994, *Music of the Mind*. Sydney: Hill of Content.

Sheldrake, Rupert 1996, *Natural Grace: Dialogues on Science and Spirituality*. London: Bloomsbury.

Zukav, Gary 1980, *The Dancing Wu Li Masters: An Overview of the New Physics*. London: Fontana.

PSYCHOANALYSIS

Rieff, Philip 1987, *The Triumph of the Therapeutic*. London: Chatto & Windus.
Symington, Neville 1994, *Emotion and Spirit: Questioning the Claims of Psychoanalysis and Religion*. London: Cassell.

PSYCHOLOGY, AND PSYCHOTHERAPY

Claxton, Guy 1996, *Beyond Therapy*. Newton, Dorset: Prism Press.
Coxhead, Nona 1991, *Beyond Psychology*. London: Mandala.
Jones, Caroline 1998, *An Authentic Life: Finding Meaning and Spirituality in Everyday Life*. Sydney: ABC Books.
May, Gerald 1992, *Care of Mind, Care of Spirit*. San Francisco: Harper.
Moore, Thomas 1992, *Care of the Soul: A Guide for Cultivating Depth and Sacredness in Everyday Life*. New York: HarperCollins.
——1996, *The Re-Enchantment of Everyday Life*. New York: HarperCollins.
Pennington, Basil 2000, *True Self/False Self*. New York: Crossroad.

RITES OF PASSAGE

Eliade, Mircea 1965, *Rites and Symbols of Initiation*. New York: Harper & Row.
Jung, C.G 1960, 'The Stages of Life' (1930/1931). *CW* 8.
Newton, Miller 1995, *Adolescence: Guiding Youth through the Perilous Ordeal*. New York: Norton.
Raphael, Ray 1988, *The Men from the Boys: Rites of Passage in Male America*. Lincoln: University of Nebraska Press.
Van Gennep, Arthur 1960, *The Rites of Passage* (1908). University of Chicago Press.

SEXUALITY AND THE BODY

Connor, Randy 1993, *Blossom of Bone: Reclaiming the Connections between Homoeroticism and the Sacred*. San Francisco: Harper.
Eisler, Riane 1995, *Sacred Pleasure*. San Francisco: Harper.
Gudorf, Christine 1994, *Body, Sex, and Pleasure*. Cleveland, Ohio: Pilgrim Press.
Moore, Thomas 1994, *Soul Mates*. New York: HarperCollins.
——1998, *The Soul of Sex*. New York: HarperCollins.

SOCIOLOGY

Berger, Peter 1967, *The Sacred Canopy*. New York: Doubleday.
Carroll, John 1998, *Ego and Soul: The Modern West in Search of Meaning*. Sydney: HarperCollins.
Griffin, David Ray (ed) 1988, *Spirituality and Society: Postmodern Visions*. Albany: State University of New York Press.
——1989, *God and Religion in the Postmodern World*. Albany: State University of New York Press.
Spretnak, Charlene 1991, *States of Grace: The Recovery of Meaning in the Postmodern Age*. San Francisco: Harper.
Tacey, David 2000, *Re-Enchantment: The New Australian Spirituality*. Sydney: HarperCollins.
York, Michael 1995, *The Emerging Network*. Lanham, Md: Rowman & Littlefield.

WESTERN CULTURE AND EASTERN THOUGHT

Batchelor, Stephen 1994, *The Awakening of the West: The Encounter of Buddhism and Western Culture*. London: Aquarian.
Bishop, Peter 1994, *Dreams of Power: Tibetan Buddhism and the Western Imagination*. London: Athlone.
Jung, C.G. 1958, 'Yoga and the West' (1936). *CW* 11.

WOMEN

Anderson, Sarah 1997, *The Virago Book of Spirituality: Of Women and Angels*. London: Virago Press.
King, Ursula 1993, *Women and Spirituality: Voices of Protest and Promise*. Basingstoke, UK: Macmillan.
Sewell, Marilyn 1991, *Cries of the Spirit*. Boston: Beacon Press.

GENERAL

Johnston, William M. 1996, *Recent Reference Books in Religion*. Downers Grove, Illinois: InterVarsity Press.
Lao-Tzu 1972, *Tao Te Ching* (6th century BC).Translated by Gia-fu Feng and Jane English. New York: Vintage.
O'Donohue, John 1998, *Eternal Echoes: Exploring Our Hunger to Belong*. London: Bantam.
O'Murchu, Diarmuid 1997, *Reclaiming Spirituality*. Dublin: Gill & Macmillan.
Tacey, David 1988, *Patrick White: Fiction and the Unconscious*. Melbourne: Oxford University Press.
——1995, *Edge of the Sacred: Transformation in Australia*. Melbourne: HarperCollins.
——1997, *Remaking Men: Jung, Spirituality, and Social Change*. London and Philadelphia: Routledge. In Australia and NZ: *Remaking Men: The Revolution in Masculinity*. Melbourne: Viking Penguin.
Whitehead, A. N. 1926, *Religion in the Making*. Cambridge University Press.
——1929, *Process and Reality*. Cambridge University Press.

INDEX

cults, 28
culture, creation and experience, 76
Cupitt, Don, 163
cynicism versus hope, 55

Dalai Lama, 134
'Death by Water' (Eliot), 27
deconstruction, 86, 128–129, 130–131
Deepak Chopra, 142
depression, health problem of, 220
Derrida, Jacques, 23, 61, 62, 127,
129–131, 137
development, sustainable, 220,
222–223
devotion and creativity, 33
devotionalism and spirituality,
193–194
dialectics, Marxian, 71
disconnectedness and
connectedness, 70–73, 218, 223,
224–226
discourses, liberation, 59–60, 70–73
diseases as Gods, 218
disenchantment and re-enchantment,
97, 180–181
diversity in spirituality, 44–45
Divine (the) and heaven, 72
doctors and spiritual patients,
201–202
Dostoyevsky, Fyodor, 137
'Dover Beach' (Arnold), 21
dualism of spirit and world, 67–68,
84, 103–104, 213–214

earth, healing wholeness of, 186–188
Eastern religions, 76–77, 99, 121, 167,
180. see also Buddhism
Eckhart, Meister, 33
eco-centrism and ego-centrism, 183
ecologies, spiritual and natural, 66,
181–188, 219–223
economic rationalism, 222
education
    academia, 57, 60
    boredom and frustration, 57
    holistic, 104–105
    imagination and art in, 160–161
    interest in spiritual, 58–59
    religious educators, 78–79
    revolution in, 73–74

secular, 94–95
spiritual, 92–93, 203–204
teaching spiritual, 76–78, 95–97,
100–101
universities, 59–60, 73–74
ego and the spirit, 66, 83, 89–90,
146–147, 211–212
ego-centrism and eco-centrism, 183
Eliade, Mircea, 20, 106, 137–138
Eliot, T.S., 27, 78, 110, 111, 177
email, 224–226
enchantment, disenchantment and
re-enchantment, 97, 180–181
Endgame (Beckett), 134
engaged spirituality, 65–67
enlightenment, 18, 62
environment, 66–67, 181–188,
219–223
escapism, 65–67
esoteric mysteries, 68–70
European Yearbook, 129–130
evangelisation, 101
evil and good, 84–86
experience, culture and creation, 76
experience, spiritual, 78

faith
    demands of, 119–120
    family and, 191
    letting go, 143–144
    loss of, 106–107
    mystical, 170–171
    natal, 109–110
'Faith and Knowledge' (Derrida), 23,
62, 130–131
family, 32, 43, 191
fascism, 28
fear of the sacred, 117–118
fellowship and community, 194–195
feminism and spirituality, 99
Ferraris, Maurizio, 132
five-fold path, 106–107
form and spirit, 31, 33–35, 42,
158–159
'Four Quartets' (Eliot), 110, 111
Francis of Assisi, 33
Freud, Sigmund, 24, 156–157
fundamentalism and spirituality,
11–12, 97–101, 210, 212–213